MW01252898

Consumer Culture in Latin America

Consumer Culture in Latin America

Edited by

John Sinclair and Anna Cristina Pertierra

palgrave
macmillan

CONSUMER CULTURE IN LATIN AMERICA

First published in 2012 by
PALGRAVE MACMILLAN®
in the United States—a division of St. Martin's Press LLC,
175 Fifth Avenue, New York, NY 10010.

Where this book is distributed in the UK, Europe and the rest of the world,
this is by Palgrave Macmillan, a division of Macmillan Publishers Limited,
registered in England, company number 785998, of Houndmills,
Basingstoke, Hampshire RG21 6XS.

Palgrave Macmillan is the global academic imprint of the above companies
and has companies and representatives throughout the world.

Palgrave® and Macmillan® are registered trademarks in the United States,
the United Kingdom, Europe and other countries.

ISBN: 978-0-230-34073-2

Library of Congress Cataloging-in-Publication Data is available from the
Library of Congress.

A catalogue record of the book is available from the British Library.

Design by Newgen Imaging Systems (P) Ltd., Chennai, India.

First edition: December 2012

10 9 8 7 6 5 4 3 2 1

Contents

Illustrations

Acknowledgments

The idea for this edited collection first arose from a conference panel at the 2009 Congress of the Latin American Studies Association, held in Rio de Janeiro. The panel was organized by Anna Cristina Pertierra, with John Sinclair and Diana Lima as discussants. The editors wish to thank Marc Figuerola Delgado for editorial assistance.

Understanding Consumer Culture in Latin America: An Introduction

John Sinclair and Anna Cristina Pertierra

This collection brings together recent work from across the humanities and social sciences on consumption, consumers, and consumer culture in Latin America. It presents original research by sociologists, anthropologists, media and cultural studies scholars, geographers, and historians; contributors range from the most senior scholars working on these topics today, to emerging early career researchers, and includes academics based in Latin American institutions as well as others working in North America, the United Kingdom, and Australia. Although the strength of the volume derives from this diversity of contributors and that of the approaches and topics they cover, it can make understanding the relationship between the various papers, and even understanding what "consumer culture" might be, whether in Latin America or in any other region of the world, a challenge. Chapters in this book consider consumption practices and consumer culture in places as diverse as Mexico, Central America, the Caribbean, the Andean region, Brazil, and Chile, covering topics such as media, cultural production and creative industries, household consumption, tourism, shopping, and environmental and economic consequences of globalization among other things. The goal of this introductory chapter, then, is to explain how such varied studies of consumption might be relevant to scholars and students of Latin America, as well as to demonstrate and explain the particular importance occupied by Latin American societies, and the Latin American region as a whole, in the growing world scholarship on consumption and consumers.

As an object of study, consumer culture in Latin America has to be constructed in retrospect. Whilst anthropologists, historians, sociologists, and others in the past have taken note of certain consumption patters or the use of particular kinds of goods, this has always occurred, appropriately enough, within the framework of their own respective disciplines, not the study of consumption as such. That is not to say, these are not rich sources of data for consumption studies. On the contrary, we have, for instance, Lévi-Strauss's descriptions of the use of the herb *mate* and the preparation of the stimulant *guaraná* by colonists in Brazil in the 1930s, along with ethnographic descriptions of the foods and artifacts of Amazonian Indians at that time (Lévi-Strauss 2011 [1955]). Similarly, Oscar Lewis's study of family life in Mexico in the 1950s includes observations such as how manufactured bread and the use of tableware were replacing the tradition of eating food wrapped in *tortillas* (1979 [1959]). However, these researchers subordinated such observations to the traditional anthropological objective of building up a detailed and holistic description of a particular way of life. In those decades, while anthropologists dealt with cultural meanings in general, the study of consumption was quite separately pursued in a narrower sense within economics; as we will discuss later, this volume forms part of a more recent movement to see consumption as being both economic *and* cultural.

Outside of Latin America, the region is not necessarily thought of as part of the global consumer society. On the contrary, it is more likely to be seen, in popular understanding at least, as the ostensible source of certain kinds of goods and consumption experiences, such as enjoying tequila and tacos in the local Mexican restaurant. Even then, such consumer experiences may be mediated through another country: in Australia, for instance, there are Mexican restaurants not because Australia is close to Mexico, but it is close to the United States, at least in a cultural sense. Yet, Latin America has long been central to the global development of mass consumption, ranging from the export of raw commodities in colonial times, through the rise of middle-class consumers in the nineteenth and twentieth centuries, to the contemporary involvement of many Latin American people in global networks of consumption. Take, for example, the development of modern global media culture: Latin American popular music has been a notable cultural export to the world for decades, going back at least to the classic *boleros*, like *Bésame mucho*, from between the World Wars, and a host of dance genres—*tango, samba, salsa*—to the more recent fashion for the US Hispanic crossover styles of Ricky Martin and Jennifer Lopez. In many countries of the world, even beyond the West, Latin America is known through its characteristic television exports, notably in the *telenovela* genre, usually, though inaccurately, referred to as a Latin soap opera. As well, Latin America is an exotic tourist destination, whether for the North Americans who venture no further south than Tijuana on the US-Mexican border, or for the European backpackers who trek to Machu Picchu in the Andes of Peru. Indeed, another whole book could be produced on these kinds of consumption of Latin America in the rest of the world, but in this collection, rather than engage with partial and exoticized appropriations of an imagined Latin American repertoire of cultural production, we intend to explore actual patterns of consumption and consumer culture within the region itself, and hope to do justice to the depth and variety it exhibits across both time and place.

Even in academic circles, at least in the dominant English-speaking world, Latin America might not be seen as a region in which consumption studies could find much of interest. Rather, Latin America's history of colonization and subsequent economic dependence on the United States identifies it with what used to be called the "Third World," or latterly, the "developing world." Notwithstanding the relatively recent emergence of Brazil as one of the world's fastest-growing economies, the region as a whole is seen as poor, and the presumption is that consumption studies are irrelevant in poor countries. We have two responses to such assumptions, both of which are dealt with more extensively across chapters in this volume. In the first place, as anthropologists of consumption have argued extensively, poor people do, in fact, have patterns of consumption and modes of participation in consumer culture that are well worth academic attention. Thus, the consumption of Coca Cola is important to study not only in the communities of the United States but also in such places as Papua New Guinea (Foster 2006), and cell phones may be more important to (and certainly more popular amongst) Jamaicans or Filipinos than Western Europeans (Horst and Miller 2004; Pertierra et. al. 2002). Even supposedly "high end" consumer goods such as designer fashion labels may be studied in the Congo rather than in Paris (Friedman 1994). It has by now become quite accepted within the qualitative consumption literature that the struggles of contemporary poor people to consume more and better goods should be researched empathetically as sets of cultural practices that are no less authentic than other practices more frequently associated with "traditional" lifestyles in poor or marginal communities (Miller 2001; Schor et. al. 2010). Secondly, while we no have intention of denying that Latin America is a poor region, the extraordinary range of socioeconomic conditions to be found in Latin America mean that the experiences of consumers across the region cannot be simplistically generalized, and vary from among the richest of the world's elites, to enormous middle classes, and of course to the very poor. As Latin America is "the most unequal region in the world" (Székely & Montes 2006, 589), sites for the study of Latin American consumption can range from the

Ecuadorian Andes (Colloredo-Mansfield 1999) or the Mexican low-income households in the shadow of the US border (Campbell & Heyman 2009), to the fancy shopping malls of São Paolo (O'Dougherty 2002) or the multiplex cinemas of Buenos Aires (Wortman 2003). Such complex class structures in Latin American countries can be brought to light in part through the study of consumption: peasant, tribal, urban poor and middle-class consumers bring their distinct values, histories and aspirations to the active appropriation of material goods and cultural forms in ways that require very localized unpacking, even while their documentation makes important contributions to international research questions.

Far from making it peripheral to the world emergence of consumer culture, it is precisely Latin America's postcolonial condition that makes consumer practices in the region so interesting and variable. The economies and cultures of Latin American peoples have been deeply influenced by longstanding relationships with other parts of the world, including the initial colonial relationships with Europe, the cultural history that links much of the Americas to Africa, and the interconnections of trade, commerce, and culture between distinct parts of the region itself. Perhaps above all, the economic rise of the United States in the nineteenth and twentieth centuries, and its political and military engagements with, and pursuit of its economic interests in many countries of Latin America, has shaped—for better and for worse—the economic and cultural parameters of most Latin Americans' lives. Relative to Asia and Africa, Latin America is the world's oldest former colonial region, dating from the early 1500s, and although its nations have had their independence for the longest period of time, it also experienced the longest period under colonization, for independence did not begin to happen until some three hundred years after settlement had begun. Colonial modes of production were established under which the native peoples, and also slaves from Africa, worked on the estates and in the mines. Consumption options in this era were thus restricted to the quasi-feudal class of plantation and mine owners, and in the absence of local manufacturing, merchants who prospered through importing goods of all kinds from Europe. Conversely, the colonial system bound in Latin America to consumption in Europe, through the export of its minerals and the valuable plantation crops of coffee, sugar, and tobacco (Galeano 1973). As the work of anthropologist-historian Sidney Mintz among others has established, the history of plantation economies in the Americas is effectively a history of contemporary transnational capitalism, intimately shaping the everyday lives of people across the transatlantic region not only through labor and economics, but also through the changing consumption patterns that both prompted and resulted from modern global trade (Mintz 1986).

Thus, by the time of independence, the seeds of contemporary consumer culture in Latin America had already been sown. This period began with Napoleon invading the Iberian Peninsula in 1808, deposing the Spanish monarchy, and causing the Portuguese royal family to flee to Brazil. Independence struggles were initiated throughout all of Spanish America, so that most of the colonial territories were independent by 1825 (Williamson 1992). Most of the new nations abolished slavery around this time, paving the way for free immigrants to come from Europe, especially in the second half of the century, thus further transforming their economies and social structures, although slavery did continue in Cuba and Brazil until the 1880s. Having lost its empire, Spain had to stand back and watch Britain and France and other nations become the leaders of the new industrial age. First the European powers and later the United States set up neocolonial relationships with the new nations through trade and investment. The initial trade with Europe laid the basis for the postcolonial indebtedness and dependency that have continued to characterize the region. Yet, the United States had also declared its interest in the many lands reaching far away to its south. In 1823 President Monroe had warned off European powers, which might have had colonial ambitions in the region, and pledged US support for any country so threatened. As the century wore on, this "Monroe Doctrine" was used to legitimize US intervention in Latin America whenever it saw its interests were either at risk or could be advanced, culminating in 1898 in a war against Spain, out of which it acquired protectorate rights over Puerto Rico and Cuba, Spain's first and last colony in the Americas (Williamson 1992). This opened up Cuba to US investment, which we can see as a clear example of how international trade and politics has shaped consumption in Latin America. Notably, along with Panama and Mexico, Cuba was one of the first countries outside of the United States where Coca-Cola established a market, ushering in a period of rapid expansion throughout the hemisphere between 1906 and 1938 (Coca-Cola Corporation 2006). Retail chains from the United States set up stores, which introduced US fashions and sold refrigerators and radios, and later television sets, to the emergent middle class (Pertierra 2011,26–29, 111–112). Meanwhile in Brazil, General Electric was opening its own stores, while Ford dealers were offering "bumper to bumper modernism" to aspirational urban elites (Stearns 2001, 112).

Although there were also certain European companies, such as Nestlé and Philips, who sought to cultivate Latin America as a market in the early decades of the twentieth century, US corporations were favored by their government's political stance towards the hemisphere. Throughout the century, the US government pursued policies of direct and indirect

military intervention; support for client states led by repressive dictator-
ships and juntas; and engagement in "covert operations" and "low inten-
sity conflicts." These tactics were motivated by the government's resolve
to protect the massive private investment by US corporations in Latin
America, and a determination to maintain the "security" of the region
against whatever forces the US government perceived to be inimical to
those interests, especially during the "Cold War" decades. Proceeding
with both force and diplomacy (as in the Good Neighbor Policy between
the World Wars, or the Alliance for Progress in the 1960s), the United
States clearly and consistently asserted its political as well as economic
hegemony over the entire region in the postcolonial era (Williamson
1992). Often denounced within the region as "US imperialism," this
influence was seen to have a cultural dimension, "cultural imperialism"
which worked through advertising and the media to achieve "the export
of consumerism," a force threatening the diversity of national cultures
with homogenization (Schiller 1979, 24). So, as with many other aspects
of life in Latin America, understanding the character of consumers and
consumption practices there requires an understanding of the region's
particular relationship with the United States, both past and present. However, we do not wish to deny in any way the agency of Latin
American consumers—in all their diversity—to make use of commodities
in very local ways despite the larger political and economic restrictions
that placed them in relative subjugation to the needs of foreign governments and markets. In an influential edited collection on the importance of imports to colonial Latin American societies, Orlove and Bauer
(1997) argue that studying the internal social factors that shaped Latin
Americans' use of imported goods offers important historical insights
that an excessive focus on exports and production as the only noteworthy
features of Latin American economic history precludes. In other words,
while it is important to acknowledge the interests and influences of colonial and postcolonial powers, such an acknowledgment is a necessary
but only partial explanation of how and why Latin American consumers
make use of commodities in specific cultural and political contexts.

The decades following World War II saw great expansion in investment by private US-based manufacturing corporations in the establishment of foreign subsidiaries and affiliates. Between 1953 and 1973, there
was a six fold increase in the book value of direct overseas investment
by US companies, most of it in manufacturing (Schiller 1979, 24). Latin
American countries attracted high rates of penetration, relative to other
less industrialized world regions. Several Latin American governments
had adopted protective "import substitution" policies following the Great
Depression, intended to reduce imports and stimulate national industries,

but by allowing the setting up of foreign manufacturing subsidiaries and affiliates, it seemed to these governments that they could gain the benefits of foreign capital, manufacturing plants, and technology, and that the goods would be produced in the country and not imported. The contradictory result of such "internationalization of internal markets" was "a simultaneous process of dependence and capitalist development" (Salinas and Paldán 1979, 88). The critique of such "dependent development" or "dependency," in which economic development was tied to that of the investor nations, became a dominant feature of economic thought in Latin America in the 1960s. Meanwhile, many of the brands made and marketed by what were then called "transnational" or "multinational" corporations became firmly established in these countries.

By no means has all transnational investment gone into consumer industries, nor has it all come from the United States, but the establishment of subsidiaries, partnerships, and licensing arrangements by US consumer goods corporations has been of particular significance in fomenting a consumer culture in Latin America, because of the demand thus created for advertising, and the preference for television in particular as an advertising medium. While the press has had its role historically in the emergence of a consumer culture in Latin America, it has been commercial broadcasting, first radio and then television (Fox 1995), which was decisive in ensuring that the dominant media have been formed as a "consumer delivery enterprise" (Bunce 1976, 106). Unlike the regions of Europe, Asia, and Africa, where television was established on a state run and/or public service model, most countries in Latin America adopted the US commercial model from the start, and this has resulted in a thoroughgoing commercialization of popular culture, the *telenovela* being the most obvious example. The *telenovela* is to Latin America as the Hollywood film is to the United States (López 1995), for while film production in Latin America has been spasmodic and largely dependent on state subsidy, the *telenovela* has evolved as a form—most strongly in Mexico and Brazil, but also elsewhere—that is commercially successful yet regarded by many Latin Americans as a valid and cherished expression of their cultures.

In contrast to other major regions of the world, there often seem to be greater similarities between one nation and the next in Latin America, and there is the apparent common bond of the Spanish language, with the notable exception of Portuguese-speaking Brazil. However, these similarities are deceptive. While there are cultural goods, such as the *telenovela*, which are traded within the region, Latin America does not form a single market. Indeed, even within nations, there are significant variations from one province to the other. This is particularly evident in music.

In Mexico, for instance, quite distinct genres flourish in different parts of the country, from *música norteña* in the border states to *música tropical* on the southern coasts. On a regional scale, MTV has found it must offer different channels to subscribers not only in Brazil, but also in Mexico, Colombia, and Argentina. Nevertheless, much popular culture in Latin America—from television to music and beyond—does seem to feature a degree of transnational movement that could be described as a sort of pan-Latino consumer culture formed in part because Latin American people and Latino communities of the United States have been identified in popular and business circles as an increasingly important "market" for the consumption of goods and services (Dávila 2001; Sinclair 2003). Many Latin Americans, rich or poor, urban or rural, interact frequently with people from abroad whether they be tourists, employers or family members, and many are themselves frequent world travelers whether for leisure or for labor. Perhaps even more than in other world regions, due to their historical role in the engagement of so-called Old and New Worlds, Latin Americans constantly and frequently experience consumption as part of a globalized process that has been developing for centuries and continues to evolve.

The Rise of Consumption, and of Consumption Studies

Until the late 1970s, the term "consumption" or "consumer" would mostly be found only in the work of economists and marketing scholars. In other fields, such as anthropology, sociology and history, the influence of Marxian or other political economic models seemed to emphasize the role of industry, production, and the state as being the main areas that constituted the objects of social theory, and at a more qualitative level turned to topics such as tradition, ritual, and language to understand the constitution of individuals' identities in the world. But in recent decades, the study of consumption has moved from being something periph- eral that was vastly outweighed by the study of production, to becom- ing a central topic of research across the humanities and social sciences. A number of academic developments in the 1980s and 1990s seemed to create a "perfect storm" of elements that would bring consumption to the fore of topics for cultural research. In France, following the lead of Roland Barthes' work on the cultural meanings of consumption, philosophers and sociologists such as Pierre Bourdieu, Jean Baudrillard and Michel de Certeau—each in different ways—produced social theory that was based upon the politics of interior decoration, the importance of Disneyland, and the individual's everyday practices in eating, shopping, and dressing, respectively. In the United Kingdom, the rise of the Birmingham School of cultural studies, and the related emergence of media studies as an important interdisciplinary field encouraged British scholars to take seriously the theoretical (and political) importance of wide ranges of people as creative actors who produce "culture" in all of its forms, high or low, elite or popular. Anthropology, too, increasingly moved beyond a tendency to specialize in "exotic" cultures that were expected to represent extreme difference from global capitalism—both by taking their ethnographic methods to explore urban, industrialized, mass-market communities, and by recognizing the ever expanding role played by global networks of producers and consumers in the previously less globally integrated societies. Mary Douglas and Baron Isherwood led the way in this field, arguing that goods are significant in all societies not so much for their usefulness, but "for making visible and stable the categories of culture" (1979, 59), meaning that goods are endowed with value by their place in a social understanding of them. Thus, for contemporary anthropology as for consumption studies, goods do not so much derive their meaning from culture, but on the contrary, provide culture with meaning. Along the way, historians also reminded everyone else that actually such global networks had, in many places, long been in existence. In particular, Western European histories of the birth of consumer culture have played an important role in the development of consumption studies (McKendrick et al 1982; Campbell 1987), and although such literature is necessarily partial in its coverage, historians such as Frank Trentmann (2004) are actively engaged in building a more nuanced global understanding of the distinct though interrelated developments of consumer cultures in modern history.

Of course, Latin American scholars have had their own roles to play in this unfolding of academic developments to turn towards consumption; many of them have long been interlocutors with social theorists in Europe and North America but perhaps more importantly have also directed their research to more specific national and regional debates. In larger Latin American countries—most notably Mexico and Brazil, but also in Argentina and Chile—clusters of researchers have emerged devoted to consumption research, and in particular to the consumption of popular cultural forms and media often described as cultural consumption (*el/o consumo cultural*). Among many others, notable scholars working within and across Latin American institutions include Livia Barbosa, Fatima Portilho, and Ruben George Oliven in Brazil; Guillermo Orozco and Ana Rosas Mantecón in Mexico; Beatriz Sarlo and Ana Wortman in Argentina; and Guillermo Sunkel in Chile. But two Latin American scholars stand out as making particular innovations in contemporary Latin American thought, both in specifically addressing consumption and in bringing

Latin American scholarship to a broader international audience in the humanities and social sciences; these two are Jesús Martín-Barbero and Nestor García Canclini. Both are prominent among the Latin American scholars who sought new ways to account for inequality, injustice and social division within Latin American societies that moved beyond theses of dependency and cultural imperialism. While retaining a Marxian interest in accounting for power and injustice as a key reason for understanding culture, such thinkers wanted to acknowledge that Latin American peoples and institutions themselves had been, and continue to be, active agents both in perpetuating inequalities and in forging cultural meanings through their everyday lives. García Canclini argues that in Latin America, particularly since the 1980s, political, economic and technological changes have transformed "Latin American civil societies into atomized ensembles of consumers"; such cultural changes have "impeded the constitution of identities through national symbols. Now, they are shaped by the programming of, say, Hollywood, Televisa, and MTV" (2001,5).

Already it is clear, then, that Latin American consumption studies may be thought to take a more explicitly political position than some European alternatives: if researchers such as García Canclini largely share the strategies of European social scientists in terms of using ethnographic or other qualitative data to develop an understanding of actual consumer practices, their involvement in public debates and their explicit addressing of theorizing consumption as an avenue for redressing social inequalities is perhaps more akin to some British and North American forms of cultural studies. Another characteristic much Latin American scholarship shares with Anglophone cultural studies has been the prominence of studying media—television, film, and increasingly new media technologies—as a way to generate theoretical and political arguments about the state of contemporary life. Martín-Barbero's proposal that media in itself is less important to study than the process of mediation—the circulation of images and texts between people in everyday life—has been especially productive in media and cultural studies internationally (Martín-Barbero 2004). Both García Canclini and Martin-Barbero, in their distinct but connected ways, look at the changing practices of cultural consumption to produce new understandings of how modernity is playing out in Latin America in ways that are part of, but not controlled by, the international forces of neoliberalism and globalization.

Having outlined where the study of consumer culture in Latin America has taken us to date, we can now turn to the chapters of this volume to consider recently emerged key questions and issues that represent the current state of play in this interdisciplinary field of consumption research. Of course, there are innumerable ways in which the 14 chapters

compiled in this collection could have been ordered: we have made efforts
to include something of every region, and to include chapters that recognize transnational, national, local, and ethnic identities. Differences
of class and gender are also considered from multiple angles, and while
the focus of the collection is clearly on consumption, the importance of
consumption not only to identity, but also to everyday practice, to politics, to governance, or to the natural and built environments, is many
times made clear throughout these different contributions. Despite the
connecting ideas that weave through the chapters, we have grouped them
according to certain key themes that, as this introduction has described,
have become particularly important to the study of consumer culture in
Latin America. Part 1, *Transnational Developments,* acknowledges the
flows of capital, culture, and people that move across the Latin American
region in complex and uneven ways. This section takes a more wide-
scale approach than most others, looking at industries and movements
across multiple countries. Part 2, *Getting and Spending* (a title we owe
to Ruben George Oliven and Rosana Pinheiro Machado), examines the
role of money; how people think about it, what people do to get it, how
they use it when they have it, and how they cope when they lose it. Part 3,
Domestic Practice shows how across different Latin American places and
times, the material products of everyday life in and around the home form
a primary site for the incorporation, innovation and maintenance of consumer practices. This section demonstrates even more clearly than others
how home making and housekeeping, as a locus for consumption, also
require considerable labor, both actual and symbolic. Part 4, *Images and
Soundscapes,* turns to what Latin American scholars have often described
as "cultural consumption" (*el/o consumo cultural*), taking three different
approaches to understand the role of visual and aural culture and considering how the cultural forms of photographs, advertisements and songs
might contribute to national as well as regional or local identities. Part 5,
Spaces and Places, reminds us that the various ways in which consumption is understood and enacted are always dependent upon relationships
with the world around us. Frequently, we are quite literally consuming
the natural environment in order to attain the world of consumer culture
we desire. Relatedly, the section shows how Latin Americans are often
required to demonstrate and package their "Latin American-ness" for the
consumption of others in order to get by.

Far from being a conclusive guide to research on consumer culture
in Latin America, we see this volume as a starting point, or an invitation to researchers and readers to think about how consumer culture is
both distinctive within Latin American communities, and is connected
to the wider world of consumption in late modernity. The contribution of

the region to global consumer culture, both historically and in the present, is soundly articulated through the chapters of this collection, while the importance of scholars working within and upon Latin American culture should also become apparent as an exciting focal point of new consumption research that is not always given sufficient attention in the Anglophone academy. We hope and expect that the collection inspires as many new questions as it provides answers, and we look forward to an unrolling of ever greater exchanges between scholars of consumer culture in the English, Spanish, and Portuguese speaking worlds.

References

Braudel, Fernand. (1993) *A History of Civilizations*, New York: Penguin Books.

Bunce, Richard. (1976) *Television in the Corporate Interest*, New York: Praeger.

Campbell, Colin. (1987) *The Romantic Ethic and the Spirit of Modern Consumerism,* Oxford: Basil Blackwell.

Campbell, Howard, and Josiah Heyman. (2009) "The Study of Borderlands Consumption: Potentials and Precautions." In *Land of Necessity: Consumer Culture in the United States-Mexico Borderlands.* Edited by Alexis McCrossen, 325–332. Durham, NC: Duke University Press.

Coca-Cola Corporation. (2006) *The Centennial of Coca-Cola in Latin America.* Available at: http://www.thecoca-colacompany.com/citizenship/pdf/Centennial_Coca-Cola_Latin_America_English.pdf. Accessed 20 February 2012.

Colloredo-Mansfield, Rudi. (1999) *The Native Leisure Class: Consumption and Cultural Creativity in the Andes.* Chicago: University of Chicago Press.

Dávila, Arlene. (2001) *Latinos Inc: The Marketing and Making of a People.* Berkeley: University of California Press.

Fox, Elizabeth. (1995) "Latin American Broadcasting." In *Latin America Since 1930: Ideas, Culture, and Society.* Edited by Leslie Bethell, 519–568. Cambridge: Cambridge University Press.

Friedman, Jonathan. (1994) "The Political Economy of Elegance: An African Cult of Beauty." In *Consumption and Identity.* Edited by Jonathan Friedman, 120–134. Amsterdam: Taylor & Francis.

Galeano, Eduardo. (1973) *Open Veins of Latin America: Five Centuries of the Pillage of a Continent.* New York and London: Monthly Review Press.

García Canclini, Néstor. (2001) *Consumers and Citizens: Globalization and Multicultural Conflicts.* Minneapolis: University of Minnesota Press.

Horst, Heather, and Daniel Miller. (2006) *The Cell Phone: An Anthropology of Communication.* Oxford: Berg.

Lévi-Strauss, Claude. (2011 [1955]) *Tristes Tropiques.* London: Penguin.

Lewis, Oscar. (1979 [1959]) *Five Families.* New York: Basic Books.

López, Ana. (1995) "Our Welcomed Guests: Telenovelas in Latin America." In *To Be Continued...Soap Operas Around the World.* Edited by Robert Allen, 256–275. London and New York: Routledge.

Martín-Barbero, Jesús. (2004) "A Nocturnal Map to Explore a New Field." In *The Latin American Cultural Studies Reader*. Edited by Ana Del Sarto; Alicia Ríos, and Abril Trigo, 310–328. Durham: Duke University Press.

McKendrick, Neil, John Brewer and J.H. Plumb. (1982) *The Birth of a Consumer Society: The Commercialization of Eighteenth-Century England*. London: Europa Publications.

Miller, Daniel. (2001) "The Poverty of Morality," *Journal of Consumer Culture* 1: 225–243.

O'Dougherty, Maureen. (2002) *Consumption Intensified: The Politics of Middle-Class Daily Life in Brazil*. Durham, NC: Duke University Press.

Orlove, Benjamin, and Arnold J Bauer. (1997) "Giving Importance to Imports." In *The Allure of the Foreign: Imported Goods in Postcolonial Latin America*. Edited by Benjamin Orlove, 1-30. Ann Arbor, MI: University of Michigan Press.

Pertierra, Anna Cristina. (2011) *Cuba: The Struggle for Consumption*. Coconut Creek, FL: Caribbean Studies Press.

Pertierra, Raul., Eduardo Ugarte, Alicia Pingol, Joel Hernandez, and Nikos Dacanay. (2002) *TXT-ING Selves: Cellphones and Philippine Modernity*. Manila: De La Salle University Press.

Salinas, Raquel., and Leena Paldán. (1979) "Culture in the Process of Dependent Development: Theoretical Perspectives." In *National Sovereignty and International Communication*. Edited by Kaarle Nordenstreng and Herbert Schiller, 82–98. Norwood, NJ: Ablex Publishing Corporation.

Schiller, Herbert. (1979) "Transnational Media and National Development." In *National Sovereignty and International Communication*. Edited by Kaarle Nordenstreng and Herbert Schiller, Norwood, NJ: Ablex Publishing Corporation.

Schor, Juliet, Don Slater, Sharon Zukin, and Viviana Zelizer. (2010) "Critical and Moral Stances in Consumer Studies." *Journal of Consumer Culture* Vol. 10(2): 274–291.

Sinclair, John. (2003) "The Hollywood of Latin America: Miami as Regional Center in Television Trade." *Television and New Media* 4(3): 211–229.

Stearn, Peter. (2006) *Consumerism in World History*. London: Routledge.

Székely, Miguel, and Andrés Montes,. (2006) "Poverty and Inequality." In *The Long Twentieth Century*. Edited by Victor Bulmer-Thomas, John H. Coatsworth, and Roberto Cortés Conde. Cambridge: Cambridge University Press.

Trentmann, Frank. (2004) "Beyond Consumerism: New Historical Perspectives on Consumption." *Journal of Contemporary History* Vol. 39(3): 373–401.

Williamson, Edwin. (1992) *The Penguin History of Latin America*. London: Penguin Books.

Wortman, Ana. (2003) "Viejas y nuevas significaciones del cine." In Ana Wortman, (coord.), *Pensar las clases medias: Consumos culturales y estilos de vida urbanos en la Argentina de los noventa*, 23–128. Buenos Aires: La Crujía.

Part I

Transnational Developments

New Social and Business Models in Latin American Musics

George Yúdice

This essay focuses on the production, distribution, circulation, and consumption of music in Latin America. These different dimensions of the music sector of the culture / creative industries cannot be fully separated, since it is consumption that drives both commercial and alternative strategies to reach audiences, and, increasingly, participation in social networks (which also increases revenues).[1] Music cannot be separated from other media, particularly radio, television, video, videogames, mobile telephony, and a number of Internet applications, making it increasingly a multimedia experience. New forms of circulation and distribution are tailored to consumption patterns, something which the traditional music industry ignored, to its disadvantage, and for which it is now trying to play catch-up belatedly vis-à-vis new business models that have appeared over the past decade. The large global media conglomerates, with their focus on bestsellers and blockbusters, and the concomitant mega marketing and publicity budgets to ensure profitability, lost sight of what consumers want and how they go about getting it. This is an observation that many enthusiasts of Web 2.0 concepts and technologies see as indicative of a sea change in the market *and* in society.

Traditional business enterprises, and particularly the entertainment and media industries, sought to capitalize on the few bestselling offerings on the "head" of the L-shaped statistical distribution curve; the Internet, however, has made it possible to focus profitably on the innumerable low-selling items on the "long tail" (Anderson 2006). In contrast to the relatively few stars promoted by the majors, the long tail is the domain of diversity, where people may find cultural offerings that interest them but that the entertainment industry does not provide. As we will see, new technologies seem to enhance the possibilities that cultural producers in small regions and countries—such as those of Central America, or off-the-beaten-path areas in otherwise media-top heavy countries like Brazil—will be able to better connect with interested public. User activity is necessary for the economics of the long tail to work, since it identifies those items that recommender software programs connect with others on the network (e.g., Amazon, eBay). "Participants," "users," "interactants," and so on, are thus a source of value.[2] I shall review a number of cases of what Brazilian anthropologist and television producer Hermano Vianna calls "parallel music," which operates precisely where the majority of Latin American consumers are: in informal markets. As we will see, gauging consumer behavior is not so easy in Latin America because there are numerous heterogeneous markets and they are not usually brought together into a comprehensive study or public policy.

The Latin American music industry has a disproportionately low share of the world media market: 3.8 percent, which is less than half of Latin America's share of the world population, 8.4 percent (see Figure 1.1). Market share is unlikely to grow significantly in the next five years due to broadband penetration, few licensed services, and one of the highest rates of digital piracy in the world (Wikofsky Gruen Associates 2010, 325).

However, there are means of access to music that are not fully addressed in large-scale industry reports, including the sharing of MP3 files via burned compact discs, external hard disk drives, flash drives, secure digital cards, and USB MP3 players. People with an Internet connection can also listen to music for free on Internet radios like Spotify, Pandora and Last.fm, some with up to 100 million users. Such radio stations can also be accessed by cell phones, a means of access by streaming that makes the issue of downloading increasingly irrelevant. Revenue does not come from payment for purchase of music but through publicity, and, in some cases, subscription fees.

Piracy is often simplistically condemned by the mainstream music industry without any concern whatsoever for the complexities of how popular classes in Latin America may access music. But as we will see below, what might be called "piracy"—or more accurately "parallel music" in the nonjudgmental phrase that Vianna uses for the reproduction and distribution of phonograms in a range of musics of the popular classes[3]—is an integral part of informal, albeit legal forms of music consumption in a diversity of thriving music scenes across the Americas, among them dancehall, Rio funk, tecnobrega, huayno pop, cumbia villera, and champeta.

Type of Music	Main feature	Profile of the main actor	Type of Artist	Consumer profile	Rights management	Main source of revenue	Business model
Major Record Labels	Contract for all possible revenues from music	Conglomerates	Blockbuster	Masivo o "Corta cola"	Copyright	360° services	Monopolize production, distribution, shows
Fine Arts	Claims cultural superiority	Museums, national theaters, philharmonic orchesters,	Virtoousos, geniuses	Elite	Copyright	Box office, subsides, branding	Governmebt-funded, non-profit
"Art Music"	Artistic elaboration	Singer songwriter, e.g., Música Popular Brasileirra (MPB)	Artist	Middle class, educated, intellectuaIor Intellectualoid	Copyright	Records Concerts Rights Management	Small & Medium Labels, e.g., Biscoito Fino or Papaya Music
Indies	Alternativ production & distribution	Small & Medium labels (SMEs), DJs, independent artist	Traditionally rock and punk, now techno & all artists	All kinds of niches	Copyright Creative Commons CC	Records digital sales DJ services	SMEs, DYI, festivals, pay for service (DJ)
Anaroo-punk	Rejection of values	Individual	Artiste maudite	Underground Elite	No rights, copyright	Self-subsidy Sales at shows	Contestatory
Popular Culture	Integration with a community	Informal groups	Community master musicians	Locally sanctioned spaces, occasionally plays in national venues	No rights,	Community &/or Church support, cultural tourism	Self organized
Art-in-action	Social commitment, inclusion, integral development	Collective, a particular group	Community artist	Streets, plazas, cultural centers	No rights,	Subsidies, pay for service	NGO, non-profit or informal group
Mixed Model	Profits earned used for social activism	Artist-managed, eg Afro Reggae, CUFA, Nós do Morro	Socially responsible artist	Performances or work in cultural centers, work with youth	Copyright, CC o gigt economy	Sales, subsidies, commissions, sell line of products, services	Combination of for-profit and non-profit organizations, festivals
Parallel Music	Mass concerts, prevalence of digital technologoes	Informal groups, eg, Champeta, Cumbia villera, Tecnobrega, Huayno Pop	Technified, urban popular groups	Larges spaces, sports fields, parking lots, dances	No rights, distribution in pirate sale venues	Concerts, % of beer sold	Revenues distributed among the various actors in the production chain
Networks, circuits	Organized & managed via Web 2.0	Networks e.g., Circuito Fora do Eixo, SCI	Bands, theater and dance groups	Shows, services	CC, copyright, & no rights	Sales, subsidies & comissions	Solidarity economy w/links to market, festivals

Figure 1.1   Latin American music industry

Source: Yúdice (2012a and 2012b).

The music panorama is quite varied across Latin America, with major record labels still having privileged access to radio and television, but there is a vibrant independent music scene in rock, fusion, so-called folklore, hip hop, and "art" (singer-songwriter) genres. Moreover, the music scene has diversified even more as new actors have emerged to transform it. The following table gives just a hint of this diversity.[4]

This paper presents four such examples, to throw some light on what is missed by formal music and audiovisual industries and censuses.

From Parallel Music to New Business Models: 4 Case Studies[5]

Huayno Pop, Peru

In Peru, huayno pop music is a hybrid of traditional huayno music with other genres such as cumbia, rock, pop, and techno. While the origin of huayno in the Peruvian highlands dates back to the time of the Incan empire in the twentieth century, as migrants from the highlands populated coastal Peru and particularly Lima, the flourishing music and video industry of huayno pop developed in the popular classes of Lima.[6] As Santiago Alfaro, author of a study on huayno pop, writes, it was considered by José María Arguedas—Peruvian novelist, linguist, and musicologist—as "the most legitimate voice and expression of the Peruvian indian and mestizo throughout time" (cited in Alfaro 2009, 6), but through the processes of urbanization, industrialization, and globalization it has become a commercial success in the music and television industries, "recreating it and making it relevant to the mestizo and indigenous majorities rather than occasioning its disappearance" (Alfaro 2009). Its hybridization, moreover, has enabled it to become the rage throughout all of Peru as well as in Bolivia and Ecuador and beyond the Andean region.

One of the genre's distinctions is that it succeeded without the involvement of the mainstream music labels, in great part because it is a music of the popular classes without the cachet of industry-promoted pop stars (one of the majors' costly risk reduction strategies to ensure profitability). Moreover, as is characteristic of other similar phenomena (Champeta in Cartagena de Indias, Tecnobrega in Belém do Pará, or the Nigerian film industry or Nollywood), it was nurtured and sustained by very small enterprise capital (most often informal) and (non-Internet) social networks. As Alfaro explains, music production is conducted by "family economic units with very little division of labor, driven by people involved in the music industry or who decided to get into that business on account of the low cost of digital equipment and the widespread ownership of DVD players in Peruvian homes, after having cut their teeth taping *quinceañera* parties, baptisms and other private events. Many of these businesses are located in the Mesa Redonda shopping center in Lima; there are other similar shopping centers in various regions of Peru. The masters are handed over to pirate copiers who circulate them via street vendors on every corner of the more populous areas of the country" (Alfaro, pers. comm. November 12, 2009).

As huayno pop and other huayno hybrids gained popularity, they made inroads into radio and even television. Revenues are earned both by the sale of CDs and DVDs (sold by street vendors) and at concerts either held regularly in designated dance halls or in makeshift places, such as parking lots, football fields, empty lots, markets, recreational centers, and after-hours industrial spaces (Alfaro 2009, 74). These concerts are the main source of income. Musicians get a percentage of the tickets and beer sold. As Alfaro states: "Our *Billboard* [(i.e., economic measurement] is based on entrance charges and amount of beer consumed" (Alfaro 2009, 76).[7] In contrast to the increasingly concentrated concert industry in the United States, Europe, and mainstream spaces throughout the world, the structure of the concert industry in Peru is decentralized, with numerous promoters, as well as radio and TV stations, and newspapers that use concerts as an alternative income stream (Alfaro 2009, 77).

Some of the huayno pop stars become so popular that radio programs and even television stations seek them out. This is the case of Dina Páucar, the "'beautiful goddess of love,' [who was] venerated massively much before being filmed in a highly successful TV mini-series" (Alfaro 2009, 7). Páucar's and other huayno pop stars' popularity has to do with their embodiment of their audiences phenotypes, ethnicity, and class belonging, something which had been relatively absent in the mainstream media in a society in which white elites treat the indigenous and mixed-race populations with condescendence, if not disdain.

As in other examples that I will mention below, huayno pop and associated media may be alternative to mainstream media but they are not outside the domain of capitalism, at least at the level of micro and small enterprises. They require capital, technology, and in some cases the Internet and the media. Small concerts need to attract at least a thousand people. An entrepreneur will invest about 10,000 soles (US$ 3,500) to rent sound and light equipment, buy flyers and radio publicity, pay the singer(s), hire an announcer and security guards, pay for municipal permissions, taxes on ticket and beer sales, and rights to APDAYC, the Peruvian music rights collection society. Ticket and beer sales will earn the entrepreneur between 3,000 (US$ 1,000) and 5,000 soles (US$ 1,750).

The popularity of the musicians helps sell CDs and DVDs, which operate totally outside of the copyright regime. While there is rampant piracy of foreign music and film—the piracy rate is 98 percent and almost all music stores and large film rental outlets like Blockbusters have gone out of business—the reproduction and distribution of Andean music CDs and videos is not illegal because producers negotiate directly with copiers (who also happen to be pirates) to engage in legitimate business. Musicians make very little from CDs—the prices are very low, about $0.65 to $1.00, because the producer, copier, and vendor get almost all of the profit—but they function more as promotion for where the artists make their earnings: concerts.

Tecnobrega Music and the Overmundo Initiative, Brazil

In modernity, emerging youth cultures often develop cultural clashes around music, such as those between zoot suiters and big band fans in the 1940s and 1950s, rockers and folk music lovers in the 1960s, punks and disco infernoists in the 1970s, *salseros* and *nueva trova* fans also in the 1970s, and *salseros* and *mergenueros* in the 1980s. The clash between "purists" and the down-'n-dirty iconoclasts of the hood is also played out in tecnobrega music from Belém do Pará in northern Brazil. Tecnobrega is the techno version of what came to be considered "tacky rock"—derived from early rockers like Roberto Carlos who became soupy crooners—mixed with indigenous and afro rhythms. As anthropologist and music TV producer Hermano Vianna tells it, tecnobrega musicians who once used vinyl records to mix their songs, have now migrated to MP3 technology. "In this sense they are completely different from Brazilian middle-class DJs of electronic music who organize themselves in pro-vinyl movements that attempt to maintain the analogue tradition of night clubs. The sound-systems musicians do not hesitate to throw away the old equipment. They want to be recognized as pioneers, as the first ones to adopt innovations. The audience valorizes this attitude" (Vianna 2003). Like Peruvian huayno pop and other genres of parallel music, tecnobrega consists of computers, mixers, electronic keyboards, microphones, and walls of dozens and even hundreds of speakers. DJs rip tracks from MP3s downloaded from the Internet, mix in the lyrics and instrumentation characteristic of tecnobrega. They perform their innovations at sites similar to those of huayno pop (from dance halls to parking lots and markets) competing with other sound systems. CDs (usually collections of a sound system's hits in MP3) are mainly promotional accessories, although they are also part, albeit minimal, of the production chain.

In contrast to the traditional music industry, the final product is not a recording. It is the dance, where fans dance and groove to the creativity of the producers and DJs who remix inventive, hip-gyrating sounds that attract the audience. Although copyright is totally absent from tecno-brega, there is a system of payment for creativity: the more inventive the songs, the more DJs and producers derive their income from sound systems that play them. The power and the profits are spread out among a range of actors in a decentralized production chain: musician, producer, go-between, home industry of CDs, distributors, street vendors, radio programs, owners of sound systems, DJs.[8]

Vianna was inspired by this model of music production and dissemination to invent Overmundo, a new platform for circulating music and other forms of culture. In 2000, he traveled over 80,000 kilometers to 82 cities to map the various musics of Brazil for a documentary video for MTV Brasil and a book and 4 CD boxed set titled *Projeto Música do Brasil* (Vianna 2000). The MTV program and the set of CDs were but the tip of the iceberg of an enormous amount of music that he had never heard in the Rio-São Paulo axis, where the media production and administrative offices are concentrated, and which disseminate what Brazilians get to see and hear in a country the size of the United States. In association with open source technicians, alternative intellectual property lawyers, and cultural activists, Overmundo makes it possible for anyone in any state and municipality of Brazil to upload their music, or their literature, art, film, and video, in networks that can be appropriated in keeping with the particular preferences of the musicians, thus making what is available on Overmundo amenable to the kind of remixing characteristic of tecnobrega and other open business models. Launched in March 2006, Overmundo used and made available to users a range of open source web 2.0 tools for social networking. It has over a million visitors and 1.7 million page views per month, and 46,000 active users who upload content, as well as representatives in each state of the country who interact with users. Its financing comes from the Ministry of Culture and a matching grant from Petrobras, the Brazilian oil company, which is one of the major funders of culture in the country. As web 2.0 platforms like Facebook and YouTube became ever more popular, Overmundo created its own research institute in open business models of all kinds, including tecnobrega, funk, cumbia villera, champeta, and other musics, as well as providing open business services (see Lemos and Castro et al. 2008).

Culture and Integración Program (C&I), Central America

The Central American Culture and Integration program (C&I) created a platform for bringing into contact all the cultural producers from the seven nations of the Isthmus (Belize, Guatemala, El Salvador, Honduras,

Nicaragua, Costa Rica, and Panama) to map, make visible, and facilitate cultural work so that it may be visible to regional venues and institutions, and thus better disseminate that work. In a previous incarnation the program was an ancillary Internet tool to bring together the dispersed and heterogeneous Central American cultural sector for a regional integration campaign funded by the European Union. The portal Mucho Gusto Centroamérica—a directory of cultural directories—was part of a publicity campaign of series of spots and communicational material to "create conditions of identification among Central Americans that would facilitate social, economic, and cultural integration in the Isthmus." The campaign included spots and printed material featuring noted figures, including musicians and other cultural producers from neighboring countries, as well as a promotional CD for the tourism sector, a concert of musicians from all the countries of the Isthmus, and airtime on radio and cable TV. This experience showed the financial and strategic challenges that institutions face when they attempt to promote local contents: investment in media exposure is expensive and difficult to get and activism does not compensate for it: structural issues need to be addressed.

As a follow-up strategy, C&I developed as a more civil society-oriented proposal with the support of Spanish Agency for International Cooperation and Development (AECID), seeking to make visible and assist projects of cultural actors and networks in the region. The project brought together cultural producers to gather information and strategize while new interconnections are developed in order to explore all aspects of the cultural value chain, including consumption, in order to have a greater impact in dissemination and markets. One of the main sectors addressed by C&I have been music starting with an already existing network: the Network of Independent Central American Record Labels.

The Central American mainstream music industry is captive to the media and entertainment conglomerates from the United States and Mexico, which leave virtually no space for local production. But Central America is teeming with diverse musics and numerous musicians whose existence is mostly ignored in the rest of Latin America. Yet, despite the absence of these musicians on the airwaves, local fans flock to their concerts and sing along to their songs, a phenomenon that requires research to figure out how this takes place, the institutional and market infrastructure not being very visible.

Music research companies do not do a very good job of measuring consumption in countries with low sales and a high level of informality, such as those of Central America. According to the industry association IFPI, recorded music sales were a mere $20.8 million for all Central American countries, about $0.50 per capita for the region's 43 million inhabitants; of that digital sales totaled $6.3 million. The big surprise is that half of all ring back tone sales in Latin America came from Central America, despite the weak economies of these countries (Cobo 2009). But to analyze such a partial set of statistics is to ignore the many other ways in which Central Americans consume music: at concerts, in dance clubs, in pubic spaces, at numerous festivals, and on radio. Moreover, as the C&I conceptual frame and strategy shows, actors working with or representing social interests related to youth, rural people, and other people are less likely to be taken into consideration by IFPI, PWC, or Billboard. Yet they need to be taken into consideration in order to understand the sustainability of music in the region and to have a better sense of how music and cultural production and consumption work in the region, from local expressions and festivals (which are now part of the tourist attractions) to the more formal and urban stage scene. C&I understands that there is a relation of codependence with other sectors (tourism, art-in-action with youth at risk, environmentalism, etc.) and that this is what helps ensure the cultural rights of Central American citizens to enjoy, recreate, and empower themselves through a stronger connection and access to their cultural heritage and expressions while providing opportunities to get work into the public and to gain income from it. C&I's goal is that the market should reflect regional cultural values, awareness, and self-esteem.

Among other important tasks such as gathering data on the region's cultural agents, C&I has also been working with record labels from Belize, Honduras, Nicaragua, and Costa Rica that comprise the Central American Network of Independent Record Labels. C&I is helping to establish new connections in support of a long-standing aspiration: a Central American conglomerate and branding platform that will present the region as a player on a Latin American and international scope.[9]

The first step was to support the Central American Independent Record Label Network in their first regional appearance in a world-class event (WOMEX). For that purpose, the Network produced the *Central American Music Box*, with tracks from four labels: Stonetree Records (Belize),[10] Costa Norte Records (Honduras),[11] Moka Discos (Nicaragua),[12] and Papaya Music (Costa Rica).[13] Its first incarnation was a demo for international promotion; it subsequently became the first collaborative commercial production. Given the small size of each country's market, the labels are working together in the Isthmus and networking in world music circuits and seeking funding for a long-term strategy. The goal is to expand the number of venues and opportunities for their artists.[14]

The network of labels is working to promote Central American music among Central Americans in the Isthmus and in the diaspora, among tourists, and world music fans, especially in Europe, where there are greater sources of revenue. The strategy reveals that local musics in small countries with low GDP must: (1) develop new forms of promotion, (2) work the social networks just like the majors are increasingly doing, (3) generate new income streams, including with neighboring sectors, such as working with youth, tourism, or environmentalism, (4) provide services such as composing music for the public and private sectors, (5) lobby governments to require and enforce Central American music quotas, just as is now the case in Argentina and Uruguay. Proof that Central American musicians have a significant public are the packed concerts wherever musicians like Guillermo Anderson (Costa Norte Records, Honduras), Perro Zompopo (Papaya Music, Nicaragua), or the rock fusion group Malpaís (Papaya Music, Costa Rica) perform. These and other musicians played at the first Central American Music Market fair in San José, Costa Rica in March 2012,[15] organized by the label network, C&I, and the Ministry of Culture, through the International Festival of the Arts. The event brought together music professionals like Gerald Seligman (president of Caravana Arts Consultancy and former director of WOMEX), Octavio Arbeláez (director of the art market CIRCULART and a founding member of ADIMI—Association of the Development of the Music Industry), Alvaro Abitia (academic director of the International Music Fair, Guadalajara, the Universidad Libre de Música and creator of the most important independent music publishing company in Mexico—Bonsai Publishing), as well as music programmers from North and Latin America and Europe.

A number of very interesting alternative business models were discussed, including Autómata Records downloading service, which is competitively priced with pirate sales: for $2.00 you can download an album. You buy a card, available at concerts and many stores and sites and on the Internet, and you enter a code on the website: www.automatarecords.com.

Figure 1.2   Central American Music Market

Source: Images provided by Papaya Music / Simbiosis de Centroamérica, SA.

Fora do Eixo (FDE), Brazil

Fora do Eixo Circuit ("Outside the Circuit") is a network of small initiatives in peripheral areas of Brazil, that is, beyond the Rio-São Paolo corridor where the central offices of the media and culture industries are located. It has become one of the most controversial and innovative initiatives that uses the Web 2.0 as a space for collaborative work. The precursor to the Circuit is the Cubo Mágico, a collective of communications students from the two major universities in Cuiabá, a small city in the central-west Brazilian state of Matto Grosso. In 2001, they created a video and events production company and later took over the organization of the first rock festival, Calango, in the city, whose mission was to give visibility to local bands. Given the lack of access to recording studios, rehearsal spaces, and other resources necessary to bring off the festival successfully, they regrouped, studied successful festivals in other peripheral cities, and brought in a consultant to who helped them plan subsequent events. Rebaptized Espaço Cubo, they established a rehearsal space and organized a series of yearly events with local bands, putting to work their research into all aspects of event organization and management. The Internet and open source applications in administration, accounting, communication, and other functions were also crucial to their success. Each year the number of bands increased as did the audience.

Given the lack of funding, group members began to exchange services among each other and with providers of space, sound engineering, equipment rental, video, design, publicity, and so on, and soon were able to include other business such as restaurants in their solidarity economy. As they earned income from their concerts and from the provision of other services, the solidarity economy expanded and incorporated more businesses such as hotels, English language schools, stationery shops, communications agencies, producers, stores, a range of different performance venues, and so on. Where there were no resources before, and no place in the regular economy, the exchanges of the group oriented to producing music on a professional level, generated economic value that could operate alongside the regular Brazilian currency. In time, the group created their own alternative currency—the Cubo—for the services exchanged and that would be accepted in all of the above enterprises. Moreover, as the solidarity economy spread to other groups in other cities, they formed a network with its own bank with collateral for convertibility of the Cubo and eventually created a Cubo Card.[16]

This solidarity economy required administration, accounting, and other management activities that were provided through exchanges and were professionalized. From this activity, they developed a methodology and shared it with groups in other cities and, by 2005, created the network Circuito Fora do Eixo (FDE) with three other collectives from Rio Branco (in the Amazonian extreme west state of Acre), Uberlândia (a secondary city in the south-central state of Minas Gerais), and Londrina (in the southern state of Paraná). The main activity of the network is to work synergistically to foment the creation of bands and festivals, and to exchange new production and administration technologies. Today FDE has more than 100 nodes in all 27 Brazilian states and has even attracted affiliates from Argentina, Bolivia, Central America, and Uruguay. Collaboratively, FDE circulates over 2000 bands and they organize more than a thousand events and initiatives per year. Hundreds of people work with FDE to ensure the sustainability of this alternative production and management enterprise. Initially, all of their activities and accounts, including those having to do with their finances, were archived on the Internet to guarantee transparency, using open source software.[17] This is becoming more difficult as they expand and as they are criticized for their handling of public funds (see below). They also hold weekly and sometimes daily meetings from numerous nodes via Skype and similar communications technologies. At their last assembly in December 2011, 1400 FDE delegates attended, along with another 600 invitees.

FDE has moved beyond music to organize dance, design, film, and performing and visual arts. It was also instrumental in organizing the Occupy Wall Street–like Marcha da Liberdade (Freedom March in 2011), and the Partido da Cultura (Culture Party), which does not promote its own candidates but lobbies politicians to support open access and other progressive policies for culture.[18] Together with many other dissatisfied music and cultural activists, FDE has opposed the reversals of the current Minister of Culture, Ana de Holanda, in particular her espousal of traditional copyright law and accommodation to US sponsored laws, such as ACTA and SOPA.[19] The Universidade Fora do Eixo, which researches the kinds of activities—social technologies, solidarity economy, new distribution initiatives, and so on—that the network has developed in order to better organize, systematize, and disseminate them.[20] The FDE leadership calls these initiatives simulacra, meaning by that parallel institutions (bank, party, university); through these they seek to gain influence and thus expand.

FDE is not without controversy.[21] Capilé and other leaders hold on firmly to their use of resources to expand the capacity of the network to create events and initiatives, all of them founded on open source principles and a solidarity economy. Some musicians feel shortchanged because FDE does not pay for performances at festivals, although the Circuit has increasingly been able to get millions of dollars in government and paragovernmental funds. Capilé explains that that the main purpose of the festivals is to showcase bands and to create publics. He adds that the funds that FDE uses are invested in infrastructure to make those functions possible. But FDE is criticized because large portions of those funds are used to support the central nucleus of the network. Also controversial is the use of Creative Commons licenses that allow works to be appropriated, again following the principle of openness and also of the principle that creativity is in part the reworking of materials. Since the main business of FDE is concerts, and the sale of CDs is dwindling anyway, FDE is betting on the use of music made available for free on the Internet as promotional tools.[22] More recently, FDE ran into difficulties with partners in Central America when the time came to formalize a series of joint initiatives: FDE sought to subsume these initiatives under its own brand although the local networking process and events had already been organized by locals throughout the region for years and the joint events in the region were organized equally by both partners and obviously made possible by the Central Americans. This maneuver is a symptom of its penchant to continually expand not only throughout Brazil, but also throughout Latin America. Similar criticisms have been raised in connection with ABRAFIN—the Brazilian Association of Independent Festivals—in which FDE has played a protagonist role, and with the vibrant digital culture movement, whose projects have been promoted by FDE as their own. The point, however, is neither to demonize nor romanticize these movements as the incarnation of a Negrian-Virnian multitude but to understand that they operate in a field of force in which power-plays cannot always be obviated, that there isn't sufficient funding for all initiatives, and that the rhetoric of egalitarian collaboration is a utopian horizon to be aspired to. Consumption is best understood as operating in a complex and contradictory field of force that includes all of these considerations.

Conclusion

The diverse cases of alternative business models that I have reviewed all show that it is possible to think outside the box that research on the music and culture industries constructed, both in the business world of record labels and in academia. Sales figures, numbers of subscribers, and website hits are important elements in understanding production, distribution, and consumption, but they are not the only or even the principal factors. Social organization—evident in these four case studies and many other examples that I do not have the space to examine—is one of the most important factors in a music experience more integrated in social life. Music has always been a social experience, and new interactive technologies enhance these social aspects of the music experience. Rose Marie

Santini's analysis of Last.fm, one of the world's largest music websites, is instructive in understanding the potential value of such technologies; far from resulting in isolated consumer niches, Santini's work indicates that music websites and Internet radio stations promote knowledge of various musics through interaction with others whose preferences we encounter in social networks. Santini writes: "the repertoires transmitted via the traditional communications media represent the catalogues of products offered and imposed by the culture industries—which control the principal channels of mass diffusion and distribution—and conceal information on the tastes of different individuals and groups" (Santini 2010, 304). Moreover, collections of music on Internet sites also do not faithfully reflect user's tastes, as witnessed by a high number of songs never accessed by users; only 2 percent of music heard on sites is ever purchased (Santini 2010, 305). Factoring in these provisos, Santini analyzed the playlists of Last.fm users and data on the number of times that they listen to songs—which include all music on their computers or that they link via MP3 players and iPods—and was able to get a more accurate picture of what users listen to. The results raise more questions than they answer; the website claims 56 million users, but 16 million artists, suggesting that one in four users is also an artist.

Clearly, the music industry, and especially its methods of measuring what is consumed, do not jibe with this more varied experience of consuming music in contemporary Latin America. Information on the production, circulation, distribution, and consumption of music and other culture industries cannot be left in the hands of industry alone, or even in the hands of academics accustomed to protocols of objectivity that are belied by the very arrangement of the object they study. There should be public policy entities, working together with initiatives like Overmundo, C&I, Circuito Fora do Eixo, all of which have their own research initiatives. It is often said that in the Internet age producers and consumers can dispense with intermediaries. That is a tall order, or rather a tall fiction. As we have just seen, platforms like Google or Last.fm that presumably dispense with intermediaries in fact are just another generation of intermediaries. One never gets rid of them. That is the reason why the alternative initiatives I reviewed have entered the field of intermediation, on behalf of specific interests (those of huayno pop, tecnobrega, cumbia villera artists, and producers) and on behalf of those "open source" and "open end" intermediaries like Overmundo and C&I that seek to open public space to whomever would like to occupy it.

The upshot: consumption cannot be discussed without examining every aspect of the production chain and the relations of power that hold in the context in which it operates. Then, hopefully, we will be on firmer ground in understanding how our choices are constructed.

Notes

1. I use the word "participation" with caution since many recent commercial strategies to increase revenues, particularly by entertainment and media enterprises, involve technologies whereby users are presented with cultural products and services to access and/or purchase based on the preferences they exhibit by their activities on the web (Santini, 2010). In other words, "participation" is monitored, channeled, and harnessed to increase profitability such that the scope of agency—active engagement in decision-making oriented to governance—implicit in the term is diminished.

2. Blogs, social networking sites, discussion boards, music sites, e-zines, experience or photo sharing sites, customer review sites, citizen journalism, fanfiction, and so on, are examples of venues for user-generated content, which according to International Data Corporation, an information and technology research and analysis firm, account for 70 percent of all content on the Internet (Cooper, 2007).

3. "Popular classes" is the Latin American term for a range of class fractions from the urban working classes, peasants, informal workers, the unemployed, and ethnic groups (indigenous peoples, Afrodescendants), which overlap with these class fractions.

4. This table was published in Yúdice, 2012b.

5. The analysis of these 4 cases studies draws in part on work published in Yúdice, 2012a.

6. The best known huayno is "El condor pasa," largely because it was recorded by Simon and Garfunkel in 1967 and became an international hit. Many versions were made since then, some of them anticipating the instrumentation used by Simon and Garfunkel, such as the version by Los Incas in 1963.

7. The amount of beer consumed is also used in many economic impacts of culture studies as a surrogate indicator of revenues earned in live music venues in some Latin American countries where the data are not available.

8. The segment "About tecnobrega" excerpted from the documentary on copyright *Good Copy, Bad Copy*, gives an excellent explanation of the phenomenon. http://www.youtube.com/watch?v=xo2sv3jjJi8. Accessed on 8/3/10.

9. A first meeting of regional labels was held in 2006 for that purpose.

10. www.stonetreerecords.com

11. www.costanorterecords.com

12. www.mokadiscos.com

13. www.papayamusic.com

14. Stonetree Records' efforts in this regard have been exemplary. In 2007, musician Andy Palacio won the Womex award for best world music album. He was the best-known musician of the Garifuna people, a mixture of Africans and Caribbean Indians, whom the British resettled in 1797 from Saint Vincent in the extreme southeast of the Caribbean, to the extreme west off the coast of Honduras, form where they traveled north to Guatemala and Belize and south to Nicaragua. Unfortunately, Palacio died soon after receiving the award and was not able to leverage the exposure that it gave him. See

"'Watina': A Look Behind the Music of Andy Palacio" at http://www.youtube.
com/watch?v=nt6oOzyG9ec. Accessed on April 22, 2012.
15. http://centralamericanmusicbox.com/blog/2011/10/23/central-american-
music-market-2012/
16. See http://picasaweb.google.com/cubocard/CuboCard02# for an explanation
of the development of the Cubo Card. Accessed on April 22, 2012. Other collectives that form part of CFE have also created their currencies and cards.
For an account of the Fora do Eixo Card, see Poljokan, et al. More recently
it is becoming increasingly evident that it is not the alternative currency but
government, paragovernmental funding (e.g., the state petroleum conglomerate Petrobrás), and private foundations (e.g., that of the second largest mining company in the world Vale do Rio Doce) that is increasingly enabling
FDE to conduct its work.
17. See https://spreadsheets.google.com/spreadsheet/pub?key=0AnYs0B2jKJs-d
GpzVkxRMXU4Z0NieVdTUG5mWWlqc0E&gid=21
18. http://partidodacultura.blogspot.com/
19. http://foraanadehollanda.blogspot.com/2011/03/se-ana-de-holanda-quer-
guerra-por-que.html
20. See http://foradoeixo.org.br/profile/universidade Accessed on April 22,
2012.
21. I would like to thank Alvaro Santi for bringing to my attention this set of
critiques of CFE.
22. For an in-depth set of critiques of CFE, see Argüelles, 2012.

References

Alfaro Rotondo, Santiago. 2009. "Economía y cultura de la música andina en Lima
Metropolitana." Licenciature Thesis. Pontificia Universidad Católica del Perú.
Facultad de Ciencias Sociales. Sociología.
Alfaro, Santiago. 2010. "La nueva economía de las industrias culturales: Escenario
para la integración andina." Paper presented at the Conversatorio "Liberando
la creatividad: Nuevas visiones sobre los derechos de autor en la era digital."
Sala Roja del Centro Cultural de la Pontifica Universidad Católica del Perú,
Lima, February 25.
Anderson, Chris. 2006. *The Long Tail: Why the Future of Business is Selling Less
of More*. New York: Hyperion.
Argüelles, Régis. 2012. "O pós-rancor e o velho Estado: uma crítica amorosa à
política do. Fora do Eixo." Passa Palavra, February 2. http://passapalavra.
info/?p=51886. Accessed on April 22, 2012.
Cobo, Leila. 2009. "Glimmer of Light: Surging Ringback Sales in Central America
Point to Mobile Opportunities." *Billboard* August 1. http://www.billboard.biz/
bbbiz/others/glimmer-of-light-1004076959.story. Accessed on April 22, 2012.
Cooper, Lucy. 2007. "Will the Growth in User Generated Content Swamp Our
Ability to Monitor It?" Econsultancy March 15. http://econsultancy.com/

forums/other-topics/will-the-growth-in-user-generated-content-swamp-our-ability-to-monitor-it?page=1. Accessed on April 22, 2012.

Lemos, Ronaldo, Oona Castro et al. 2008. *Tecnobrega: O Pará reinventando o negócio da música*. Rio de Janeiro: Aeroplano. Available for download at: http://overmundo.com.br/banco/ pesquisa-o-tecnobrega-de-belem-do-para-e-os-modelos-de-negocio-abertos. The English-language translation is available for download at: https://www.google.com/url?sa=t&rct=j&q=&esrc=s&sour ce=web&cd=1&ved=0CFEQFjAA&url=http%3A%2F%2Fwww.overmundo. com.br%2Fdownload_banco%2Fthe-tecnobrega-business-model-arising-from-belem-do-para&ei=TIuUT8eaM8X56QGh16i-BA&usg=AFQjCNF QqnVNh0WUvb38uON6qKgk9XxUfg&sig2=A1d3qHjJb_JbElc-T46lRw. Accessed on April 22, 2012.

Santini, Rose Marie. 2010. "Os Usuários e a Desorganização da Cultura: Os Sistemas de Recomendação e as conseqüências da classificação para os usos sociais da música na Internet." PhD Dissertation Universidade Federal Fluminense, January.

Vianna, Hermano. 2000. *Música do Brasil*. São Paulo: Abril Entretenimento. And CD-22316.

Vianna, Hermano. 2003. "A música paralela: Tecnobrega consolida uma nova cadeia produtiva, amparada em bailes de periferia, produção de CD piratas e divulgação feita por camelôs", *Folha de S. Paulo*, 13 de octubre. http://www. overmundo.com.br/banco/a-musica-paralela. Accessed on April 22, 2012.

Wikofsky Gruen Associates. 2010. *Global Entertainment and Media Outlook, 2010–2014: Industry Overview*. PriceWaterhouseCoopers. https://www. materialogic.com/webapps/ CUSTOM/ORDERSITES/bin/OrderSites/pwc_ gemo_emedia?action=downloadItems&branch_no=OUT0091112&userNam e=null&refSiteId=pwc_gemo_emedia. Accessed on April 22, 2012.

Yúdice, George. 2012a. "La innovación en la acción cultural." In *La cultura en tiempos de desarrollo: violencias, contradicciones y alternativas*. Edited by Nuria Girona Fibla, Anejo n° 78 of *Revista Quaderns de Filologia*. Valencia: Universidad de Valencia.

Yúdice, George. 2012b. "Table of Types of Music." Miami Observatory on Communication and Creative Industries. http://www.miamiobservatory.org/ en/music/creative-industries/music/table-of-types-of-music. Accessed on May 12, 2012.

2

The Advertising Industry in Latin America: A Contemporary Overview

John Sinclair[1]

To say that advertising has a crucial role in the making of consumer culture is to state the obvious, yet the actual working of advertising as an industry is not widely understood. Although advertising as a cultural institution is certainly a metonym for the pervasive commercialization of social life being experienced across the world in the era of triumphant capitalist modernity, this chapter will show that as an industry, advertising needs to be conceived of more as an intricate and contingent set of relations between advertisers and the media, with advertising agencies as key intermediaries.

Like so many of their biggest clients, the advertising agency business is itself highly globalized in its organization, and a force for globalization in national media and consumer markets. Since advertising is an industry at the service of advertisers, whether global or local, the constant quest by advertising agencies to reach and cultivate markets for their clients has a profound effect upon the development of the media, and hence also on popular culture and social communication. Accordingly, research into the workings of the advertising industry can expose the grounds on which various dialectics intersect: global and local, production and consumption, economy and culture. The set of institutional relations that form the advertising industry can be thought of as forming a "manufacturing-marketing-media complex" (Sinclair 2012). Yet, not all advertisers are manufacturers. Traditional critiques of the advertising industry have tended to focus on the global manufacturers of branded products, ranging from automobiles to everyday packaged goods, or FMCG ("fast moving consumer goods"). However, significant global and also "local" (national or regional) advertisers increasingly come from consumer-oriented service sectors such as retailing, telecommunications, and banking. The complex includes "marketing" rather than advertising per se, because advertising is just one aspect of what the industry likes to call "integrated marketing communications," encompassing all kinds of sales promotion as well as media advertising, though our interest here is in the impact of globalization upon the media in particular.

The research presented in this chapter outlines the recent state of play within the complex of advertiser, agency, and media interests in the biggest national markets of Latin America: Brazil, Mexico, and Argentina. It inquires into how far, and in what ways, the advertising industry has been globalized in each of these countries and assesses the impact of these interests upon the development of the media. The chapter presents detailed information on the largest advertising agencies in each nation, their local and global corporate connections, and their relative influence over the business. As for the advertisers, the largest ones in each country are identified, with particular attention paid to both the relative incidence of global, regional, and national corporations, and also to each one's field of service or production—FMCG, retail, or whatever. To assess their impact on social communication, some data on the distribution of advertising expenditure is also presented, taking special note of how well television is faring in the defense of its customary dominance against the challenge of online advertising. In these ways, the chapter provides a comparative empirical account and analysis of the mode in which the advertising industry, through its influence on the media, is an "agency" that binds the leading nations of Latin America into both economic and cultural globalization.

From Americanization to Globalization

Latin America began to experience the impact of the "manufacturing-marketing-media complex" between the world wars of the twentieth century. When General Motors was expanding its activities from the United States to key foreign markets in the 1920s, its advertising agency in the United States, J. Walter Thompson, was motivated to open up offices in Argentina, Brazil, and Uruguay. Similarly, McCann Erickson opened up offices in Latin America and elsewhere to serve its client Standard Oil, and also commenced a long association with Coca-Cola in the region. Other major US-based corporations that became clients for advertising services in new markets around this time include Ford, Gillette, Kraft,

Kellogg's, and Procter & Gamble. This initial period has been called the "imperial" phase in the internationalization of advertising. The second phase came with the intensification of corporate expansion after World War II, which prompted many governments to impose restrictions on foreign investment. For this and other reasons, American advertising agencies seeking access to foreign markets in the 1960s and 1970s tended to adopt a "nationalization" strategy: that is, entering into some kind of partnership arrangement with a local agency (Mattelart 1979, 252–259).

The globalization era began in the 1980s, when UK-, France-, and Japan-based agencies rose to challenge the hitherto US domination of the industry at a global level. The British agency Saatchi & Saatchi was pivotal. They foretold of a global future in which there would be fewer and fewer agencies serving fewer and fewer clients. However, this raised the thorny issue of "client conflicts." Advertisers will not accept a situation in which their advertising agency also holds a competing account. Saatchi & Saatchi managed this problem by creating separate agencies under the one corporate group structure, in which the different agencies in the group could take on competing brands but quarantine their marketing strategies from each other.

To raise the capital needed to acquire the additional agencies to build these group structures, however, Saatchi & Saatchi floated their company on the stock market, a notable break with the industry's tradition of private ownership (Goldman 1997). This was the beginning of true "globalization," in the sense that the national origin of these new international agency networks became less significant than their actual coordination at the completely new and truly global level of ownership and management which the group structure made possible, and that it was all sustained by stock market capital from indeterminate national origins. In 1987, another British firm, Wire and Plastic Products (WPP) entered the fray with an audacious takeover of the US-based international agency, J. Walter Thompson, and a year later, the revered Ogilvy & Mather.

Soon after, two French agencies, Publicis and Eurocom-Havas, also launched themselves as global groups, the former by taking over a US agency and the latter a UK one. Meanwhile, in the United States itself, Omnicom was formed, based on the US and international operations of BBDO Worldwide and DDB Needham. Omnicom's competitor in the United States was Interpublic, which had created itself as a global group in 1978, based on the McCann Erickson agency network. A little later, Dentsu of Japan, the largest single agency in the world throughout the 1970s, entered global arrangements with WPP and Publicis (Mattelart 1991).

The formation of the global groups, and their capitalization on stock markets internationally, was the definitive leap into globalization. It is

Table 2.1   The two-tiered structure of leading global groups and their major advertising agency networks

WPP (UK): JWT, Ogilvy & Mather, Young & Rubicam, Grey, *Group M*
Omnicom (US): BBDO, DDB, TBWA, *OMD*
Publicis (France): Saatchi & Saatchi, Leo Burnett, *Starcom, ZenithOptimedia*
Interpublic (US): McCann Erickson, DraftFCB, Lowe, *Universal McCann*
Dentsu (Japan): Dentsu, Dentsu Young & Rubicam (+ 15 per cent Publicis)
Aegis (UK): Media agencies only: *Carat, Aegis Media, Isobar, Synovate*
Havas (France): Euro RSCG, Arnold, *Havas Media, MPG*

Source: Agency Family Trees 2010.

important to understand that these "megagroups" are not in themselves global advertising agencies, but corporations or holding companies that are composed of global advertising agency networks. They are networks of networks, a higher tier of financing and management, which furthermore incorporate major international companies in related marketing communications "disciplines," such as public relations, direct marketing, and "digital" agencies for online advertising.

Another aspect of the contemporary global marketing communications industry's structure that should be mentioned is that there has been a specialization of functions within the practice of advertising itself, with the advent since the 1980s of "media-buying" agencies. These specialize in the original business function of advertising, which is the brokerage of space and time. In effect, they operate as wholesalers of pages in print media, and spots in broadcast media. This is a profitable business that has been spun off from the other traditional advertising function of preparing advertising content: advertisements. That job is done by "creative" agencies. Typically, the global advertising groups will include both media and creative agencies under their umbrella. Table 2.1 sets out the global groups in order of size, with the main international agency networks that belong to each. Media-buying agencies are included, shown in italics.

The Commercialization of the Media

Just as the expansion of US-based consumer goods manufacturing companies into Latin America attracted advertising agencies along with them, in the same way a demand was created for commercial media to carry their ads and generate markets. In the first instance, this meant radio, and so the foundations of a commercial broadcasting regime were laid in the main markets well before World War II. By the 1960s and 1970s, the crucial stage at which US-based corporations were in the process of transforming themselves into what were then called "transnational" (or "multinational," but not yet "global") corporations, television had arrived to offer these advertisers ever greater access to their markets in the making. Whereas most of Europe, Asia, and Africa had opted for some form of state-controlled television system, the US model of advertiser-supported, privately owned commercial broadcasting predominated in Latin America. Even where the television system was owned by the state, such as in Colombia at that stage, the commercial model became the norm.

The "sponsorship" system, which had characterized commercial radio in both the United States and Latin America, became transplanted to the new medium. In this system, instead of buying advertising time as "spots" within programs provided by the network, which is still predominantly the usual practice today, advertisers would actually provide the programs themselves, complete with advertising. This was a common function of advertising agencies over this period: to produce such programs for sponsors. Significantly, this was the system under which the *telenovela*, like the *radionovela* before it in the 1940s, flourished in countries like Brazil, thanks to sponsors such as Lever and their then in-house advertising agency, Lintas (Luis López 1998; Mattelart and Mattelart 1990).

However, more characteristically, the dominant networks in each national market have produced their own programming, thus integrating the production of programming with its distribution, a very profitable formula. Notably, TV Globo in Brazil, Televisa in Mexico, and Artear and Telefé in Argentina all have established and defended a strong position within their domestic markets, and in some of these cases, penetrated international markets with their production of commercially popular programs. These are predominantly *telenovelas*, the genre which is at once a true artifact of vernacular culture, and a commercial vehicle for advertising. Although the corporate advertisers and their agencies may be for the most part global, television is still the major advertising medium, and remains firmly in the hands of Latin American entrepreneurs and companies, but both groups of interests benefit by it being run as a "consumer delivery enterprise" (Bunce 1976, 106).

Major Markets of the Region

According to the most recent comparative data available from the advertising trade associations of Argentina and Chile as presented in Table 2.2, the major markets of the region are Brazil, Mexico, Argentina, Colombia, Venezuela, and Chile, in that order. Each of the first three markets, which

Table 2.2   Major advertising markets of Latin America, by estimates of key indicators, 2006

Country	Population (Millions)	GDP (Billions US$)	Total ad spend (US$)	Spend per capita (US$)
Brazil	186.8	784.5	7,244,276,000	38.8
Mexico	104.9	811.0	3,933,600,000	37.5
Argentina	39.1	187.0	1,748,870,000	44.7
Colombia	46.8	108.5	1,498,577,000	32.0
Venezuela	27.1	134.6	898,638,000	33.1
Chile	16.4	107.7	890,271,000	54.2

Source: ACHAP 2007b, 2007c; United Nations Statistics Division 2008.

attract 80 percent of the total advertising expenditure of the region, is examined below, having regard to the biggest advertisers and agencies, and the degree and mode of globalization evident in each case. First, however, it is worth noting that as a world region, Latin America attracts a comparatively small share of global advertising expenditure. In 2009, this was 6.9 percent, ahead of Eastern Europe at 6.2 percent and the Middle East at 4.2 percent, but well behind the Asia-Pacific's 23.4 percent (AAAP 2009b). Nevertheless, it has shown strong growth in relative terms. Indeed, Latin American advertising survived the global financial crisis of 2008–2009 and subsequently grew much more than that of any other world region (Johnson 2010).

Brazil

Brazil, in fact, is not only the largest national advertising market in the region, but also one of the world's ten largest (ZenithOptimedia 2008). As Table 2.3 shows, not one agency is 100 percent Brazilian. Each of the four biggest global groups has at least one agency amongst the top-ranked ten, either wholly owned or in Brazilian partnership. The mix of agencies on the list reveals the major phases of the internationalization of the industry in Latin America: as noted, J. Walter Thompson and McCann Erickson arrived early, in the "imperial" phase; AlmapBBDO and Giovanni FCB represent the era of the 1970s and 1980s when partnership arrangements became favored; while the global group ties of Neogama or Lew Lara clearly signify the present era of globalization. On the question of splitting or "unbundling" formerly "full-service" agencies into creative and media-buying specialisms, it is instructive to note that this has been

Table 2.3   The biggest ten advertising agencies in Brazil, as ranked by 2008 billings, expressed in Brazilian Reais, where 0.56 Reais = US$1

Agency	Billings	Global Affiliation
Y&R Brasil	R$2.9 bn	WPP
Grupo JWT	R$1.1 bn	WPP
AlmapBBDO	R$1.1 bn	Omnicom/Brazil
DM9DDB	R$814 m	Omnicom/Brazil
McCann Erickson	R$813 m	Interpublic
Africa	R$727 m	Omnicom/Brazil
Ogilvy e Mather	R$715 m	WPP
Grupo Giovanni FCB	R$679 m	Interpublic/Brazil
Neogama BBH	R$655 m	Publicis/Brazil
Lew Lara TBWA	R$601 m	Omnicom

Source: Adbrands 2010.

prevented from happening in Brazil by regulations designed to protect the television industry (which means especially TV Globo), from global groups gaining a monopoly over media buying (Ferriera Simões, Demartini Gomes, and Fernando Jambeiro, pers. comm.).

Brazilian researchers calculate that the top ten agencies bill around half the total media expenditure in the country (C. Ferriera Simões, N. Demartini Gomes, and O. Fernando Jambeiro, pers. comm.). In terms of how this expenditure is distributed across the various media, data cited by Brazil's Internet Advertising Bureau (2010) puts free-to-air television at over 63 percent. Unsurprisingly, the major beneficiary of this very large proportion of revenue going to television is TV Globo, while Globo's share of this revenue is estimated at 70 percent (Carugati 2007). Internet advertising has not made as many inroads in Brazil as it has in other major world markets, amounting to only 4.2 percent in 2010 (Internet Advertising Bureau, Brazil 2010).

Looking now at the advertisers, Table 2.4 shows Brazil's ten largest advertisers ranked by their 2008 expenditure, according to data from Ibope as published in *Advertising Age*. (In order to have a common basis for comparison, this same source is used for data on the largest advertisers in all three countries examined in this chapter). There are three Brazilian and seven foreign-owned advertisers, of which five are based in Europe, and two in the United States. The Brazilian advertisers are Casas Bahía, a retail chain; Bradesco, a major private bank; and the national savings bank, Caixa Econômico Federal. Of the foreign-based advertisers, Unilever has been either the second, or more often, the largest advertiser in Brazil at least since 1996, while Ford has been consistently in

Table 2.4   Ten largest advertisers in Brazil, ranked by expenditure, in millions of US$, 2008

Advertiser	Field	Ownership	Expenditure
Casas Bahía	Retail	Brazilian	605.0
Unilever	FMCG	Anglo-Dutch	363.8
Ambev	Beverages	Belgian	136.2
Ford	Auto	US	134.5
Fiat	Auto	Italian	133.0
Bradesco	Private bank	Brazilian	131.4
Caixa	State bank	Brazilian	127.0
Vivo	Telecoms	Spanish	105.4
Volkswagen	Auto	German	103.5
Colgate-Palmolive	FMCG	US	99.8

Source: Global Marketers 2009, 2009a.
Ranking and figures reprinted with permission from *Advertising Age,* "Global Marketers 2009," (2009). Copyrighted 2011 Crain Communications. 75587-nlpf.

the top ten since 1999 (Global Marketers Index 2009). Ambev was not formed until 1999, out of a merger of the Brazilian brands Antarctica and Brahma, and subsequently created as the region's division of Inbev, one of the world's biggest brewers. Vivo is a leading cell phone company, owned by Telefónica of Spain.

To sum up, Brazil's profile is that of a relatively diverse and sophisticated advertising market by regional standards. Brazilian companies maintain a presence both within the advertising agency business, even if with global partners, and amongst the leading advertisers. However, the high proportion of advertising revenue going to TV Globo suggests that the alleged benefits of globalization are being sequestered by a company which is still deeply entrenched as a beneficiary of the traditional mass commercial broadcasting paradigm (Sinclair 1999).

Mexico

Mexico established its broadcasting system on the American model in the early days of radio, and has attracted foreign advertisers and agencies since long before World War II (Sinclair 2012). Table 2.5 presents the ranking for 2010 of advertising agencies in Mexico, as calculated by the trade journal, *Merca 2.0* ("185 agencias de publicidad en México" 2010). Clearly, direct global ownership predominates, but there is one wholly owned Mexican agency, and four with ownership participation by Mexicans. Although these kinds of agencies tend to have rather more

Table 2.5 The biggest ten advertising agencies in Mexico, by rank in 2010

Agency	Global Group
McCann Worldgroup	Interpublic
Ogilvy Mexico	WPP
JWT México	WPP
Young & Rubicam	WPP
Vale Euro RSCG	Mexico/Havas
Terán/TBWA	Mexico/Omnicom
Olabuena Chemistri	Mexico/Publicis
Euro RSCG Beker	Mexico/Havas
Pauta Creativa	Mexico
Publicis México	Publicis

Source: "185 agencias de publicidad en México." *Merca* 2.0. 2010.

Mexican clients than some of the US-based agencies, most agencies on the list do have both global and national clients on their books (García Calderón, pers. comm.).

Mexico's list of largest advertisers is exceptional, in that the largest advertiser is also the media corporation which garners the most advertising revenue. Grupo Televisa is one of the biggest media conglomerates not only in Latin America, but also in the whole Spanish-speaking world. Like TV Globo in Brazil, it has interests across most major media divisions, with its greatest strength being in television, where it lords it over its only national competitor, the second largest advertiser shown here in Table 2.6, Televisión Azteca (Sinclair 1999). Azteca was launched to challenge Televisa in the early 1990s, and the subsequent competition in this television duopoly for audiences, and hence advertisers, has given stimulus to their own advertising expenditure (Gonzalez Amador 2006).

There are four other Mexican corporate advertisers in Table 2.6: Genomma Labs manufactures a host of pharmaceutical brands, while América Movil is the holding company of Mexican telecommunications mogul Carlos Slim. Orfeón is a significant producer and distributor of recorded music, in the top ten since 2006, while Bimbo, a Mexico-based international company, is a perennial major advertiser of its bread and other baked packaged goods.

The four US- and Europe-based advertisers on Table 2.6's list are outnumbered by the Mexican ones, but they are all involved in marketing on a major scale worldwide, some for decades. Procter & Gamble has headed *Advertising Age*'s annual list of the largest 100 global marketers

Table 2.6   Ten largest advertisers in Mexico, ranked by expenditure, in millions of US$, 2008

Advertiser	Field	Ownership	Expenditure
Grupo Televisa	Media	Mexican	459.2
Televisión Azteca	Media	Mexican	171.7
Procter & Gamble	FMCG	US	118.5
Genomma Lab	Pharmaceutical	Mexican	88.1
Unilever	FMCG	Anglo-Dutch	76.0
Bimbo	FMCG	Mexican	72.7
América Movil	Telecoms	Mexican	67.3
Nestlé	FMCG	Swiss	60.2
Colgate-Palmolive	FMCG	US	59.8
Orfeón	Media	Mexican	58.0

Source: Global Marketers 2009, 2009a.
Ranking and figures reprinted with permission from *Advertising Age*, "Global Marketers 2009," (2009). Copyrighted 2011 Crain Communications. 75587-nlpf.

since 2000. In 2009, Unilever was next, with Nestlé tenth, and Colgate-Palmolive, a company which has been in Mexico since the 1930s, at thirty-sixth rank. All of them market a host of brands farmed out in complex arrangements with various global agencies in different countries (Global Marketers 2009).

In terms of the distribution of advertising expenditure in media, an indicative figure from Ibope in Mexico puts free-to-air television's share at 60 percent (Mejía Guerrero 2006), a proportion similar to that of Brazil, and as in Brazil, the dominant network takes the lion's share. That same year Televisa took 71.2 percent of television advertising revenue, while Azteca got 28.2 percent (Gonzalez Amador 2006). Notwithstanding competition from recent growth in pay TV and continuingly rapid Internet growth, television viewing in Mexico continues to increase, with *telenovelas* remaining by far the most popular genre ("Ibope: Telenovelas, the Most Watched in Mexico" 2010). However, Internet advertising has not kept pace, standing at only 5 percent of advertising expenditure as of 2009 (Internet Advertising Bureau, Mexico 2009).

To sum up, Mexico is Latin America's second largest advertising and media market, characterized by some Mexican ownership still to be found amongst the largest advertising agencies, though with a strong presence of Mexican companies amongst the largest advertisers. Remarkably, the nation's dominant media conglomerate and its competitor are the largest two advertisers, yet at the same time, they are the beneficiaries of the globalization of advertising.

Argentina

From its heyday as a prosperous trading nation, Argentina became attractive to US-based advertising agencies: JWT arrived at General Motors' request in 1929, NW Ayer for Ford in 1931, and McCann Erickson for Standard Oil in the mid-1930s (MacLachlan 2006, 60–61). Today, all of the full-service or creative agencies linked to the global groups as listed in Table 2.1 are to be found in Argentina. Although official published ranking of agencies appears to have ceased in 2001, researchers in Argentina have provided the list given in Table 2.7.

As in Brazil and Mexico, agency networks linked to global groups dominate, with WPP being particularly strong. There is one fully owned agency, CraveroLanis, a successful creative agency, while Publicis Graffitti is majority owned by Publicis. As in Mexico, the advertising industry in Argentina has been challenged by the activities of media-buying agencies.

There is an obvious predominance of global firms based in the United States and Europe in Table 2.8, although there is one large Argentine company, as well as two regional companies. Topping the list is Danone Group, the Paris-based packaged foods company, which has its regional base in Argentina. Following are Procter & Gamble and Unilever, the world's two biggest global advertisers of FMCG brands, as mentioned, and SC Johnson, the US-based cleaning products marketer. Other large advertisers of note are the UK-based pharmaceutical conglomerate GlaxoSmithKline, and Mexico-based América Móvil. Also from

Table 2.7   The biggest ten advertising agencies in Argentina, by estimated rank in 2006, showing national and global ownership affiliations

Agency	Global Group	Association
Ogilvy & Mather	WPP	Fully global
Young & Rubicam	WPP	Fully global
JWT	WPP	Fully global
McCann Erickson	Interpublic	Fully global
BBDO	Omnicom	Fully global
Euro RSCG Worldwide	Havas	Fully global
CraveroLanis		Argentine
Draftfcb	Interpublic	Fully global
Publicis Graffiti	Publicis	Global/Argentine
Grey Worldwide	WPP	Fully global

Source: C. Aguerre, pers. comm.

Table 2.8 Ten largest advertisers in Argentina, ranked by expenditure, in millions of US$, 2008

Advertiser	Field	Ownership	Expenditure
Danone	FMCG	French	91.9
Unilever	FMCG	Anglo-Dutch	59.8
Procter & Gamble	FMCG	US	30.9
PepsiCo	FMCG	US	27.5
SC Johnson	FMCG	US	25.3
Cencosud	Retail	Chilean	22.7
Telecom Argentina	Telecoms	Argentine	22.2
América Movil	Telecoms	Mexican	19.8
Editorial AGEA	Media	Argentine	17.1
GlaxoSmithKline	Pharmaceutical	UK	15.3

Source: Global Marketers 2009, 2009a.
Ranking and figures reprinted with permission from *Advertising Age,* "Global Marketers 2009," (2009). Copyrighted 2011 Crain Communications. 75587-nlpf.

elsewhere in Latin America is Cencosud, a Chilean retailing corporation. Telecom Argentina, a major telecommunications provider, is majority-owned by Telecom Italia. AGEA is the newspaper publishing division of the country's foremost media conglomerate, Grupo Clarín

As with Mexico, global FMCG manufacturers figure largely in Argentina, but when it comes to the distribution of advertising expenditure across the media, Argentina has a quite distinct profile, in that the proportion of advertising expenditure going to print in Argentina is the highest among the three countries examined here, and indeed, in the region as a whole, while expenditure on television is the lowest. This said, print has a narrow lead: in 2009, free-to-air television took 33 percent of ad revenue, while print had 35 percent. The Internet, it should be noted, scarcely obtained 3 percent (AAAP 2009a).

Discussion

Saatchi & Saatchi's self-fulfilling prophecy of a global advertising industry in which fewer agencies serve fewer clients is clearly evident in the major markets of Latin America. Looking firstly at the agency side, the tables for each national market show massive dominance by agencies linked to the global groups, although Mexico and Argentina each can claim a fully nationally owned agency in the top ten. Because the global advertisers like to have the same agency handling the same brand in every country where it is marketed, this means that the globally linked agencies have a competitive advantage over national agencies in gaining and maintaining global clients. Such a practice, known as "global alignment," makes global alliances attractive to the national agencies, for without a global partner, they have less access to the largest accounts. For this reason, the successful local-global ventures gravitate toward the top of the agency lists.

On the advertisers' side, it must be conceded that while taking the top ten advertising clients in each country may be a concise, convenient, and comparative indicator, obviously it can be only a partial one. By definition, any top ten excludes many more large advertisers, both global and national, as well as a host of small advertisers, in each country. That said, it is interesting to note that the top ten lists do not manifest the degree of domination by US-based advertisers that would have been found in past decades, and which then attracted the condemnation of "cultural imperialism" critics. In each list, there is an equal or greater number of Europe-based advertisers as US ones, while in Mexico there is a majority of national advertisers in the top ten, and Argentina features two top advertisers from other countries in the region itself. These figures may be taken as evidence of the globalization, as distinct from the "Americanization," of Latin American economies.

In reference to the advertisers' fields of business, we find categories that tend to characterize the advertising markets of more developed world regions, such as retail, automotive, telecommunications, and media. Yet, the global FMCG conglomerates' influence should not be underestimated. Notably, half the advertisers in both the Mexican and the Argentine lists are in FMCG, a label which covers scores of product types and hundreds of brands: personal care products, household goods and cleaners, packaged food and drinks, patent medicines, and so on. Such goods can be and are heavily advertised and distributed widely, not just to the "middle class," but also to the masses, even where there is little purchasing power. Speaking globally and historically, FMCG companies have had a pronounced preference for television as their core advertising medium, and this is particularly true in countries with relatively low levels of literacy, as is still the case in most of Latin America. This tendency is particularly significant when it comes to assessing the influence of advertising on media development and a popular consumer culture in Latin America.

It has been noted that free-to-air television attracts around 60 percent of advertising expenditure in Brazil and Mexico, and 32 percent in Argentina, while the average for the region is 52.7 percent (ACHAP 2007a). Free-to-air television continues to be a true mass medium, while pay TV is an elite one: that is, access to television in Latin America corresponds to the sharp social stratification which still characterizes the region. In Mexico, pay TV is in a third of TV homes, and just over a quarter in Brazil

("Web reach rises in Latin America" 2010). As for the Internet, penetration varies considerably: from 64.4 percent in Argentina, to 37.8 percent in Brazil, and 27.2 percent in Mexico ("Internet Usage Statistics for the Americas" 2010). As seen in the data presented above, the share of advertising expenditure going to the Internet is small, around 3, 4, and 5 percent respectively, though future growth can be expected off this small base.

While there may indeed be an emergent "middle class" in Latin American countries, the rhetoric of neoliberal modernity conceals the huge gap still to be found between the elite minority's access to the ostensible benefits of globalized capitalism, and that of the vast mass of the people. Rather, Latin American dependency theory still seems to apply. In particular, Raquel Salinas and Leena Paldán's concept of "the internationalization of the internal market" provides a useful understanding of how advertising serves to create consumer markets on a national basis, and opens them up to the global marketers, while at the same time enabling certain national companies to benefit as they become taken up in the process. Furthermore, the analysis in this chapter of the cases of Globo and Televisa bears out the view that "the sector of the national bourgeoisie that owns the media is closely tied to the industrial bourgeoisie and constitutes a central link to metropolitan interests" (Salinas and Paldán 1979, 90). In brief, the corporate ecology of the region is one in which deep-rooted, nationally owned media oligopolies, often dynastic in character, continue to prosper from advertising revenue derived from the large global (though also major national and regional), companies that are given access to mass audiences through free-to-air television, the medium which is not only the most popularly accessible, but also the most pervasive in its cultural influence.

Note

1. This chapter is an output from a program of research under Discovery—Project, DP0556419, "Globalisation and the media in Australia," funded by the Australian Research Council 2005–2009. The author gratefully acknowledges the ARC's financial support. Thanks are also due to research correspondents in Latin America: Cassiano Ferriera Simões, Neusa Demartini Gomes, and Othon Fernando Jambeiro in Brazil; Carola García Calderón in Mexico; and Carolina Aguerre in Argentina.

References

"185 agencias de publicidad en México." (2010). *Merca 2.0*, July. Accessed February 8, 2012. www.merca20.com/este-mes-en-merca-julio-2010/

AAAP (Asociación Argentina de Agencias de Publicidad). 2009a. "Informe Oficial Argentina de Inversión Publicitaria 2009." Accessed November 25, 2011. http://190.220.150.93/webaaap/wp-content/inversion_publicitaria/2009/argentina/informe_inversion_publicitaria_2009.pdf.

AAAP (Asociación Argentina de Agencias de Publicidad). 2009b. "Informe Oficial Latinoamericano de Inversión Publicitaria 2009." Accessed November 25, 2011. http://190.220.150.93/webaaap/wp-content/inversion_publicitaria/2009/latam/informe_inversion_publicitaria_latinoamerica_2009.pdf.

AAM (Asociación de Agencias de Medios). 2010. "Agencias Afiliadas." Accessed September 8, 2010. www.aamedios.com/agen.htm

ACHAP (Asociación Chilena de Agencia de Publicidad). 2007a "Cuadro Comparativo de Inversión Publicitaria Latinoamérica 2006." Accessed November 25, 2011. http://www.achap.cl/estudios.php.

ACHAP (Asociación Chilena de Agencia de Publicidad). 2007b. "Informe Global de Inversión Publicitaria Año 2006." Accessed May 7, 2008. www.achap.cl/estudios_05.php.

ACHAP (Asociación Chilena de Agencia de Publicidad). 2007c. "Relación Entre Inversión Publicitaria/PBI." Accessed May 8, 2008. www.achap.cl/estudios_05.php

Adbrands. 2010. "Brazil's Leading Agencies in 2008." Accessed August 23, 2010. www.adbrands.net/br/index.html.

"Agency Family Trees 2010." *Advertising Age*, 2010. Accessed August 23, 2010. http://adage.com/agencyfamilytrees2010/.

Bunce, Richard. 1976. *Television in the Corporate Interest.* New York: Praeger.

Carugati, Anna. 2007. "Globo's Roberto Irineu Marinho." Accessed May 1, 2008. www.worldscreen.com/print.php?filename=irineu0107.htm.

"Global Marketers 2009." *Advertising Age,* 2009. Accessed September 2. http://adage.com/globalmarketers09/#10.

"Global Marketers Index." *Advertising Age,* 2009. Accessed September 3, 2010. http://adage.com/datacenter/article?article_id=106350.

Goldman, Kevin. 1997. *Conflicting Accounts: The Creation and Crash of the Saatchi & Saatchi Advertising Empire.* New York: Simon & Schuster.

Gonzalez Amador, Roberto. 2006. "Televisa y TV Azteca, aliadas para bloquear a nuevos competidores." *La Jornada*, December 13, 2006. http://www.jornada.unam.mx/2006/12/13/index.php?section=economia&article=028n1eco

"Ibope: Telenovelas, the Most Watched in Mexico." *TodoTVNews.* Accessed September 8, 2010. http://www.todotvnews.com/scripts/templates/estilo_nota.asp?nota=eng%2FTV+Abierta%2Fratings%2F2010%2F02_febrero%2F26_ibope_anuario_mexico_telenovelas_lo_mas_visto_2009

Internet Advertising Bureau, Brazil. 2010. "Participação dos Meios em Abr/2010." Accessed August 27, 2010. http://www.iabbrasil.org.br/arquivos/doc/Indicadores/Indicadores-de-Mercado-IAB-Brasil.pdf

Internet Advertising Bureau, Mexico. 2009. "Inversión Publicitaria Online 2009." Accessed September 10, 2010. http://www.iabmexico.com/

"Internet Usage Statistics for the Americas." 2010. Accessed September 10, 2010. http://www.internetworldstats.com/stats2.htm

Johnson, Bradley. 2010. "Top 100 Global Advertisers See World of Opportunity." *Advertising Age*, December 6, 2010. Accessed November 25, 2011. http://adage.com/article/global-news/top-100-global-advertisers-world-opportunity/147436/

Luis López, Oscar. 1998. *La Radio en Cuba*, 2nd corrected edn. La Habana, Cuba: Editorial Letras Cubanas.

MacLachlan, Colin M. 2006. *Argentina: What Went Wrong*. Westport, CT: Praeger Publishers.

Mattelart, Armand. 1991. *Advertising International: The Privatisation of Public Space*. Translated by Michael Chanan. London: Routledge.

Mattelart, Armand and Michele Mattelart. 1990. *The Carnival of Images: Brazilian Television Fiction*. New York: Bergin & Garvey.

Mejía Guerrero, Angelina. "Desplaza publicidad exterior a la radio." *El Universal*, November 17, 2006. www.eluniversal.com.mx/finanzas/vi_54876.html

Salinas, Raquel and Leena Paldán. 1979. "Culture in the Process of Dependent Development: Theoretical Perspectives." In *National Sovereignty and International Communication*. Edited by Kaarle Nordenstreng and Herbert I. Schiller, 82–98. Norwood, NJ: Ablex.

Sinclair, John. 1999. *Latin American Television: A Global View*. Oxford and New York: Oxford University Press.

Sinclair, John. 2012. *Advertising, the Media and Globalization*. Oxford and New York: Routlege.

United Nations Statistics Division. 2008. *Population, Latest Available Census and Estimates (2005–2006)*. New York: United Nations.

"Web reach rises in Latin America." *WARCNews*, December 10, 2010.

ZenithOptimedia. "Advertising Boom in Developing Ad Markets Compensates for Credit-Crunch Gloom in the West." Accessed May 7, 2010. www.zenithoptimedia.com/gff/pdf/Adspend%20forecasts%20March%202008.pdf

Part 2

Getting and Spending

3

From "Country of the Future" to Emergent Country: Popular Consumption in Brazil

Ruben George Oliven and Rosana Pinheiro-Machado

Popular consumption is currently at the heart of public debate in Brazil. It has been approached as a truly national phenomenon, directly related as it is with public policies for distributing income. In effect, the latter's most immediate outcome has been to increase the purchasing power of a substantial part of Brazilian society.

Despite the absence of a particular focus on consumption, Brazilian anthropology does have a significant tradition of research on the working and popular classes (Duarte 1986; Fonseca 2000; Sarti 1996). This scholarship has rejected scarcity, necessity, and the logic of survival as the main categories for explaining consumption in this population strata. It proposes, on the other hand, to approach it as a unique (albeit not isolated) analytical sphere in which holism, honor, and family solidarity figure as prominent aspects in one (or many) popular culture(s). The anthropology of consumption emerged as a disciplinary field from another scholarship tradition, which is different but shares some of the former's arguments. It calls attention to the symbolic dimension underlying the choice and use of objects, thus breaking away with the economic, neoclassic bias according to which need is the cardinal explanatory variable for demand (Douglas and Isherwood 1996 [1979], Sahlins 1978 [1976]).

Beyond academia, popular consumption has since long been the object of prejudice. Statements such as "The poor rather have a TV set than a plate of food at home" circulate in common sense as an accusation, an argument corroborating the supposed irrationality of popular consumption. In effect, this example makes evident the strong moral character underlying the logic of survival—or practical reason (Sahlins 1978)—which is reproduced in Brazilian elites' longstanding discourse about low-income groups. During the last decade, however, this picture began to change in Brazil. Public policies fostering income distribution spurred the economic emergence of the lower classes by increasing their purchasing power, thus favoring the growth of various economic sectors. Business professionals now acknowledge that they have for long ignored the taste of popular groups. Various surveys have tried to catch up with understanding the material aspirations nurtured by the so-called pyramid base (Data Popular 2010).

Drawing on this social context, this chapter discusses popular consumption based on ethnographic research carried out in the city of Porto Alegre, capital of Brazil's southernmost state, Rio Grande do Sul. Since 2005, we did participant observation in the living and working environments of people whose income ranges from 500 to 1,500 reais (about US$280 to 842). Our research was carried out in the poorest part of Morro da Cruz, a slum located in the Eastern periphery of Porto Alegre, in the Partenon neighborhood. It aggregates various small slums, known as *vilas* (villages). Moreover, we catalogued and analyzed news about the topic in the country's chief media outlets. Our main argument revolves around the importance attributed by our informants to buying products they consider to be expensive and of good quality, and what this means in terms of their reciprocity networks. But before plunging into the ethnographic analysis, a discussion about the recent socioeconomic context in Brazil is in order.

The Emergent Brazil

With almost two hundred million inhabitants and continental dimensions, Brazil has been traditionally portrayed as the "country of the future"—the title of a 1941 book by the Austrian writer exiled in Brazil, Stefan Zweig (Zweig 1960). Historically, Brazil has always lagged behind most countries in terms of income distribution. In 1989, its Gini index—which measures a country's degree of inequality in terms of family income (ranging from 0 to 1: the closer to 1, the higher the inequality)—was one of the world's highest, 0.634. That year, the 20 percent richest Brazilians concentrated 67.5 percent of all income, whereas the 20 percent poorest had only 21 percent (World Bank 2005). For a long while, the monthly minimum wage in Brazil remained below one hundred dollars. This caused the Brazilian economy to be directed toward a consumer group relatively small in number, but sufficiently large in absolute terms.

In 1994, the federal government launched the Real Plan, which introduced a new currency and succeeded in curbing inflation, thus eliminating the negative impact it had on the popular classes. In January 2003, Luis Inácio "Lula" da Silva, a founder of the Workers' Party, acceded to the Brazilian Presidency. The new administration benefited from the previously achieved economic stability and a favorable international scenario. One of the new government's actions was to distribute income by effectively raising the minimum wage, which amounts today to around US$300. Another was a series of social programs—among them the notorious "Bolsa Família" (a financial aid program that encourages poor families keep their children in school)—which awarded financial bonuses to low-income people. This led to a fast and steep decline in Brazil's income inequality, reflected in a reduction of the country's Gini coefficient to 0.566 in 2005 (Barros 2007).

These policies had a powerful impact on the economy. All of a sudden, a large portion of the so-called Class D (which, for marketing purposes, includes those with a monthly family income between 768 and 1,065 reais [or about US$431 to 598]) migrated to "Class C" (comprising families with a monthly income between 1,065 and 4,591 reais [or US$598 to 2,579]). It is estimated that, within six years, 20 million Brazilians migrated from Class D to Class C (Mioto 2010). A study by the Getúlio Vargas Foundation, based on data from the Brazilian Institute of Geography and Statistics, showed that in 2008, for the first time in history, the total income of the 91 million people in Class C was greater than the sum total of Classes A and B (that is, those with income above 4,591 reais [or US$2,579]). Today, Class C households account for 46 percent of the total national income, versus 44 percent of Classes A and B, which have traditionally prevailed in the Brazilian economy (O Globo 2010).

This substantial movement of people from Class D to Class C had a ripple effect, causing consumption to increase significantly. In a way, Brazil is undergoing today what took place in other countries a century ago. When, in 1914, Henry Ford decided to double his employees' wages and pay them five dollars per working day, he claimed that he wished they would earn well enough to be able to buy the automobiles produced by his company at the lowest possible cost (O'Toole 1998). Inasmuch as the Workers' Party is fostering the development of the domestic market and incorporating to it historically excluded sectors of the population, one may say that the Party is, ironically, triggering the bourgeois revolution that the Brazilian elite has failed to carry forward.

Brazil is currently the sixth world economy, with a GDP of US$1.57 trillion. Growth estimates point to a 7 percent figure for 2010. The swift wave enjoyed by the Brazilian economy is reflected in the perceptions held by many Brazilians about their country's future. A survey by Datafolha in late 2009 showed that 57 percent of Brazilians evaluated their own economic situation as being positive. In December 2009, 42 percent of the interviewees believed their salaries' purchasing power would go up, compared to 34 percent of those who had the same opinion in March that same year (Folha de S. Paulo 2010).

The popular classes have always been consumers—chiefly, of basic food products, clothes, and other essential items. The novelty is in the consumption of goods that were not typically purchased by the poor, such as new refrigerators, stoves, television sets, and so forth. Previously, these were either bought second hand or gifted by others who discarded them as outdated. This recent spur in popular consumption is reflected in many sectors. The chief one is that of durable goods (appliances, electronics, and furniture), which has expanded significantly. It has grown twice as much as the overall market: 30 percent per year since 2005. The new members of Class C are copiously buying furniture and appliances, suggesting that there was a repressed demand for these goods (Sverberi and Betti 2009, 180–184). Expansion of credit is an important part of this process.

Other economic sectors are also benefiting from the rise of Class C. Sales in drugstore chains increased 37.5 percent in 2009, compared to the previous year. Such increase is driven by the growing income of the members of popular classes, who are spending more on hygiene and beauty products (Rolli 2010). Several other sectors have recently released products geared towards Class C, such as energy drinks (Fusco 2010) and gyms (Cirilo Junior 2010). One novelty is air travel by Class C. People who have never travelled by plane are beginning to do so, and the companies have had to adapt to it (Rolli 2010). Stores specializing in popular products are also improving and providing better service for their clients, as a result of the popular classes' increased purchasing power (Forneti 2009).

Another important sector is construction. Construction suppliers have credit lines specific for members of the popular classes who wish to improve their homes. Moreover, the construction of residential compounds targeting Class C is an emerging phenomenon. With the support of state credit—such as the governmental program "My House, My Life"—popular groups can now afford real estate by paying small monthly installments. Many compounds reproducing the lifestyle of luxury ones are being built in the vicinity of popular neighborhoods. The rationale for such enterprises is that individuals from the popular groups wish to rise socially, but without breaking away with their territorial identity. This is because they would not be acknowledged as such had they moved out of their original neighborhoods (Data popular 2010).

The banking system is also beginning to adapt to this new economic picture. In order to attract clients who never had a bank account, some banks are creating reward programs that provide prepaid cell phone credits (Barbosa 2010). Opinion surveys show that Class C members aspire to higher education. The university diploma is regarded as a symbol of those who wish to overcome poverty (Dimenstein 2009). The Lula administration created the ProUni program, which offers free positions in private universities for poor students. Moreover, a growing number of banks are offering educational credit for members of Classes C and D who wish to take undergraduate courses in private schools, and therefore have to pay for it (Sciarretta 2010). As Classes C and D are increasing their participation in consumption, banks feel encouraged to raise the amount of money lent to them, charging high interest rates. (Cirilo Junior 2010). Historically, Brazilians have resorted to credit for making purchases. Many interest rates are abusive, but this is often the only way to acquire some products.

In Brazil, popular consumption has changed radically during the last few years. Traditionally, the poorest did not have access to credit, as they were not trusted to honor their debts. The new consumption scenario shows that the poorest groups do make timely payments, as they cannot afford to have a bad credit record. The term *emergent* is used in Brazil to indicate groups that have risen socially. It may be employed either pejoratively—when one refers, for instance, to the parvenu who does not have cultural capital and therefore mastery over the higher classes' social codes—or in a positive sense when referring to hitherto poor people who are now able to afford previously inaccessible goods and services. As in other countries, in Brazil, too, consumption is a sign of upward social mobility, so to be emergent is usually regarded as being successful.

Sacrifice and Reciprocity: Festivities and Brands

New job opportunities for the young and government allowances received by housewives during the last decade in Brazil have enabled many of the poor to consume goods they had always wished for, be it for themselves or as a gift for somebody else. This new picture caused the circulation of gifts to become even more pronounced in places like Morro da Cruz. Consumption needs therefore came to be seen as part of a circuit of gifts and sacrifice (Mauss 2002; Miller 1998). As Miller (1998) has argued, consumption, love, and devotion are interrelated categories. He understands consumption as a ritual act of sacrifice in the strict sense. This sacrifice act marks the end of a productive process (savings) and the beginning of a transcendental phase, which evokes subjects of devotion. For him, in modernity, divinities have been replaced by individuals, with whom one entertains a relation of romantic love. The work of this author is elucidating for understanding consumption among popular groups, as the notion of sacrifice takes on an even more paradigmatic meaning in this case. It has the double meaning of both ritual and straining effort, inasmuch as these groups' average monthly income is lower than the national minimum wage. Thus, for various reasons (be it love, devotion, appearances, affirmation of citizenship, social assertiveness, or ostentation)—motives which practical reason cannot explain—these subjects value buying products that are considered "good" even if this means refraining from having other things considered as "basic" by the middle classes. Herein lies the moral value of sacrifice, and thus the object's economic value—as indicated by George Simmel's (1990).

In many situations where our informants showed significant effort for making a purchase, this was directed towards "subjects of devotion"—as also found by Miller in his critique of the individualistic and superficial aspect of consumption. As explained by 47-year-old Dona Marisa, "when it's for somebody else we really make the sacrifice; if it's for ourselves it's not that important, especially when one is a mother." Even though this idea may be true of all social classes (including the Northern London middle classes studied by Miller), it is undeniable that, among popular groups, the "family value," as part of a more holistic social universe (Duarte 1986), is particularly salient.

Marisa works as an attendant in a city hospital. She got this job thanks to a professional training program in the Morro da Cruz. For two years, she saved her earnings in order to afford a good gift for her daughters—who, differently from most other girls in the neighborhood, did not want a fifteenth birthday celebration[1]. One of her daughters, Julia, chose a modeling portfolio that cost, in 2007 figures, 1,200 reais (or US$675). She felt like a model indeed: she had her hair and makeup done, and her pictures taken. Even though this was a few years ago, these photographs are still in her profile on the social website Orkut, and she shows them off to everyone who comes to her house. Ana, Dona Marisa's other daughter, did something she always dreamed of: "I've spent it all on clothes, I spent the entire day buying, buying, everything on clothes, I love clothes!" she said. Marisa explained that she saved money for Ana's gifts, but that her daughter also relied on her mother's installment plans in various department stores for buying the clothes she wanted.

A young neighbor of Julia and Ana, Paula, got a fifteenth birthday party, but she blames herself for taking too long to choose her gift (only one year ahead) so her mother was not able to save as much as she expected. Nonetheless, the party took place as idealized by the family, and the photo album is still proudly displayed. These are *rituals of devotion* by mothers who spend all their savings on their daughters' coming of age rituals. These sacrifices are not forgotten by their children. In due time, they are reciprocated when the children grow up and have their own job and income. "A mother is a mother," said Paula. "I had to pay in twelve installments for what she asked for in Mother's Day: a gold medal with her children's names engraved, which cost 350 reais."

This kind of sacrifice is also made by women such as Norma, a 42-year-old cleaning lady who had 17 children, but lost 5 of them. She earns a minimum wage and invests whatever she can in clothes for her 12 children. After all, in her words, "appearance is all they have, they have to look good… I cannot afford to give them a house, to pay for their college, so all I can do is to make them look good and I think I should offer them that."

In general, to buy brand products has become mandatory among young people from the Brazilian peripheries. This desire, which emerges in school, is supported by parents, who see themselves as obliged to provide "good things" for their children as a way to secure for them a better fate than their own. When these teenagers leave school and get a job, they are free to consume whatever they want; however, what one finds is that they invest their earnings in brand products, not for themselves, but for their partners. This is a form of returning love.

Therefore, besides the mother-child relation, gift giving between young couples is also prominent in Morro da Cruz. The emergent share of popular groups is usually made up of young people, and for them consumption of international brand goods has become an important diacritic mark of upward social mobility. Julia, Dona Marisa's daughter, plays soccer in a Porto Alegre team. Once, when leaving the field, she showed the sneakers she got from her boyfriend. "Look, it's original, it cost 350 reais," she said, while proudly exhibiting the tag on the shoe's tongue. The influence of Nike in Morro da Cruz is huge. Three 19-year-olds we interviewed declared they were looking for jobs just in order to become consumers of this brand. Moreover, they pointed out that they would never date a girl who did not wear Nike shoes, even if she were otherwise perfect. Therefore they buy such shoes for their girlfriends so they may one day reciprocate with an equivalent gift.

Technologies and Cell Phones

We understand consumption of certain brands and products as a major identity act by individuals from popular groups in contemporary Brazilian society. It is the objectification of broader symbolic structures. In a society that discriminates by class and color, to dress well is extremely important, as it is to own state-of-the-art technological gadgets. Consumption objectifies an urge for belonging and social inclusion by popular groups, and is a way to express citizenship. During fieldwork, we recorded numerous stories of subjects who would go great lengths to buy a product considered good, with the sole purpose of showing it off in their networks (computers, cell phones, plasma TV sets). Ultimately, "good" and "expensive" products bolster one's prestige vis-à-vis the community and/or specific social networks. Following Friedman (1990), they are at the same time a political assertion, a way to demonstrate the fact of belonging to the global order.

Of those publicly acknowledged signs, one of the most important is the cell phone. Today, cell phones in Brazil outnumber the total population. During fieldwork, interviewees were often surprised and questioned why we, as members of the middle class, owned such ugly cell phones. This was something they could not understand. Girls from Morro da Cruz have colored cell phones and master all the technology they carry, from MP3s to MP7s. A cell phone is therefore a fundamental object: it is part of one's body and attire; it is an extension of the self, a portable locus of modernity. In Marta's words, "it is very important to have a pretty cell phone. It rings, you make a charming move and say *heloooooooo*; it's awesome!" The purchase of a cell phone is made, even if it need be in many installments.

It is interesting to remark that, in this social setting, the cell phone is a form of bodily expression, an accessory, an alternative way of communicating. Rarely do such devices have enough prepaid credits for making a phone call; they most often work as a phonebook or for receiving calls. Calls are made from phone booths, the so-called *orelhão*—as also found by Silva (2008) in a slum in the Brazilian city of Florianópolis. We found that the cell phone ornament is more important in the Morro than in the *camelódromo*, where functionality is valued over design. Communication between our informants from the Morro takes place chiefly through web chats and virtual social networks accessed through computers in the so-called *lanhouses*—currently, major sites of consumption and sociability in the Brazilian urban peripheries (Lemos 2007; Dornelles2008; Scalco 2008).

Intra- and Extra-Class Distinction

Many of the examples included in this discussion highlighted the importance of sacrifices made for acquiring original and expensive goods. Following Friedman's (1990) analysis of the use of French brands by popular groups in the Congo, we do not believe this kind of consumption is a mere emulation of the taste of the elites; or a cheaper imitation, as suggested by Bourdieu's "Distinction." All these objects and purchases, as well as the ways they are put to use, confer distinction on consumers inasmuch as they operate as class markers (Bourdieu 1984). In this case, however, the symbolic struggle for prestige takes place less inter- than intra-class. In other words, distinction matters for a particular local and relational context.

There are two reasons for this. First, the category of social emergent, to which our informants declare to be proud to belong, only makes sense among peers: their achievements are only meaningful for a particular, affective social group. In these circuits of consumption and meaning making, goods are not merely copied from the upper classes, but are also re-signified according to local taste and representation. Second, Brazilian society's biased classificatory forms do not legitimate popular consumption. "It's a poor people's thing" is still a powerful category in Brazil for defining consumption among the popular classes.

This is how Paula explained the fact that their parents chose to build a larger house inside the same slum—still marked by violence and drug trafficking—rather than buy an apartment in another neighborhood. Paula had just entered a private college with the aid of a government-funded program, and worked as a secretary. She lost a relative during a police strike against drug dealers in Morro da Cruz. Thus, to leave the peripheries would have been a logical unfolding of this family's trajectory. The family's decision, however, was another:

> *Paula*: Even with all this, my father preferred to stay. What is the point of going to a fancy apartment compound if, there, we are nobody? My father preferred to invest the money in construction supplies and enlarge our house. But I do think about leaving the Morro.
> [*Researchers*]: Where would you want to live?[2]
> *Paula*: Ah, when I graduate I want to buy an apartment in that luxury apartment compound on Bento [an enterprise directed to Class C]. Think about it: me, going swimming in the pool!
> [*Researchers*]: Don't you think about moving out of this neighborhood?
> *Paula*: No. Never.

This statement clearly shows that the idea of social emergence is coupled with a particular social universe, but that younger generations are widening the horizon sustained by their parents. Even if Paula wishes to move out, such change is deflected symbolically and territorially. Thus, the distinction afforded by new purchases and achievements is more intense within the social class one belongs to. This is less about the upper layers of Brazilian society, which still entertain a tense relation with the rising consumption of lower income groups. Class distinction was put in the following terms by Paula's boyfriend, Gerson:

> Rich people are disturbed by the fact that we're using the same things they use. I think they want to remain distant from us, they should do like us, work hard in order to become even more rich and even more distant from us. We are conquering things, and this shouldn't bother them.

Distinction across classes shows how ruthless Brazilian classificatory systems can be. *Who* is wearing (that is, the *habitus* incorporated in the subjects) is still a key factor in the extra-class struggle for authenticity. This is what make original goods appear as *counterfeit* ones, or vice-versa, when they leave the shops and enter social life. A keen look at Marisa's networks delegitimizes and deauthenticates her "authentic" object. By the same token, an elite woman in a particular social interaction would perhaps look authentic even while wearing a Ray Ban copy. The point is that Marisa is happy with her glasses; she thinks she looks "hot" and "powerful" with them, and "doesn't care" about anything else. She knows she is being looked at, and is sorry for other people's ignorance and prejudice. When she returns to the Morro, her glasses become original again. There are, therefore, (individual and collective) meanings operating in such usages, meanings that go around external discrimination and underscore the importance of understanding the local context wherein objects are used.

Final Remarks

Brazil is not the only country where groups belonging to the urban peripheries accord high status to "expensive," brand goods, or to state of the art technology. Similar examples have been found in other countries, such as brand consumption by low-income groups in the Congo (Friedman 1990) and in England (Lemos 2008). Thus, what happens in Brazil today may be viewed as part of this movement of "global and inter-connected peripheries" (Lemos 2008). But, above all, the facts approached in this chapter lead to the conclusion that they are more than instances of a global phenomenon; they also showcase deep changes in Brazilian society during the last years. In this sense, the country's current situation points to the significant upward mobility of the poor, especially due to their increased purchasing power. Scholarships, allowances for poor families, rising credit in retail and real estate are some of the events that have helped change the profile of the Brazilian consumer. It is undeniable that there is today a larger share of low-income people in the consumer market, and that this has contributed to the health of the national economy at large.

This chapter sought to understand consumption among a particular low-income community in which some families are benefiting from new consumption opportunities. Thus, from an anthropological perspective, more than ascertaining this scenario of changes it is vital to understand how it affects the local dynamics of one community: which goods are desired, why they are desired, and how they are exchanged. In this sense, we found that new opportunities for consumption reassert local networks of affect and belonging, strengthening gift circuits and improving the presents that circulate.

In this new national political and economic context, material achievements (be it a brand piece of garment or the renovation of one's home) are only meaningful in terms of local realities. To be a "social emergent" brings distinction and prestige within one's own community. It is thus about a distinction that occurs inside a class rather than between classes. After all, as the national economy grows along with consumption, other forms of keeping the distance between the social classes also emerge.

But our informants do not feel victimized by the Brazilian elite's prejudice against them; they are people who are proud of their achievements and who are not interested in accessing highbrow circuits of material or symbolic goods. In other words, to purchase branded shoes and exhibit them in school or around the neighborhood is a dream to be fulfilled; to attend restaurants, theatres, and cinemas is not. This is therefore a particular process of social mobility: one driven by the increasing purchasing power of a significant share of the Brazilian population, but one that does not necessarily jeopardize Brazil's class structures.

Finally, it is important to remark that this study approached a phenomenon that is ongoing in Brazil. Ethnographies of consumption by low income groups are fundamental for Brazilian anthropology if it is to refine its understanding of how macro social structures are re-signified by everyday practice. There is still a long way to go in this field of study, which should keep pace with the rapid changes in low-income consumption in Brazil.

Notes

1. In all social classes in Brazil, a tradition is maintained of throwing a big coming of age party—or some other rite of passage—when a girl turns fifteen.
2. The names of all those interviewed have been changed to preserve their anonymity.

References

Barbosa, Mariana. 2010. "Recarga no celular estimula novas contas." *Folha de S. Paulo,* August 30.

Barros, Ricardo Paes de. 2007. "The Recent Decline in Income Inequality in Brazil: Magnitude, Determinants and Consequences." Ciudad de Guatemala. (Powerpoint presentation).

Bourdieu, Pierre. 1984. *Distinction. A Social Critique of the Judgment of Taste.* Cambridge, MA: Harvard University Press.

Cirilo Junior. 2010. "12 percent das famílias devem 5 vezes a sua renda." *Folha de São Paulo,* September 1.

Cirilo Junior. 2010. "Body Tech lança academias visando clientes da classe C." *Folha de S. Paulo,* August 19.

Data Popular. 2010. *O mercado da base da pirâmide.* Available at: HTTP://www. datapopular.com.br Last accessed, June 23, 2010

Dimenstein, Gilberto. 2009. "Dr. Classe é o personagem do ano." *Folha de S. Paulo,* December 27.

Dornelles, Jonatas. 2008. "Vida na Rede. Uma análise antropológica da virtualidade." PhD Diss., Federal University of Rio Grande do Sul (UFRGS), Porto Alegre, Brazil.

Douglas, Mary, and Baron Isherwood. . 1996. *The World of Goods,* London: Routledge.

Duarte, Luiz, Fernando Dias. 1986. *Da vida nervosa nas classes trabalhadoras urbanas,* Rio de Janeiro, Zahar Editora.

Financial Times. 2010. "Retails Find New Custumers in Brazil's Favela." November 13.

Folha De S. Paulo. 2010. "Cresce otimismo do brasileiro com economia." January 1.

Fonseca, Claudia. 2000. *Família, Fofoca e Honra,* Porto Alegre, Ed. da UFRGS.

Forneti, Verena. 2009. "Lojas da 25 de Março mudam para atender novo público." *Folha de S. Paulo,* December 20.

Fraga, Érica. 2010. "País ficará estagnado em ranking de renda." *Folha de S. Paulo,* August 16.

Friedman, Jonathan. 1990. "Being in the World: Globalization and Localization." In *Global Culture.* Edited by Mike Featherstone, 311–328. London: Sage.

Fusco, Camila. 2010. "Grupo Convenção desenvolve energético voltado à classe C." *Folha de S. Paulo,* July 29.

Guimarães, Larissa. 2010. "Brasil ocupa 9º lugar em desenvolvimento na América Latina." *Folha de S. Paulo,* July 24.

Horst, Heather A., and Daniel Miller. 2006. *The Cell Phone.* Oxford: Berg.

Lemos, Ronaldo. (2007) "From Legal Commons to Social Commons—Brazil and the Cultural Industry in the 21st Century." Working Paper. Center for Brazilian Studies, University of Oxford. Accessed January 20, 2009. http://dlc.dlib.indiana.edu/archive/00002304/

Mauss, Marcel. 2002. *The Gift. The Form and Reason for Exchange in Archaic Societies.* London: Routledge.

Miller, Daniel. 1998. *A Theory of Shopping.* Ithaca, NY: Cornell University Press.

Mioto, Ricardo. 2010. "Para especialista nova classe C ignora sustentabilidade." *Folha de S. Paulo,* January 1.

O Globo. 2010. "Classe C do Brasil já detém 46 percent da renda." Fevereiro 6.

O'Toole, Patrícia. 1998. *Money and Morals in America. A History.* New York: Clarkson Potter.

Rocha, Ângela da, and Jorge Ferreira de Silva. 2009. *Consumo na Base da Pirâmide.* Rio de Janeiro: Mauad.

Rolli, Claudia. 2010. "TAM vai vender bilhete nas Casas Bahia." *Folha de S. Paulo,* August 4.

Rolli, Claudia. 2010. "Varejistas investem R$ 2bi em classes CD." *Folha de S. Paulo,* July 13.

Rolli, Claudia. 2010. "Venda em redes de drogarias crescem 38 percent." *Folha de S. Paulo,* August 5.

Sahlins, Marshall. 1978. *Culture and Practical Reason.* Chicago: University of Chicago Press.

Sarti, Cynthia. 1996. *A família como espelho: um estudo sobre a moral dos pobres.* Campinas: Editora Autores Associados/FAPESP.

Scalco, Lúcia. 2008. *Falakenois: etnografia de um projeto de inclusão digital entre jovens de classes populares em Porto Alegre,* MA diss., Federal University of Rio Grande do Sul (UFRGS), Porto Alegre.

Sciaretta, Toni. 2010. "Bancos apostam em crédito educativo." *Folha de S. Paulo,* July 26.

Silva, S. R. 2008. "Vivendo com celulares: identidade, corpo e sociabilidade nas culturas urbanas." *Culturas Juvenis no Século XXI,* edited by S. Borelli and J. Freire Filho, 311–331. São Paulo: EDUC.

Simmel, George. 1990. *The Philosophy of Money,* London: Routledge.

Sverberi, Benedito and Betti, Renata. 2009. "Eles Chegaram ao Topo." *Veja,* December 23.

World Bank. "Income Distribution." www.worldbank.orgdepwbeyond-beyondbeg_05.pdf

Zweig, Stefan. 1960. *Brasil, país do futuro,* Rio de Janeiro: Guanabara.

4

Chile's Forgotten Consumers: Poor Urban Families, Consumption Strategies, and the Moral Economy of Risk in Santiago

Joel Stillerman[1]

In recent years, scholars, government officials, journalists, and citizens have perceived profound changes in Chile's consumption infrastructure (retail formats, advertising, mass media, technology, and credit), and consumer attitudes and practices. Some scholars argue that lower- and middle-income groups improve their social status by imitating elite consumption styles. As a result, they argue, political participation and social solidarity have declined (Moulian 1997, 1998; Tironi 1999; Van Bavel and Sell-Trujillo 2003). Others contend that Chilean consumption patterns reflect a society-wide process of individualization (PNUD 2002; Larraín 2001). In contrast, some scholars find that women and low-income consumers exercise self-restraint in purchases, use consumption as a means to strengthen family relationships, and also that women's growing employment and consumption have made them increasingly politicized (Stillerman 2004, 2008; Tinsman 2006). In this chapter, I expand on the latter view by examining low-income consumers' experiences in two of Santiago's poorest municipalities. I argue that we can best understand low-income consumers in relation to their limited incomes, perceived gender and family roles, and financial vulnerability. These consumers limit their expenses, access resources via personal networks, and articulate modest aspirations. These patterns contrast sharply with the view of consumers as status-seeking, hedonistic individuals.

An examination of low-income consumers will provide an important counterpoint to studies that focus on their middle-class counterparts. Low-income consumers are an important exception to Chileans' growing earnings, credit use, and purchases since the early 1990s. Indeed, recent studies of lower middle–class homeowners (Ariztía 2009a, 2009b), variations in tastes among different middle class occupational groups (Stillerman 2010), and cultural consumption across social classes and generations (Gayo et al. 2009) underscore the class-specific character of consumption. However, few studies have examined how men's and women's consumption patterns differ (for exceptions, see: Tinsman 2006; Stillerman 2004; Raczynski and Serrano 1985).

The argument in this chapter is based on semistructured interviews with six adult women and two young adults (one male) who live in Cerro Navía and San Ramon, Santiago's first and fourth poorest municipalities (MIDEPLAN 2007a). I identified interview subjects via street vendors that I had interviewed in a previous study (Stillerman 2006, 2008). I conducted all but one interview in the interviewees' living rooms, permitting observation of significant household objects[2]. Additionally, I conducted 20 hours of participant observation in Cerro Navía and San Ramon street markets and at meetings of the National Association of Street Market Vendors (ASOF), including one "walkabout" with an interviewee during a shopping trip.

The data collected reveal noteworthy patterns of consumption among poor consumers. First, men's and women's perceived roles and relative earning power shape the allocation of funds and credit within the household. Second, shoppers stretch limited funds by splitting grocery shopping among multiple formats, using different forms of credit, as well as accessing and pooling resources from family and friends. Third, family health and employment crises provoke downward mobility that further limits families' purchasing power. Finally, low-income individuals hold modest aspirations for improving their social status, challenging the view that poor consumers try to imitate higher-income groups and feel frustrated when they fail to do so.

Low-Income Consumers

This chapter builds on scholarship regarding low-income consumers and research on family adaptive strategies. These analyses show how class-based socialization affects working-class taste, how poor consumers build relationships via consumer practices, as well as how low-income family members distribute earning responsibilities and allocate resources. These scholars highlight the severe financial constraints that low-income people face, their creative responses to these constraints, and the strong imprint of gender roles and ideologies on their consumption.

Bourdieu's (1984) work on class and consumption posits that an individual's learned dispositions, or *habitus*, shape their tastes for goods. These dispositions emerge from family- and school-based socialization, and determine how and to what extent individuals see consumption as a tool for status competition. Working-class consumers, who lack access to economic and cultural capital, develop a "choice for the necessary"—they adapt to their limited resources and opportunities by acquiring a taste for inexpensive and functional goods. Bourdieu's perspective suggests that workers' class-based socialization militates against their developing a desire to emulate the middle or upper classes (for a more recent analysis, see Bennett et al. 2009).

In contrast, several scholars examine the gendered character of family finances and budgets. Pahl (1989) emphasizes the persistence of male dominance over family finances, while noting the class-specific character of family budget allocation. The ideology that identifies men as breadwinners and women as caregivers either trivializes women's earnings or ties them specifically to family needs (see also Zelizer 1989). Hence, many women allow men to retain a portion of their earnings for personal consumption while they use a greater share of their own earnings for family members.

Families facing financial hardship develop "adaptive strategies" to provide members with needed resources. These include adding members to the labor force; substituting for or eliminating nonessential goods; sheltering extended family members, taking on boarders or sending children to live with others; accessing different forms of credit; or bartering goods and services with extended kin or neighbors (Stack 1974; De Oliveira and Roberts 1996; Jélin 1983; Raczynski and Serrano 1985; Gonzalez de la Rocha 1994; Moen and Wethington 1992; Finch 1989; Nelson and Smith, 1999).

With a few exceptions, research in Chile contends that individuals use consumption to gain greater social status. Moulian (1997, 1998) argues that the heightened availability of credit to low- and middle-income Chileans in recent years has permitted a new and pernicious form of social integration through which individuals accumulate debt to improve their living standard rather than seeking collective goods through political parties, social organizations or the state. This pattern undermines collective bonds and identities. Tironi (1999), in contrast, interprets this same process as reflecting the democratization of consumption.

Van Bavel and Sell-Trujillo (2003) argue that the poor are unable to save, and so they accumulate debt to improve their status and avoid stigma. In a complementary vein, PNUD (2002) and Larraín (2001) build on European conceptions of individualization. They argue that the decreasing influence of traditional institutions like the family and work on individual identities has lead Chileans to construct individual life projects via consumption.

In contrast to these individualistic views of consumption, Stillerman (2004, 2006, 2008) and Tinsman (2006) found that low-income individuals adopt an ethic of reciprocity and attempt to maintain or transform gender roles via consumption rather than seek individual upward mobility. Finally, D'Andrea et al. (2004) argue that low income consumers in Chile and other Latin American countries seek to balance their financial constraints with the purchase of desired brands, include time and transit costs in determining where to shop, prefer local stores that offer personal attention and informal credit to supermarkets, and vary in their purchasing power and attitudes.

Recent quantitative research further contextualizes low-income individuals' consumption practices. Between 1996 and 2006, poverty declined while homeownership increased, but 20 percent of Chileans still lived with extended family (MIDEPLAN 2007a, 2007b). Additionally, in 2006, members of the lowest income group still spent 37 percent of their incomes on food (INE 2008).

In recent years, consumer debts increased in tandem with incomes. The most indebted groups are the most highly educated and hold permanent jobs, though the lowest income group had the highest debt-to-income ratio (Cox et al. 2006). Poor Chileans' indebtedness is not new, however, as a study from the early 1980s found that poor Chileans used informal credit and delayed paying utility bills to make ends meet (Raczynski and Serrano 1985). Further, recent work suggests that we should expand our understanding of poverty to include individuals who are vulnerable to becoming poor due to illness, long-term disability or unemployment (Rasse and Salcedo 2008; Neilson et al. 2008).

Building on scholarship on low-income consumers, gender, and inequality, I argue that low income consumers have limited opportunities for improving their status via consumption, and many experience *downward* mobility due to accidents, illnesses, unemployment, or inadequate old-age pensions. Furthermore, poor families rely on reciprocal ties to others to make ends meet and status seeking is a secondary motivation for consumption. Finally, even more financially secure low-income families express limited aspirations for expanded consumption, supporting Bourdieu's (1984) view regarding working-class consumers.

The findings also demonstrate that consumption is rooted in family relationships, roles, conflicts, negotiations, and resource allocation patterns. I first explore gender dynamics in the household, and then examine shopping strategies, resource sharing, vulnerability, and aspirations. Women are central to families because they have historically been constructed as consumers and caregivers, even though men tend to earn more and exercise greater economic influence in families than do women (Pahl 1989). Their attitudes and practices underscore key redistributive practices and power inequities within the family.

Gender and Spending

The gendered practices noted above surfaced via several themes across the interviews. Women coded expenses into two categories—reproductive activities and leisure. Three women paid for and attempted to exert control over tasks, expenses, and products they viewed as tied to their maternal roles, while giving husbands discretion to purchase costly items and personal items. The two employed women described expenses for kitchen appliances, clothing, and children's school tuition as "my" things. Paulina, a seamstress, noted, "He pays the utility bills. I take care of my things. Sometimes if I go to buy shoes, I will pick up a pair for him…So 'my things' include him, too (laughs). I buy the children's clothing and all of the basics…When the girls were in school I paid for tuition, transportation, and food" (interview, June 15, 2007). Women conflate their consumption with that of their children, making their own needs and desires less visible.

Women view their own consumption as illegitimate in the face of children's needs. Graciela, a housekeeper, comments, "When I think about buying something for myself, I think about what my children need and then I decide not to buy it." In contrast, her husband does have personal expenses. "He works Monday to Saturday and then goes out drinking with his friends" (interview, June 9, 2007).

Women and men outline distinct priorities for household expenses. Paulina comments, "He has been updating our car over the years. He bought a used car two years ago. Now he says he wants to buy a new one at the end of the year, a Toyota, so that he knows he will not have problems with it for four or five years" (interview, 15 June 2007). Nonetheless, he ignored her desire to remodel their home: "The house is too small for all of us. I told my husband we need a second bathroom and he said, 'Why do you want a second bathroom since our adult children will be leaving soon?' In fact, the opposite occurred: our adult children returned to the house" (interview, June 15, 2007).

Women and men often disagreed about credit use. Aurelia, who is unemployed, comments: "He doesn't like credit cards. He saves money, and when he has enough, he will buy something." She later recalled nostalgically that when her daughter was employed, she purchased all the household furniture and appliances using department store credit cards (interview, June 15, 2007). Paulina also comments, "If I used all of my credit cards, my husband would kill me…If he buys something for me with a credit card, he says, 'don't run up any more credit card debt' " (interview, June 15, 2007). Hence, women see credit cards as means to purchase needed goods while men seek to control and limit women's credit card purchases.

Shopping Strategies

All interviewees were very conscious of their tight budgets and attempted to reduce shopping expenditures to a minimum. Several couples split purchases between street markets (for produce), butchers, and supermarkets. As Graciela explains: "I go to the street market on Saturday for produce, and once a month to the supermarket to get dry goods. I go to the butcher to buy meat…Produce is more expensive at the supermarket and the meat has too much fat." Other couples purchased food and clothing in street markets due to their declining incomes, their desire to limit transit expenses, or in an effort to avoid the temptation to overspend. Lucia, an unemployed woman, notes, "We buy vegetables, fruit, and dry goods at the feria…We can't afford the bus fare to the nearest supermarket" (interview, June 15, 2007). As D'Andrea et al. (2004) note, when determining where to shop, low-income consumers look at the total cost of purchases in price, travel time, and transit cost as well as at issues of quality and service.

Families also stretch family resources by using various forms of credit. Aurelia comments, "I take home my dry goods from the street market and pay the vendor the following week" (interview 15, June 2007). China, who lacks access to credit cards, uses informal credit to buy clothing: "I pay 1000 pesos per week rather than 6, 7, or 8,000. That's why I keep my regular vendors…If you don't have money one week, they will not increase the price; but if you miss a credit card payment, they increase your interest rate right away. I know it's more expensive here: they charge you two or three times what you would pay in a department store" (interview, June 15, 2007). Higher interest charges in street markets led Paula, a street vendor, to use credit cards: "I don't use credit in the street market because they give better payment options at HITES and La Polar" (interview, June 11, 2007).

Others use informal credit and credit cards depending on how much cash they have on hand: *Graciela stops at a stall to look at a teapot:* "I want to buy a tea pot because mine is worn out." ... *She says to the vendor,* "I'll take that one. I'm not going to give you any installment payment today, though." *She turns to me:* "When I am out of money or I have to pay my credit card bill, it doesn't make sense to spend money. I don't have 11,000 pesos plus interest to spend all at once. So, I pay this off little by little" (field notes, June 11, 2007). While women develop different strategies for accessing credit, most used credit cards sparingly, as Graciela comments: "I try to use the card for something I can pay for in three to six months at most ... If you miss a payment they double the amount due—no way! I'd rather avoid eating than skip a credit card payment" (interview, June 9, 2007).

These families access goods and services available to most of their peers rather than seek to emulate higher social strata. During conversations in interviewees' homes, I observed the array and expense of goods they owned as well as the condition of their homes. Most families own standard appliances for Chilean homes—a TV set, stereo, kitchen appliances, and a computer (often without internet access). A 2001 survey found that over 75 percent of low-income families had refrigerators, washing machines, and color televisions (CEP 2001). Some families did not even have computers.

Vacations are another significant expenditure. Several interviewees commented that they had not gone on vacation in years, only visited family outside Santiago, or children were the only family members who could take vacations. Victoria, an unemployed young adult, comments: "My 17-year-old sister is in the girl scouts. She goes camping every year. She is the only one who goes on vacation" (interview, June 12, 2007).

Pooling Resources

In contrast to the view of Chileans as increasingly individualistic, all of the interviewees exchanged scarce resources in order to assist family members or neighbors. Interviewees reported giving or receiving small amounts of food, handmade clothing, or assistance with childcare. As Lucia comments: "I knitted this sweater and I will give it to our neighbor's baby ... I help people when they ask—I make things for them, I take care of the neighbors' children sometimes ... Our son works on a farm and he gives us fruit" (interview, June, 15 2007). Paulina, a seamstress, also reported making specialty clothing for her adult children when they had job interviews (interview, June 15, 2007).

Several interviewees also provided housing for adult family members in need. As China comments, "My brother and his child who is sick live with us practically as *allegados* (doubled-up). He is separated from his wife and never got along with our father, so he lives here...He has been here for almost a year" (interview, June 15, 2007). All of the households included adult children and several included three generations in the same home. Indeed, from 1990 to 2006, across social classes, 19 percent of Chilean households included extended family members (MIDEPLAN 2007b).

Several families also lent or borrowed credit cards, which directly contradicts the image of *individuals* using credit cards for personal expenses. China, whose husband lost his job and could not pay off their credit card bill, comments: "My sister has cards from most of the major stores. She purchased most of our kitchen appliances with her card" (interview, June 15, 2007). This practice can be risky, as Victoria comments: "My father lends his card to family or friends and some have taken a long time to pay him back...He is superresponsible about making payments, so now he's reticent to lend his card" (interview, June 12, 2007). However, consumers may obtain cards with the goal of assisting family members, as Paula notes: "Having the card is good because my daughter was able to use it to buy her son a computer" (interview, June 11, 2007). In these cases, a formal market relationship gets reinscribed into the moral economy of family life so that individuals can access costly goods. Individuals insert formal market media into primary relationships (Zelizer 1989).

Vulnerability

Several families described emergencies that forced them to significantly scale back expenditures, underscoring the objective barriers to upward mobility for low-income families. Aurelia comments: "My daughter was working but she got hit by a bus and is now disabled. I take care of her...I haven't been to the supermarket in years. When she was working...we would spend 60 or 70,000 pesos at the supermarket...I used to buy food for the month; now I buy daily...I'd like to work, but no one will take care of my daughter out of the goodness of their heart...We spend half of our money on medicine" (interview, June 15, 2007). Others receive inadequate pensions: "I worked in the plastics industry and then was unemployed for four years. I got screwed on my pension. My employer did not contribute to the fund from 1974 until 1980 and I lost 24 years' credit for years of service...I sued them and won but I was not awarded a settlement." Individuals who are victims of theft or who lack job security often experience credit problems: "My husband is a subcontractor for a private water company...We had a credit card, but when they stole his pickup truck, we had to stop making payments. The interest rates increased and now our debt is handled by a collections agency. To get out of debt, we need to pay our entire balance…His truck is a necessity for his job, not a luxury. He had to rent a truck, which costs 100 or 200,000 pesos per month and that ate up all of his wages" (interview, June 15, 2007).

The interviews highlight these consumers' vulnerability to health or financial emergencies. The absence of job security exposes workers to the risk of downward mobility. These examples show that many analyses of consumption are abstracted from the challenges and risks low-income consumers face. The singular focus on formal credit use or the alleged search for upward mobility ignores the fact that low-income families face constraints that are outside their control and limit their options for luxury expenses.

Aspirations

Individuals' fantasies are a useful gauge of their aspirations for upward mobility. When asked what they would like to have if they could afford it, interviewees offered modest responses. Graciela and China, who are renters, described homeownership as "everybody's dream." This comment is noteworthy because over 90 percent of Chileans now own their homes (MIDEPLAN 2007b). Paulina, who lives with six other relatives in a modest home, wished for a larger house. Victoria, who lives with her parents, would like a newer cell phone and to live in a newer home in a mixed income community. Paula would like to have newer trucks for herself and her father (both of whom use old, unreliable cars for their jobs), and to purchase a home for her daughter so she could live nearby. Finally, Aurelia wishes for a car and Internet access to avoid bothering others. Juan and Lucía said they were happy with what they have.

These comments are striking in their modesty. They speak of these individuals' limited aspirations, which Bourdieu (1984) would describe as a "choice for necessity." These individuals have little interest in emulating others from higher social classes and may not even be aware of how other social classes live. Moreover, several of the wishes focus on either financial security for their family or on providing other family members with needed goods. They thus contradict many scholars' views that all consumers seek to increase their status via debt-financed consumption.

Conclusion

Many studies of consumption overlook low-income individuals and families. Implicitly assuming that poor consumers have simple needs and tastes, many authors choose to look at other groups. In the Chilean case, little empirical research examines low-income consumers in detail.

This chapter fills this gap by examining low-income families' consumption in its full complexity. I have found that low-income consumers are not a unified group. Indeed, men and women understand their own domains of consumption differently, assign priorities to different purchases, and vary in their degree of control over family budgets. Moreover, low-income families develop a variety of strategies to reduce expenses while strategically using credit. Additionally, family members share resources to satisfy the needs of extended kin networks. Many low-income families are at risk of experiencing downward mobility due to financial or health emergencies. Finally, low-income individuals harbor limited aspirations for upward mobility.

These findings challenge the view that all low- and moderate-income individuals seek upward mobility through consumption. Indeed, this view is far removed from the real-life challenges that low-income people face and the strategies they use to confront these challenges. They also point to the need for policies that better protect working Chileans who face illness, or long term disability, or receive inadequate pensions. Finally, these findings support the view that low-income people have distinct patterns of consumption and identity (Bourdieu 1984; Bennett et al. 2009).

Further research might identify how variations in socioeconomic segregation affect low-income individuals' and families' consumption practices, tastes, and identities. Moulian (1997, 1998) and Tironi (1999) appear to refer to the "new lower middle class"—low-income individuals who have experienced rising incomes in mixed-income Santiago municipalities such as La Florida and Maipú (see Ariztia 2009a, 2009b for a detailed ethnographic study of a similar group). Van Bavel and Sell-Trujillo (2003) examined low-income consumers in Lo Barnechea, a municipality where low-income squatters live close to affluent families and possibly emulate their consumer behavior.

Unlike the communities identified above, I conducted fieldwork in Cerro Navía and San Ramon, two homogeneous poor communities that experience large-scale segregation from other social classes and amenities like big-box supermarkets. Urban scholars argue that large-scale segregation negatively affects low-income individuals because their homes are located far from jobs, retail, services, and contacts with more affluent individuals who might employ or assist them. In contrast, those who live close to the affluent benefit from cross-class contacts (Dreier et al. 2004; Sabatini and Cáceres 2004; Salcedo 2004). Poor families experiencing large scale segregation like those I studied may be shielded from the influences of more affluent consumers and thus do not express the upwardly mobile aspirations that other studies have found among the poor and lower middle class. Comparative work on different urban communities could address this question and further specify the scope of my results.

Notes

1. Research for this chapter was conducted during July 2007 with the support of a Grand Valley State University Intercultural Studies Faculty Development Grant. Writing was supported during the 2008–2009 academic year by a sabbatical from Grand Valley State University and a US Department of Education Fulbright-Hayes Faculty Research Abroad grant (Award Number: P019A080002). I was also a Visiting Professor during that year at the Urban Studies Institute of the Catholic University of Chile. I presented an earlier version of this paper in October 2008 at the conference: "Ciencias, tecnologías y culturas. Diálogo entre las disciplinas del conocimiento. Mirando al futuro de América Latina y el Caribe" in Santiago, Chile; and in June 2009 at the Latin American Studies Association Congress in Rio de Janeiro, Brazil. I wish to thank Rodrigo Salcedo, Katherine Schulhoff, Hermann Kurthen, and volume editors Anna Pertierra and John Sinclair for helpful comments on an earlier version of this chapter.
2. Five interviewees were parents, one was a single mother, and the two young adults were single and resided with parents. All interviewees had a high school education or less, two households had two earners, and the others had a single household head. Four interviewees held blue-collar and low-level technical jobs, and two worked independently as a seamstress and market vendor respectively, and two were unemployed. All interviews were conducted in Santiago, and were transcribed and translated by the author. Interviewees are identified with pseudonyms to protect their anonymity.

References

Ariztia, Tomás. 2009a. "Arreglando la casa propia." In *SCL: Espacios, prácticas y cultura urbana*. Edited by Manuel Tironi and Fernando Pérez, 70–85. Santiago: Ediciones Arq, Pontificia Universidad Católica de Chile.

———. 2009b. "Moving Home: The Everyday Making of the Chilean Middle Class." PhD diss., London School of Economics and Political Science.

Bennett, Tony, Mike Savage, Elizabeth Bortolaia Silva, Alan Warde, Modesto Gayo-Cal, and David Wright. 2009. *Culture, Class, Distinction*. London: Routledge.

Bourdieu, P. 1984. *Distinction: A Social Critique of the Judgment of Taste*. Translated by R. Nice. Cambridge, MA: Harvard University Press.

CEP. 2001. *Estudio de Opinión Pública N° 41: Cómo hemos mejorado en los últi-mos diez años?* Accessed February 28, 2003. http://www.cepchile.cl.

Cox, Paulo, Eric Parrado, and Jaime Ruiz-Tagle. 2006. "The Distribution of Assets, Debt and Income among Chilean Households." Banco Central de Chile Documentos de Trabajo No. 388. Santiago, Chile. Accessed October 14, 2008. http://www.bcentral.cl/estudios/documentos-trabajo/pdf/dtbc388.pdf.

D'Andrea, Guillermo, E. Alejandro Stengel, and Anne Goebel-Krstelj. 2004. "Six Truths about Emerging Market Consumers." *Strategy + Business* 34: 2–12.

De Oliveira, Orlandina, and Bryan Roberts. 1996. "Urban Development and Social Inequality in Latin America." In *The Urban Transformation of the Developing World.* Edited by Josef Gugler, 252–314. Oxford, UK: Oxford University Press.

Dreier, Peter, John Mollenkopf, and Todd Swanstrom. 2004. *Place Matters: Metropolitics for the Twenty-First Century.* Rev. 2nd edition. Lawrence, KS: University Press of Kansas.

Finch, Janet. 1989. *Family Obligations and Social Change.* Cambridge, UK: Polity Press.

Gayo, Modesto, Berta Teitelboim, and María L. Méndez. 2009. "Patrones cul-turales de uso de tiempo libre en Chile. Un intento de evaluación de la teoría bourdieuana. *Universum* 24: 42–72.

Gonzalez de la Rocha, Mercedes. 1994. *The Resources of Poverty.* Cambridge, MA: Blackwell.

INE. 2008. "Resultados: Encuesta de Presupuestos Familiares, Nov. 2006-Oct. 2007." Accessed October 14, 2008. http://www.ine.cl/canales/chile_estadistico/encuestas_presupuestos_familiares/2008/resultados_EPF_2006_2007_080708a.pdf.

Jélin, Eilizabeth. 1984. "Las Relaciones Sociales del Consumo: El Caso de las Unidades Domésticas de Sectores Populares: Argentina." In *La Mujer en el Sector Popular Urbano: América Latina y el Caribe.* Edited by United Nations Economic Commission on Latin America, 175–198. Santiago, Chile: United Nations, Economic Commission on Latin America.

Larraín, J. 2001. *Identidad chilena.* Santiago, Chile: LOM Ediciones.

MIDEPLAN. 2007a. "Encuesta de Caracterización Socioeconómica: Región Metropolitana." Accessed October 14, 2008. http://www.mideplan.cl/casen/publicaciones/2006/CASEN2006-Metropolitana.pdf.

———. 2007b. "Encuesta de Caracterización Socioeconómica: Vivienda." Accessed October 14, 2008. http://www.mideplan.cl/final/ficha_tecnica.php?cenid=418.

Moen, Phyllis, and Elaine Wethington. 1992. "The Concept of Family Adaptive Strategies." *Annual Review of Sociology* 18: 233–251.

Moulian, Tomás. 1997. *Chile Hoy: Anatomía de un mito.* Santiago, Chile: LOM Ediciones.

———. 1998. *El Consumo me consume.* Santiago, Chile: LOM Ediciones.

Neilson, Christopher, Dante Contreras, Ryan Cooper, and Jorge Hermann. 2008. "The Dynamics of Poverty in Chile," *Journal of Latin American Studies* 40: 251–273.

Nelson, Margaret, and Joan Smith. 1999. *Working Hard and Making Do: Surviving in Small Town America*. Berkeley: University of California Press.

Pahl, Jan. 1989. *Money & Marriage*. New York: St. Martin's Press.

PNUD. 2002. *Nosotros, los Chilenos: Un desafío cultural*. Santiago: PNUD.

Raczynski, Dagmar, and Claudia Serrano. 1985. *Vivir la Pobreza: Testimonios de Mujeres*. Santiago, Chile: CIEPLAN.

Rasse, Alejandra, and Rodrigo Salcedo. 2008. "Progreso económico y estratificación social: ¿Cómo segmentar a los chilenos hoy?" In *Hacia una Sociedad de Derechos: Políticas públicas, titularidad y garantías. Volumen I: Serie Derechos Sociales y Políticas Públicas*. Edited by Fundación Henry Dunant, 117–126. Santiago, Chile: Ediciones Fundación Henry Dumont.

Sabatini, Francisco, and Gonzalo Cáceres. 2004. "Los barrios cerrados y la ruptura del patrón tradicional de segregación en las ciudades latinoamericanas: el caso de Santiago de Chile." In *Barrios cerrados en Santiago de Chile: entre la exclusion y la integración residencial*. Edited by Gonzalo Cáceres and Francisco Sabatini, 9–43. Santiago, Chile: Lincoln Institute of Land Policy and Pontifícia Universidad Católica de Chile, Instituto de Geografía.

Salcedo, Rodrigo. 2004. "Towards a Reconceptualization of Post-Public Spaces." PhD diss., University of Illinois, Chicago.

Stack, C. 1974. *All our Kin*. New York: Basic Books.

Stillerman, Joel. 2004. "Gender, Class, and Generational Contexts for Consumption in Contemporary Chile," *Journal of Consumer Culture* 4: 51–78.

———. 2006. "Private, Parochial and Public Realms in Santiago, Chile's Retail Sector." *City & Community* 5: 293–317.

———. 2008. "Tradition, Adventure and Pleasure in Santiago, Chile's Informal Markets." In *Lived Experiences of Public Consumption*. Edited by Daniel T. Cook, 31–49. Houndmills, UK: Palgrave Macmillan.

———. 2010. "The Contested Spaces of Chile's Middle Classes." *Political Power and Social Theory* 21: 209–238.

Tinsman, Heidi. 2006. "Politics of Gender and Consumption in Authoritarian Chile, 1973–1990: Women Agricultural Workers in the Fruit Export Industry." *Latin American Research Review* 41: 7–31.

Tironi, Eugenio. 1999. *La irrupción de las masas y el malestar de las elites: Chile en el cambio de siglo*. Santiago, Chile: Editorial Grijalbo.

Van Bavel, René and Lucía Sell-Trujillo. 2003. "Understandings of Consumerism in Chile." *Journal of Consumer Culture* 3(3), 343–362.

Zelizer, Viviana. 1989. "The Social Meaning of Money: 'Special Monies'." *American Journal of Sociology* 95: 342–377.

5

Peasants and *Pirámides*: Consumer Fantasies in the Colombian Andes

Jason Antrosio

For those accustomed to consumption norms of the US middle-class, the Latin American mix of consumer goods with small-scale agriculture can be particularly jarring. Túquerres, a highland town in Colombia's southwestern Andes, has depended on small-plot farms, manual labor, and regional peasant marketplaces. During my fieldwork in the late 1990s, people stressed these continuities at the same time as they were actively adopting new clothing styles and musical tastes, transforming cooking and kitchen spaces, and then incorporating telephones and, later, cell phones.

When I revisited Túquerres in 2009, I initially saw the combination of cell phone and agriculture as yet another instance of how people in Latin America combine elements considered "modern" and "traditional" into symbiotic appropriations that defy these conventional dichotomies (see Barbero 2006; Bauer 2001; Colloredo-Mansfeld 1999; Rowe and Schelling 1991). However, people talked about how in 2008, just one year before, everything had been different: "No one planted"; "No one worked"; "We sold our pigs"; "We lost everything." Life was interrupted by the frenzy of putting money into schemes they eventually called *las pirámides*.

In 2008, the southwestern region of Colombia became engulfed in what in retrospect were clearly gigantic Ponzi schemes, with classic pyramidal structures destined for collapse. In Túquerres the largest scheme, and perhaps the largest in Colombia, was known by its initials, DRFE, and the promise of *Dinero Rápido Fácil y Efectivo* (Fast Easy Money in Cash).

Another prominent scheme known as DMG, the initials of its charismatic founder David Murcia Guzmán, promised increasing return on debit cards based on recruiting more participants. Both still seem too much to be believed. How could these sober agriculturists—people who put money in literal pigs in lieu of banks—have been drawn into such schemes? How could they have sold their pigs in order to speculate in such ventures?

Although the scale and scope of the pyramid schemes invites ideas of novelty, this article emphasizes four points of continuity. First, the schemes are intimately linked with consumer goods and pyramidal marketing tactics: they deliberately draw from the earlier "consumerization" of cooking, leisure, agriculture, and banking that became evident during my fieldwork in the late 1990s. By highlighting this shift, I argue against explanations of pyramid schemes which emphasize peasant naiveté or absence of exposure to financial markets. Second, a key explanation for the take-off in the pyramid schemes does not come not from the desire for quick riches, but rather thrives on traditional ideals of thrift and investment, aligning consumer fantasies with peasant values. Third, the consumerization of investment tactics often makes it difficult to distinguish a scheme from a legitimate investment. Finally, the collapse of the *pirámides* led to renewed interest in peasant agriculture, and so can be seen as part of ongoing Latin American symbiosis between what is considered modern and what is traditional.[1]

Pyramidal Precursors: Consuming and Banking in the Late 1990s

In the mid-1980s, the Colombian government enacted reforms labeled *apertura económica* or economic opening, which would reduce trade barriers and tariffs. These reforms were consistent with the neoliberal economic prescriptions recommended or imposed on Latin American countries during the 1980s, and might now be seen as part of regional globalization. Túquerres, in a southwestern province bordering Ecuador, witnessed a dramatic official increase in cross-border imports. It is unclear if this amounted to an actual increase in imports—before the economic opening there was a great deal of contraband, and one of the justifications for reforms was the routine circumvention of trade laws. In any case, there was an increase in goods specifically marked and sold as Ecuadorian.

I had initially expected the economic opening to have a grave impact on agricultural production and marketing, but most people did not report large changes in agriculture. The most visible changes were in cooking practices, as many households bought Ecuadorian gas cooking ranges to supplement or replace wooden hearths. There was also a proliferation of new clothing fashions, music sales in the form of stereos and CDs, then landline telephones, followed by the now ubiquitous cell phone.

My earlier analysis of these changes concentrated on how residents adopted these items as part of what they called the modern. Many of these items spread without much of an advertising campaign or official development program. I explained this adoption by noting how residents seemed to be responding to a local system of stigma and hierarchy: urban elites had classed them as peasants or Indians, together with stereotypes about dirt, laziness, and peasant stupidity. By adopting these new consumer goods, they were overturning these stereotypes, staking a claim to a modern life that had long been denied them (Antrosio 2002).

It now seems worth highlighting that at least some of these new consumer goods, especially cosmetics and kitchen items, were promoted through a pyramid-like sales structure. Although these sales structures may not be liable to the same kind of collapse as a financial pyramid, the principle of sellers who support others at the top was becoming familiar. David Murcia Guzmán, the founder of DMG, began precisely by gaining experience as a door-to-door salesman for a US-based pyramid-marketing firm (Romero 2009). It seems hardly accidental that his scheme featured prepaid debit cards for consumer items like electronics, evolving into outlet stores and shopping malls. As Peter Cahn (2008) has analyzed in Mexico, direct selling and the recruitment of new distributors is part of a process in which people reorganize their lives around neoliberal norms while seeking and selling middle-class consumer norms.

Despite these changes, much of the income for these purchases still came largely from labor-intensive agriculture and peasant marketplaces, resulting in a new symbiosis: some of those first telephone calls were about prices for pigs and potatoes. Interestingly, the one area that seemed like what most imagine as consumer culture was the agricultural sector itself. With the neoliberal dismantling of what had once been a national system of technical attention to agriculture, some of the former technicians in Túquerres became salesmen for chemical fertilizers and pesticides. These fertilizers and pesticides were perhaps the most advertised products in Túquerres, with billboards and radio advertisements. Anyone growing potatoes could count on periodic home visits from chemical salesmen.

The dismantling of agricultural aid also led to the closure of the *Caja Agraria*, the national bank specifically devoted to agriculture. As the agricultural bank diminished in importance and finally closed, there was a proliferation of commercial banks and credit unions, with the number of banking outlets in Túquerres doubling in the 1990s. These new banks often promised loans simply in proportion to deposits. The loans could be used for agricultural or other productive purposes, but they were not tailored as such. The family I lived with received a loan to rebuild the part of the house mostly used for parties, specifically in advance of a grand first communion that the mother wanted to host for her son. These new banks were more consumer-oriented, stressing individual preferences and decisions rather than productivity growth (Antrosio 2008, 337–378).

The lure of the 2008 pyramid scheme makes more sense in the light of these changes from the 1990s. In other words, this should not be seen as a case of an unknown practice confronting innocent peasants. Rather, there were important precursors as consumer goods imported from Ecuador intersected with projects to change cooking and leisure activities; agriculture became the focus of advertising and a more consumer-oriented mentality; and banking moved from a focus on savings and productive investment to emphasize consumer-based lending. I am here arguing against interpretations, both in Colombia and elsewhere, which explain participation in pyramid schemes as a consequence of naïveté and absence of exposure to financial markets.

Pyramids and Peasant Values

"Fast Easy Money in Cash." Just the name should give the game away. Indeed, most people did not initially accept these schemes. Then a few people began putting in money and received payouts. They convinced disbelieving friends by literally showing them the money: "See, it is real." Visibility was a key component. The DRFE rented a prominent space and hired tellers with cash registers, giving out receipts. People could see the money accumulating in the rooms behind the registers. As Robert Shiller notes in a summary of Ponzi schemes, "initial investors were reportedly very skeptical about the schemes and would invest only small amounts...Investors do not become truly confident in the scheme until they see others achieving large returns" (Shiller 2000, 66; cf. Forero 2009, 7; Verdery 1995a, 5).

Much analysis of pyramid schemes tends to blame moral failings and a desire for easy money. A hidden component of these schemes is how the promoters tap into notions of frugality. People saw themselves as frugally saving up money in order to "invest." As one young woman put it, people would be proud to say they were "going to *la F.*" When the time came when they could withdraw for that month, people would at the last moment change their mind and "reinvest," again taking pride they could defer and earn more for the next month.

Together with visibility and frugality is the value of patience and even of rising early. Long lines formed outside the offices, and during the height of the scheme people had to wait all day in order to make deposits. Hawkers sold food and drink to the people in line. People camped out overnight, and some could sell a place in line; the first few places in line were worth more than a day's wage in agriculture. Others said they "woke up early" to get their place, a phrase I had usually heard associated with work and dedication, or of the virtues of going to an early-morning Catholic mass.

Another important consideration is that although raising pigs and cabbages in a small plot behind the house might seem to be the essence of subsistence agriculture, there is a great deal of risk and market fluctuation in these tiny plot activities. Raising pigs was not actually seen as a long-term, slow accumulation investment. First, there is the uncertainty of whether a pig will grow nice and fat. I realized this when I went in "halves" on a pig, only to watch the other grow while mine lagged. Second, there is the uncertainty of market price for pigs. Many people buy a pig to fatten and sell later to buy school supplies or before the holidays—thus requiring them to sell when the time may not be the right one for selling—an unfortunately timed sale can be hardly worth the months of effort. Similarly with cabbage, there would be times of windfall profits from the tiny plot, when the money could be used to buy gifts of sneakers, jeans, or CDs. On other occasions, cabbage rotted behind the house, with no buyers and too much to eat.

So although I was surprised to learn that the people I stayed with had sold their pigs in order to put their money in the scheme, on closer inspection this action is congruent with values of having something tangible and visible, of proud frugality and deferment, and of early rising patience. Moreover, the notion of putting money into a rather risky investment, which could range from windfall profits to complete loss, was a familiar feature of small-plot agriculture. In some ways the pyramids were actually more aligned with peasant values than traditional banks and their promise of constant returns.

Pyramids and Investments

The two previous sections seek to show how investing in the pyramids made sense—they were linked to changes in the consumer sphere that had also affected agricultural production, and they were also aligned with peasant values and even the boom-and-bust dynamics of peasant agriculture. This section compares the Colombian pyramids with traditional investment strategies. As jaw-dropping fluctuations in global stock markets continue and uncertainty prevails, in what respects is the pyramid scheme different from the contemporary world economy?

I am not arguing for equivalence between pyramid schemes and publicly traded corporations. However, these may be differences in degree rather than kind. It is also worth noting how much investing can be a kind of consumption activity, another theme connecting the pyramid schemes to traditional investments. Several factors are usually said to separate a fraudulent pyramid from a true investment: stability and duration; formal government regulation; the type of moneymaking activity; and diversification, or assembling a portfolio to minimize risk.

With regard to the stability and duration of the pyramid schemes, one surprise is that although these schemes were new to Túquerres, companies like DMG had actually been operating in the adjacent Putumayo province for several years (Forero 2009, 22; Ramírez 2009). Putumayo is an Amazonian region of Colombia, with notoriety as a coca-growing region. While for many highland Tuquerreños this was a conceptually distant locale, people from Putumayo came to the weekly market, and a number of people from Túquerres got work picking coca. Since these schemes had apparently been operating for years in a nearby province, their spread into the highlands could simply be seen as a business expansion. Moreover, speculation is hardly absent from normal business practices, nor does longevity guarantee escape from rapid ruin.[2]

Pyramid schemes are of course illegal, and should not receive government regulation or sanction. In Túquerres, however, people commented on the involvement of different layers of government in their functioning. At a basic level, people talked about seeing police officers, lawyers, and government officials putting money into the system. It also helped that the person who opened the branch for DRFE in Túquerres was from an already-powerful and well-connected family, and she had previously been a bank teller. Others noted that the government of Colombia seemed to be sanctioning the activity, at least passively, by not taking action against it. The Colombian government collected tax revenues from DRFE (Morales 2008). This may not add up to participation in a regulatory framework, but it is questionable how different it is from current regulatory practices.

Traditional companies are supposed to have some sort of legitimate moneymaking activity, whereas pyramid schemes are simply false fronts. It was very interesting to hear what people thought about how DRFE was making money. Some said they thought it was from a legitimate import-export business, as they saw pictures of boatloads of clothing imported from Asia. There were tales of a beneficent drug lord who now wanted to give his money to the people, perhaps as expiation for past sins. Others talked about how the pyramid scheme was "making money in dollars, euros." There is an interesting nationalistic overtone to many of these stories, spoken of as the opportunity of the common Colombian to participate in gains formerly enjoyed only by the wealthy or by foreigners (Romero 2009). In this respect, the message is not unlike those who promise that mutual funds provide access to the money-building secrets of the rich, and their activities are not unlike those of firms that simply hold trading positions rather than real assets.

It could be argued that it is unfair to compare the pyramid schemes with companies that evaporated; after all, investments are supposed to be diversified. What is interesting here is that people in southwestern Colombia developed their own form of diversification, which was to invest in multiple schemes. According to one professor, people in the region would travel from town to town, spreading money through the system to try and capitalize on rate differentials, and timing their withdrawals. While this still can be seen as an all-or-nothing approach, especially when the pyramid schemes fell in tandem, diversification across markets cannot always prevent synchronized decline.

Again, I am not suggesting that pyramid schemes are equivalent to capitalist corporations. However, in terms of stability, regulation, moneymaking activity, and diversification, the difference is one of degree, not kind. Investing can take on a kind of consumption aspect, becoming a status symbol as well as a hope for earning. In one sense, what the pyramid schemes did was to bring this status symbol to people who have usually been excluded from this realm. The vast majority in southwestern Colombia has no access to mutual funds, stock markets, IRAs, or 529 plans. Unfortunately the pyramid scheme was the closest approximation.

Consequences: Casinos and the Agrarian Bank

One morning the news ran rapidly, house to house, in the street, summed up in two words: *se fué*—it left. The classic stages of reaction to death seem applicable. Denial. Anger. Bargaining. Depression. Acceptance. For many who had believed, it became impossible not to believe. People cried in the streets, wandered aimlessly, or gathered where the schemes had been housed. There were protests in support of DMG, especially in Putumayo. Eventually, in Túquerres people broke the windows of the DRFE, burned it, and spray-painted graffiti, *ladrones, hijos de puta* (thieves, sons of bitches). Many said it was widespread knowledge that the schemes would eventually collapse, and there was simply speculation as to when. Everyone wanted to believe that they could make it for one more month. It was November—perhaps they could hold out for a Christmas payout.

In terms of the "bargaining" phase, there were rumors of ways to get the money back. One night the rumor circulated that the pyramid owners would be returning with two trucks loaded with cash for the final payout. People lined the streets, besieging any truck that passed. Classic swindles often feature a follow-up operation that poses as a way to retrieve the funds lost. I did not hear about any of these, possibly because the consequences for the original operators were potentially violent. Some of the original perpetrators were killed, others fled, some stationed permanent bodyguards, and some committed suicide. Murcia was jailed in Bogotá. His interview in the *New York Times* (Romero 2009) is eerily reminiscent of how the *Times* described Charles Ponzi in 1920: "It is almost possible, thought not quite, to believe that he was as credulous as his victims and deceived himself as much as he did them" (cited in Zuckoff 2005, 293–294). Colombia's history of personal vengeance must be considered—one professor said there was a well-known list of people drawn up who were being systematically killed (see also Forero 2009, 23). The professor spoke of how a dead body is popularly referred to as *ajuste de cuentas*, balancing the accounts.

There were some government efforts to compensate losses, but these were pittance in comparison to the enormous sums invested. Some people claimed there must have been official collusion—where did all the money go? There were also claims of video evidence of police loading bags of cash into cars just before the final collapse.

I heard of people who were in a stage of deep depression, people who had "aged" or were permanently affected psychologically, and stories of domestic violence. The people I spoke to seemed either resigned or had begun to make jokes about it. One of my friends joked he had a special connection so I could be the first investor when they returned. A city councilman said this had "now become something folkloric, humorous," the subject of mocking floats for the New Year's Eve parade. Still, there seemed to be deep anxiety about fraudulent behavior running through the town—the day I arrived in 2009 there was a church bingo, but even the church bingo cards were rumored to be falsified.

Two "casinos" had opened on Túquerres's main square, across from the main chapel. Despite promising names like "Red Dragon Casino," they looked like run-down slot-machine dives. There were also lottery-vending windows scattered through the town. The pyramid schemes seem to have spurred an institutionalization of the pursuit of luck and risk.

At the same time, the collapse of the pyramid schemes led to some very familiar activities. People were planting potatoes again, and returning to small-scale cultivation. The long line in town was outside the *Banco Agrario de Colombia*. The agrarian bank had a new name and face-lift, and was back in its former location, open for business. This was part of a national government push, in the wake of the pyramid crisis, to extend legitimate credit with a concentration on microfinance and microloans, as used in other developing countries (Forero 2009, 34). One person said the outcome of the pyramid scheme had actually "favored agriculture."

Conclusion

This chapter traces how the rise and fall of a pyramid scheme is not simply a novelty, but linked and continuous with other changes in production and consumption practices. Important precursors to the 2008 events can be found in the transformation of consumption items at home, in agriculture, and in the financial sector.

The effects of quite extraordinary losses should not be minimized, and the establishment of casinos and lotteries is problematic. However, the revival of agriculture and the agrarian bank point toward a more nuanced approach. Although consumer activities have often been either celebrated or severely criticized, they seem to be part of an ongoing process of appropriation and continuity. It is of course important to pay careful attention to inequalities of power, implications for resources, and the particular empirical elements of these appropriations: hybridization, or in an earlier era, *mestizaje*, is not necessarily cause for celebration. Nevertheless, putting Latin American consumption cases into this wider framework seems a fruitful way to understand contemporary lifeways.

Notes

1. Although there has been some analysis of the pyramid schemes from a financial point of view, there has been little formal investigation of the sociocultural aspects. This chapter draws on two unpublished analyses, a conference paper by María Clemencia Ramírez (2009) and a policy paper by Carolina Forero (2009). For anthropological analyses of pyramid schemes, a key comparison is Romania during the early 1990s (Verdery 1995a; 1995b). On a national level the Colombian schemes may have involved 8 percent of the population (Forero 2009, 1), but the regional figures were much higher; the governor of the province estimated at least 50 percent involvement (Morales 2008). When I discussed this with a professor from the region, I said I had heard that 80 percent of the population was involved. He replied, "That's a lie. 100 percent."

2. I would stress, however, that while the pyramids are in "traditional cocaine producer regions" (Forero 2009, 17), it would be a mistake to see this as part of a general pursuit of quick riches greased by cocaine. First, the real problems arose with the pyramid schemes in the highlands, where people have

generally been removed from the drug economy. Second, these may be coca-producing regions, but the farmers and laborers are not the main beneficiaries of the cocaine trade.

References

Antrosio, Jason. 2002. "Inverting Development Discourse in Colombia: Transforming Andean Hearths." *American Anthropologist* 104 (4), 1110–1122.

———. 2008. *Todo moderno: Significados de la modernización en la sierra colombiana.* Quito, Ecuador: Abya-Yala.

Barbero, Jesús Martín. 2006. "Between Technology and Culture: Communication and Modernity in Latin America." In *Cultural Agency in the Americas.* Edited by Doris Sommer, 37–51. Durham, NC: Duke University Press.

Bauer, Arnold J. 2001. *Goods, Power, History: Latin America's Material Culture.* Cambridge: Cambridge University Press.

Cahn, Peter S. 2008. "Consuming Class: Multilevel Marketers in Neoliberal Mexico." *Cultural Anthropology* 23 (3), 429–452.

Colloredo-Mansfeld, Rudi. 1999. *The Native Leisure Class: Consumption and Cultural Creativity in the Andes.* Chicago: University of Chicago Press.

Forero, Carolina. 2009. "The Problem of Pyramid Schemes: The Case of Colombia." Policy Paper, Graduate School of Public and International Affairs, University of Pittsburgh.http://www.pitt.edu/~jcf43/Policy%20paper.pdf.

Morales, Lorenzo. 2008. "La venta de trago cayó de 1.500 a 13 millones este mes en Nariño." *Semana.com*, November 25, 2008. http://www.semana.com/noticias-piramides/venta-trago-cayo-1500-13-millones-este-mes-narino/118084.aspx.

Ramírez, María Clemencia. 2009. "Complicity, Conspiracy and Legitimacy: Contesting the Hegemonic Order Through a New Corporate Formation at the Margins of the Colombian State." Paper presented at the annual meeting of the American Anthropological Association, Philadelphia.

Romero, Simon. 2009. "Where Officials see Fraud, Colombia's Masses see a Folk Hero." *New York Times*, January 31, 2009. http://www.nytimes.com/2009/01/31/world/americas/31murcia.html.

Rowe, William, and Vivian Schelling. 1991. *Memory and Modernity: Popular Culture in Latin America.* London: Verso.

Shiller, Robert J. 2000. *Irrational Exuberance.* Princeton: Princeton University Press.

Verdery, Katherine. 1995a. "'Caritas' and the Reconceptualization of Money in Romania." *Anthropology Today* 11 (1), 3–7.

———. 1995b. "Faith, Hope, and *caritas* in the Land of the Pyramids: Romania, 1990 to 1994." *Comparative Studies in Society and History* 37 (4), 625–669.

Zuckoff, Mitchell. 2005. *Ponzi's Scheme: The True Story of a Financial Legend.* New York: Random House.

Part 3

Domestic Practice

6

Decorating the New House: The Material Culture of Social Mobility

Tomas Ariztia

Although the two concepts are normally conflated into one, a house does not necessarily imply the existence of a home (Blunt and Dowling 2006). In fact, making a home often involves large amounts of "symbolic labor" expended on the house over a lengthy period of time. Home is therefore not just an idea or a space but an active cultural process (Miller 2001). Home-making practices, then, are all those by means of which dwellers ground personal and social meanings in the new residence, thus making a house into their home (Blunt and Dowling 2006). When making a home, families appropriate the new residence and make it part of their lives (Miller 1997). This chapter analyses how people deal with household possessions and decoration when moving home. By doing so, it explores the practice of decoration and arrangement of household possessions as a space in which social mobility and class cultures are assembled in contemporary Chile. Concretely, it is argued that the arrangement of possessions in the new house involves the production of individual narratives of social mobility and the performing of owner's new social position. Home possessions are described, thus, not only as material elements that mark class cultures, but also as a central dimension in the production of class cultures as such.

The chapter is based on seven months of fieldwork in a new real estate development in the suburbs of the city of Santiago in Chile called "Los Pinos."[1] I spent most of this time involved, on a daily basis, in the life of 20 families who had recently moved to the area, discussing and participating in their house-moving process. I conducted more than 60 tape-recorded interviews and compiled over 200 pages of field notes, as well as an assortment of additional material such as maps, magazines, and more than 400 photographs. This chapter relies on the fieldwork material that was related to the issue of decoration and decoration practices. Decoration and taste were a central part of interviews as well as the informal discussion over the new home. During the six months of my fieldwork, I found that this idea of homemaking as a dynamic process was pivotal. Indeed, in my fieldwork setting Los Pinos, moving to a new house was not a passive transition but an animated and dynamic process that reshaped notions of family. Many aspects of family life, such as family history, framing, projects, and everyday life practices were reshaped in such a way that boundaries between family and house were often blurred. Homemaking practices may, therefore, be seen as being at the core of the cultural repertoire that Los Pinos families deploy to make themselves feel in "place," to construct their new social and spatial position.

I argue here that homemaking practices *are*, so to speak, the material culture of social mobility. When decorating, Los Pinos neighbors produce a whole conception of social mobility. This not only relates to a shared sense of achievement and autonomy (Kaika 2004), as well as ownership and economic accumulation (Bourdieu 2001), but what is negotiated during this practice is also a new sense of attachment—of "fitting in"—through which families merge their trajectory with their current situation. The creation of home and this sense of attachment do not relate to a preexistent set of class values or positions, but are instead a consequence of an active production involving everyday practices, places, and objects. This production is executed by way of negotiation, connections, and creativity. Decorating is therefore described here as a complex and dynamic processes that often involves the articulation of delicate equilibrium between house and material possessions, family expectations and budget limitations. Improving and decorating, therefore, diverge from passive dwelling in a house designed for masses, to enact a cultural process of appropriation (Miller 1997).

Decoration and the Middle Classes in Latin America

Most of Latin American research on home cultures has focused on working-class and peasantry home[2]; indeed it is difficult to find much reflection on middle classes. One of the few pieces of research that have explored these links in the Latin American middle class is the work of O'Dougherty (2002). In her research, she shows how domestic space plays a crucial role not only in framing the family but also, more centrally, in reproducing differences between the working and middle classes. The use of domestic space (and domestic service) appears here as an important strategy for marking cultural differences. This work takes a broadly Bourdiean approach (1984) in which consumption emerges mainly as a class "marker" or the consequence of a given class position. As has been argued elsewhere (Ariztia 2009), one restriction of this approach is the marginal role attributed to the agency of objects in the production of the social and cultural forms. When it comes to class, they mostly work as signs that either "represent" social positions and their connection with the habitus or are deployed as mediums in the struggle to generate social distinctions. In most of these cases materiality is, thus, reduced to a signifier of social distinctions or structures (Rocamora 2002).

Several authors have proposed a more elaborated analysis of the connections between middle class and decoration practices. The relation between this practice and class appear in these accounts as mediated by several narratives, communities, and the objects themselves. For instance, in his research into kitchens in the UK, Southerton shows that kitchen decoration is related to "context specific practices" and the interplay of taste communities and individual narratives of taste that mediate a more extended categorization of class (Southerton 2001). In a similar vein, Woodward studied how the individual narratives of home decoration relate to wider moral boundaries that involve the production of middle-class identities (Woodward 2003). Here, people's narratives of their decoration choices appear as a space through which subjective and social identities are managed. Furthermore, other authors have explored the role of home possessions in the production of class. Clarke (2001) analyzed how furniture and home decoration help to perform social aspirations and construct an ideal "social self." Concretely, she explores how home possessions may express the tensions between owners' self-identity and their social aspirations. This account examines not only the agency of people over their home possessions—the process of symbolic labor through which people appropriate the material world—but also the capacity of these objects to have some degree of agency in shaping people's experience (Miller 2001). I take a similar stance by focusing on how decoration practice and home possessions are key elements through which people's social position is produced. It is, thus, a practice that mediates the production of class cultures.

In this chapter, I rely on this literature to analyze different ways in which decoration involves the production of new owner's social position. By taking this standpoint, I attempt to contribute to the emerging debate of the production of middle-class cultures in contemporary Chile (Mendez 2008; Barozet 2006). I do so by unpacking the complex set of narratives, objects, and practices through which class and social mobility is performed when decorating the new house. The main argument is that decoration is a practice through which newcomers perform their spatial as well as social family's new coordinates. This argument is deployed in two moments. I first describe the practice of decoration. It is described as related to the negotiation of several elements such as external references, budget considerations, and personal narratives of taste. I then go on to present two specific ways in which decoration involves the assembling of middle-class cultures. First, relying on Mendez's work (2008), I describe how decoration choices involve personal "accounts" about authenticity regarding social origin and new social position. Second, I analyze how the arrangement of old possessions in the new house involves considering and evaluating their social and residential trajectories.

The Practice of Decoration: Discourses, Stratagems and Routines

Decoration is a common topic of conversation in most Los Pinos families. Decoration is regarded as a highly enjoyable activity and usually takes up a great deal of time. In fact, during my fieldwork, I spent hours talking about detailed plans for interior decoration, furniture, colors, and style. Planning usually has its own material culture, involving maps and sketches, and an array of ideas and bargains. For example, several of my informants kept a journal of things that they liked or a wish list.

In many cases, decoration may be construed as an ongoing dialogue about style and taste between the couple. When talking about wishes and projects, couples shape what they understand and what they want to do in their house. Often, decoration is ultimately the articulation of desires or concepts emerging from a set of several different elements such as magazines, model homes, formal discourses about taste and decoration, and the values and aspirations of family members—helping to frame individual decisions.

Couples often use decoration magazines to look for deals and get good ideas. The most used in Los Pinos is *Casa y Decoración*, a Sunday supplement. None of the families I met mentioned buying any other magazine. The back pages of *Casa y Decoración* advertise sales and offers on furniture. These pages are usually regarded as a good place to find things at a reasonable price. Some people collected magazines to make a scrapbook of offers and ideas. Showhouses are also used as referents. When I asked Javier how they chose their furniture, he said: "I think it was a combination of things. We went to the model home to see what kind of lights they had used. We also looked at magazines, *Casa y Decoración*: as I am subscribed to *La Tercera* (newspaper), I get it every Sunday."

Despite the importance of these references, families very rarely take literally what they find in them. Instead, magazines and model homes help create and define a more personal sense of taste and propriety that families use to mark a distance between their final decisions and the options displayed in these media. In this sense, they take an opportunistic and pragmatic approach to the use of external references such as magazines or showhouses. The idea of adapting and borrowing ideas is highly valued, as it allows families to enhance and "personalize" the original source. In fact, none of my informants had bought a piece of furniture that was promoted in magazines or displayed in the model home. When I discussed this with Josefa, she was very clear about the distance between magazine offers and her final possibilities and choices.

> We used to have magazines that I looked at more for the garden because I haven't got a clue about gardening. A lot of people talk to me about cutting out pictures from magazines; they look for nice things in magazines. There was a time when I did that, too, but now I haven't looked at a magazine in ages. I have a house and I want to look at what I can afford to buy.

As expected, decoration projects are placed in the context of family resources and history. People must reconcile their expectations with their resources and existing objects. Different decoration possibilities are mediated by budget and pragmatic considerations. In this case, not only by budget, but also by existing possessions. The final choice is a plan conditioned by making the most of "what is at hand." Martin and Macarena, for example, defined themselves as committed to achieving a stylish and warm decoration. For them, one of the most important things in terms of decoration was to keep their house's "rustic" style. The importance they attribute to style relates to their profession as designers: "As both of us are designers and we also looked at design magazines and books."

Their house was predominantly decorated with wooden furniture and original handicrafts. In order to keep their style, they avoid receiving decorative gifts from other people, as this may soil the coherence of their decor. During one interview, however, I realized that many of their objects were not aligned with this aesthetic canon. Martin explained:

> I do not often accept pieces of furniture as a gift; this piece is just an exception. I needed it and my mother gave it to me...The one thing that is not in line is that piece of furniture there. It's my mum's, but I don't have anywhere else to keep the dishes. For that reason, we're going to buy a new piece of furniture later that has the same rustic style that we can keep the dishes in.

Thus, predictably, even the more rigorous commitment to a particular style is mediated by practical considerations.

Like house buying and home improvements, decorating is very much a matter of budget. Decorating involves two different practices: refurbishing and purchasing. On the one hand, families often refurbish and customize their furniture, trying to make the most of old things. Pamela and Joaquín, for example, worked hard to adapt their old furniture to their new house. When we talked about furniture, they told me that some of it was hard to adapt. The bed was the most difficult. They could not find a way to get it into their room, so they had to split it into parts. Now they are just using the mattress. When I asked them about buying a new bed, they told me that now they like their bedroom's style, as it has a "new-age look." As Joaquin said, "In the end we dismantled the wooden frame (of the bed) and used it to build a fence for the dogs, so that they can't get outside, and we put the mattress on the floor. We even thought about buying cushions to put on the floor permanently, the bed with cushions at the sides."

Pamela and Joaquín told me that they enjoyed making those alterations. For them, working on the furniture is also an important part of creating their new home.

On the other hand, while buying new things is not uncommon, it is usually restricted by budget considerations and is considered, overall, a second choice. In the case of decorative objects and mementoes, purchases are small and relative to the occasion. They represent very personal decisions and are not connected to more general decoration decisions. Some couples, such as Pamela and Joaquín, have made bargain hunting in flea markets one of their hobbies. They get small, cheap things there. Besides being a hobby, this is an important part of a couple's life. In the case of bigger pieces of furniture, purchases imply a larger investment of time and price comparisons. At this scale, decorating is almost as important as improving the house. I met two families for whom buying furniture was a big investment, as they had no possessions. In both cases, the purchases were planned and calculated carefully, through lengthy negotiation. The case of Josefa and Andrés illustrates this practice. The first time I met them, they had nothing in their living room. When I asked them if they had any furniture, they told me they had none, but were saving to buy everything they needed in cash. Their first purchase was a new sofa. When they bought it, they both told me that it was a difficult decision that involved balancing the sofa's use-value with considerations of style and taste:

J: It was difficult for us to choose the armchairs.
A: it is a mixture of both of us.

J: It was a mixture. The thing is that I liked, for example, this style with
      wood and fabric but Andrés didn't. I wanted something that you can
      clean easily. In the end, one day we said, "Let's go and buy the armchairs,"
      and we said, "let's go to the furniture centre, and after that, the market."

Several elements have been described here as central pieces of the decor
the new house. Budget considerations as well as practicalities play a key
role. Similarly, the use of external references such as print media and
magazines is central, though it is always mediated by individual narratives and budget considerations. The final practice emerges, therefore, as
the juxtaposition of several levels of evaluation and restrictions, such as
budget and practicalities, personal tastes, and external references.

Fitting Things in: The Material Culture of Social Mobility

In this section, I argue that decoration is one of the main practices
through which families assemble their new social and spatial coordinates.
It does so in the less visible spaces of choice and arrangement of household possessions and style decisions. I will deploy this argument in two
streams. First, the way in which decoration articulates taste, authenticity, and external referents of taste—elements that are deployed in terms
of defining new social positions. Second, I will explore how decoration
involves relating old possessions with the new house and how newcomers
reconcile old possessions and trajectories with their new residences.

Confronting Authenticity

Decoration plans are strongly related to couples' moral ideas about themselves. Decoration objectifies their personal values and aspirations and
relates to the production of their trajectories and moral frameworks
(Clarke 2001; Marcoux 2001; Woodward 2003). Decoration practices
mediate how families make sense of their process of social and spatial
change. The links between moral ideas of authenticity and the production of Chilean middle-class cultures have been explored recently in the
work of (Mendez 2008). In her work, she analyzed how different notions
of authenticity operate in the production of moral boundaries and horizontal frontiers in the middle classes. Following Mendez, but in terms
of the decoration practices explored here, I noted that decisions are also
traversed by an authenticity-related tension that relates to their social
position, particularly the tension between individual taste and what newcomers regard as mainstream decorative style.

This tension is expressed in several ways. The most common is the relation between taste and decoration and the expression of individual values and trajectories. Here, décor is understood to express "authenticity" and often opposes the "expectations" of others. During my research, I found that this quest for authenticity sometimes took precedence over the awareness of more official, "suitable" ways to decorate the house. Joaquín and Pamela, for example, told me that they preferred to base their decoration decisions on comfort and personal taste: "What we dreamt about before was old furniture, but to be honest, we thought that, as we like to lie on the sofas, both of us, and then we realized that if we bought the posh sofas, they would be too hard."

For them, mainstream style is less important than their own ideas of comfort and taste. Here, their choices diverge from more appropriate, "expected" furniture, such as old sofas. Joaquín told me that he knew that wooden chairs would have been more appropriate; however, they preferred the comfort of the big sofa.

Some people used "decorative" concepts as a way to explain their own taste in opposition to other, mainstream tastes. Here, the mainstream taste appears as a synonym of snobbism. Martín and Macarena described their own taste, based on charm and rusticity, in opposition to what they defined as a mainstream, aspirational modern taste, which they associate with modernism and minimalism. Their ideal decoration is based on wood and simple things, but with "good taste" (*elegante*) and not snobbish or cold. When I asked Martin to explain more about their taste, he compared his house with a friend's:

TA: Why do you like rustic style?

M: Because the wood is warm. Without it the house looks too cold. For example, I have a friend who has a spectacular house, full design, he has metal, glass and leather; everything simple, the place is nice but it is terribly cold.

TA: So the thing is make the house being more homey?

M: I prefer something warmer, we really like the wood.

Their style is opposed to external references and notions of "good taste" and "suitability." In this case, the definition of their own trajectories revolves around the tension between their own decorative choices and artificiality or snobbish forms. Decoration not only relates to their choices as couple, but is also held against a background defined by a mainstream and legitimate social map of taste. Within this context, the way families deal with "authenticity" is essential to the way they perform their own process of upward mobility. Unlike Mendez's findings, in which individual authenticity was connected to the production of horizontal identities among middle-class sectors (Ibid. 2008), here the comparison of personal decisions with more general taste schemes does not establish horizontal comparisons but relates to the production of couples' individual trajectories.

Other families, however, do not see "own style" as such a positive way of decorating. Óscar and Júlia, for example, told me that they feel they lack the skills to produce a coherent and harmonious decorative scheme. They construe "good taste" as an external skill that they do not possess, as they are "unskilled" in decoration. They would prefer someone *who knows how to do it* to come in and decorate their whole house. Here, the choice of being "yourself" when decorating is understood as counter to the couple's expectations, as it may lead to a nontasteful outcome or inability to cope with the new requirements. In the case of Óscar and Júlia, decorative style—or lack of it—forms part of their expectations of confirming their new social and spatial position; hence, decoration work is a space for confirming social aspirations (Clarke 2001). Mainstream good taste is regarded not as something artificial but as a desirable point of reference in the process of social and spatial mobility.

In these examples, decoration and taste is related to the management of the couple's authenticity and originality. This involves confronting their own decorative choices with a more general sense of mainstream taste, which is understood to define what is "expected" in terms of the new house. To paraphrase Savage et al. (Savage et al. 2001) in their analysis of people's relations to "class" labels in north-west England, it can be said that here the space of mainstream style decisions is not only connected with a more general view of social positions but is also used "a set of external reference points through which the individual navigates" (Ibid. 2001, 882). Mainstream style is not an explicit source of identification but a background against which couples contrast their own trajectories and style decisions. Nevertheless, within this context, not all couples regard "their own style" as preferable; indeed, while some families regard authenticity as a positive way of dealing with their new social spatial coordinates, other families recognize mainstream notions of taste and decoration as a norm they should follow in order to adapt to their new social and spatial position.

Old Things, New Life

For Los Pinos families, one of the most important decoration issues is where their old possessions will go in the new house. This is very understandable, considering that most couples have already bought most of their "essential" pieces of furniture before moving there. Based on my visits to Los Pinos houses, common possessions were: electrical appliances such as a microwave oven, cooker, TV, radio, and fridge; pieces of furniture like sofas, dining room table, bed, or chairs; and decorative objects such as pictures, ornaments, antiques, metal figures, or paintings that were displayed in the living room. The vast majority of these things had been acquired during the couple's history; often close to the start of cohabitation (marriage in the case of some couples or moving in together in the case of others). As a result, most families regarded possessions as the cornerstone in their process of accumulation. In fact, during my conversations about possessions, the expression *"nosotros hemos juntado todas nuestras cositas"* ("We've collected all our stuff") was regularly used in a quite sentimental way. Old possessions were a central part of the family's constitution. In many cases, those objects articulated and represented key points in a couple's history.

Fitting old possessions into the new house usually raised several concerns about a family's trajectory. The place of possessions mediated the change they were living. During my fieldwork, I found at least two ways of dealing with this process. On the one hand, some families planned no change or improvement of their old possessions. Old possessions were regarded as a central asset that should not be changed just because of the new house. Possessions had to be used until the end of their useful life, and would not be changed unless they really would not fit into the house or were broken during the move. As well as the cost of buying new furniture, this loyalty has to do with the belief that things should last until they no longer work. Great value was also attributed to some objects as being associated with the start of the couples' life together. In this case, keeping old possessions and adapting them to the new house offered key continuity between family history and the new house. They helped to articulate family trajectory.

When possessions are not questioned, the task of decorating has to do with making old furniture look better or shifts to details such as curtains or paint. The case of Susana and Juan illustrates this. When I asked Susana and Juan about their furniture, they told me that they had had everything they needed for a long time. They had been together for ten years and they had accumulated their things "since the beginning." Most of their things were bought at the beginning of their relationship: As Juan said, "When we moved in together we bought a dining table, the fridge, which was the most essential, someone lent us a cooker, then I won a cooker too, I also won the fridge."

Susana and Juan did not buy any more furniture when they moved to Los Pinos. As their furniture was still usable, it was not a priority. Moreover, they attached no importance to it as long as it served its purpose. Utility and durability were therefore the most important attributes of furniture for them. When I asked Juan about buying new furniture, he told me that they didn't need anything else; the investment had already been made and there was no reason to make it again: "No, no, no, we bought those armchairs and, to be honest, there isn't anything that (we need), I don't know, perhaps in the future, we could replace them, I don't know, my daughter's bed."

In contrast to Juan and Susana, other families had issues with their old possessions in the new house. For them, old possessions, particularly living room furniture, related to past times and past places that had nothing to do with the new situation. In most cases, however, the possibility of changing all the furniture was very remote given the limited resources. The case of Óscar and Júlia shows this logic. Óscar's and Júlia's living room furniture comes from their old flat. They lived in a flat that was subsidized by their company (they both work at Santiago airport) for eight years. Although Óscar recognized that the new house had given a new air to their furniture, he felt no particular attachment to it and was planning to replace all of it. When I asked Óscar what he would buy instead, he told me that if he had enough money he would buy all new furniture.

> TA: What is going to happen with your furniture? Are you going to throw it away?
> Ó: Yes, my idea was to have the new furniture immediately, but…
> TA: Is this related to moving house or do you always do it?
> Ó: Having a house is like having a new baby.
> J: Like a toy.
> Ó: More than a toy, a new baby, you want the best for your new baby.

For Óscar, things are part of past, different times and therefore need to be changed. Here, old possessions are more of an obstacle to the family's life-plan than part of their memory. Unlike other families who define their old possessions as an element of continuity between the different points of their trajectory, in this case the process of social mobility is lived more radically as involving a change in material possessions too.

Dealing with old possessions leads families to consider and evaluate their social and residential trajectories. Possessions mediate the change of family values and aspirations vis-à-vis their new circumstances. Against this backdrop, some couples, like Óscar and Júlia, were more aware and willing to embrace a new situation and lived the new house as a change in their whole cultural repertoire; others, such as Susan and Juan, articulate a sense of continuity that is not disrupted by the new house. In both cases, however, there is an active awareness of the choices that have to be made in order to be consistent with their trajectories. Decorating the new house thus involves making sense of and deciding how to live in their process of social change.

Concluding Remarks: The Material Culture of Social Mobility

By decorating their homes, families make them part of their life. Decorating helps families to make their house a home. Social and spatial mobility are also performed through decorating the new house. Elements such as magazines, model homes, or formal conceptualizations about legitimate taste are incorporated into descriptions and help families to perform and deal with their new social and spatial circumstances. It has been discussed here how some of these decisions are ordered around the tension between personal choices and "mainstream taste," therefore mediating the way in which newcomers fit into their new social and spatial coordinates. In some cases, decoration choices emerge as an individualized space of moral judgment, which is deployed against the background of mainstream style categories. In other cases, the whole process of moving into a new home is perceived to require a change in individual taste in accordance with the new situation.

The dynamic between old possessions and the new house is another essential element; it marks family trajectory and makes visible the change in living conditions. By deciding and negotiating how to adapt their old possessions, families make their own trajectory visible. Moreover, dealing with their own possessions makes the family's process of social mobility more reflexive. At all these stages, home possessions are an active part of their origin and history, so dealing with them is also a way of reordering their own narratives and projects. Based on these different elements, it can be argued, thus, that decoration work is another mediation through which newcomers attempt to negotiate and produce their new social and spatial coordinates. Links between home making practices and people's new social and spatial coordinates emerge, nevertheless, as a highly negotiated ensemble of practices, narratives and materialities. In other words, it may be said that neighbors are not alone in this process, as several external elements are involved in mediating their home-moving experience.

Materialities play an important part in this process. Indeed, household possessions are active in structuring a sense of home, family, and the whole experience of trajectories of social mobility. In fact, the entire practice of decorating may be defined, in some sense, as an effort to appropriate the new home through things (Miller 1997). Indeed, by decorating, people recontextualize the new house, making it part of the specificity of their own social trajectory. Home decoration and home possessions help thus to shape their experience of social mobility, becoming a *"source and the setting of mobility and change"* (Miller 2001: 4). In sum, families dealing with their possessions in these new circumstances not only change them but are also shaped by their material history and individual style, raising issues of how to live in their new social and spatial coordinates. Here, the new house and the household possessions help families to live particular types of experiences and relate them to certain types of decisions and practices in terms of how to live their whole home-moving process.

Notes

1. The name of the neighborhood, and the names of all participants mentioned or interviewed in this chapter, have been changed to preserve anonymity.
2. See for example: Ortega-Alcázar 2007, Ureta 2007.

References

Blunt, Alison, and Robyn Dowling. 2006. *Home*. London: Routledge.

Bourdieu, Pierre. 2001. *Las estructuras sociales de la economia*. Madrid: Manantial.

Clarke, Alison. 2001. "The Aesthetics of Social Aspiration." In *Home Possessions*. Edited by Daniel Miller, 23–45. London: Berg.

Colloredo-Mansfeld Rudi. 1994. "Architectural Conspicuous Consumption and Economic Change in the Andes." *American Anthropologist* 96(4), 845–865.

Da Matta, Roberto. 1987. *A casa e a rua: espaco, cidadania, mulher e morte no Brasil*. Rio de Janeiro: Editorial da Guanabara.

De Certeau, M. (1984). *The Practice of Everyday Life*. Berkeley: University of California Press.

Gudeman, Stephen and Alberto Rivera.. 1990. *Conversations in Colombia: The Domestic Economy in Life and Text*. Cambridge: Cambridge University Press.

Holston, James. 1991. "Autoconstruction in Working Class Brazil." *Cultural Anthropology* 6(4), 447–465.

Kaika, Maria. 2004. "Interrogating the Geographies of the Familiar: Domesticating Nature and Constructing the Autonomy of Modern House." *International Journal of Urban and Regional Research* 28(2), 265–286.

Marcoux, Jean-Sebastien. 2001. "The 'casser maison': Constructing the Self by Emptying the House." *Material Culture* 6(2), 213–235.

Mendez, Maria Louisa. (2008). "Middle Class Identities in a Neoliberal Age: Tensions between Contested Authenticities." *Sociological Review* 56(2), 220–237.

Miller, Daniel. 1997. "Consumption and its Consequences". In *Consumption and Everyday Life*. Edited by Hugh Mackay, 14–50. London: Sage.

Miller, Daniel. ed. 2001. *Home Possessions*. London: Berg.

O'Dougherty, Maureen. 2002. *Consumption Intensified: The Politics of Middle Class Daily Life in Brazil*. London: Duke University Press.

Ortega-Alcázar, Iliana. 2007. "Brick by Brick : An Ethnography of Self-Help Housing, Family Practices and Everyday Life in a Consolidated Popular Settlement of Mexico City." PhD diss., London School of Economics and Political Science.

Savage, Mike, Gaynor Bagnall, and Brian Longhurst. 2001. "Ordinary, Ambivalent and Defensive: Class Identities in the Northwest of England." *Sociology* 35(4), 875–892.

Southerton, Dale. 2001. "Consuming Kitchens: Taste, Context and Identity Formation." *Journal of Consumer Culture* 1(2), 179–204.

Southerton, Dale. 2002. "Boundaries of 'Us' and 'Them': Class, Mobility and Identification in a New Town." *Sociology* 36(1), 179–193.

Ureta, Sebastian. 2007. "Domesticating Homes: Material Transformation and Decoration among Low-income Families in Santiago, Chile." *Home Cultures* 4(3), 311–336.

Woodward, Ian. 2001. "Domestic Objects and the Taste Epiphany." *Material Culture* 6(2), 115–136.

Woodward, Ian. 2003. "Divergent Narratives: The Imagining of the Home amongst Middle Class Consumers." *Journal of Sociology* 39(4), 391–412.

7

Stitching Identities: Clothing Production and Consumption in Mexico City

Marie Francois

The 1855 essay "La Costurera" in *Mexicanos pintados por sí mismos* highlights productive, symbolic, and material connections between sewing women and the consumers of the clothing that they make. The seamstress takes her place among other typical characters that animated Mexico City in the nineteenth century, such as water carriers, female boarding house managers, auctioneers, chambermaids, coachmen, and clerks who were also illustrated and feted in essays in the *costumbrista* volume. Author J. M. Rivera identifies *costureras de cajón*, or seamstresses employed in retail workshops in the city center, as the most typical of "these workers who sustain fashion." He also identifies various *costureras domesticas*—those employed in private homes as live-in servants, those who visited the homes of regular customers, and those who sewed for others for pay out of their own homes (Perez Salas 1998) [1].

The seamstress protagonists of Rivera's narrative are treated with a sympathetic romantic tone, though the author also pokes fun, a common trope in Mexican literature (Gonzalez Casanova 1951). Rivera reserves the full satire for clients of the downtown *cajones* whose public images are built on a thin stock of respectable clothing, while he sharply indicts lecherous employers of domestic seamstresses. Consumers of clothing and employers of female clothing workers are male in the story, though of course women also purchased and wore seamstress-made clothing. Rivera's representation leaves out the most common category of women engaged in sewing clothes: mothers, daughters, sisters, wives, and aunts whose unpaid labor to maintain their families included making clothes as well as maintaining and repairing seamstress- and tailor-made wardrobes.

Two threads in this Mexican story have been taken up separately in twentieth and now twenty-first century scholarship on Latin America. First, while invisible or dismissed as unskilled in traditional labor history, professional seamstresses have become more visible in new feminist labor history. Identities are sharper for the twentieth century clothing factory sewer than for hand-work seamstresses during and before J. M. Rivera's time and women producing cloth overshadow those making clothing (French and James 1999; Hutcheson 2001; Dobles Trejos 1999). The invisibility of women's work in general in Mexican censuses, in other archival sources, and in representations in nineteenth century literature hinders a full recovery of the seamstress story from the historical record. Second, the interdisciplinary literature on material culture emphasizes the importance of clothing as a marker of wealth shaping the public identities of middle-class and elite consumers, an emphasis also found in memoirs, short stories, and novels from nineteenth century Mexico (Bauer 2001, 154)[2]. This chapter pulls these strands in the literature together in reflection on Rivera's essay and other evidence to argue that gendered producers and consumers were intimately engaged in both the physical construction of clothing as well as the more abstract stitching together of identities. The analysis of intersections between production and consumption in the case of clothing also brings in the missing thread in the 1855 story above—women sewing without pay for themselves and their families—heeding Jocelyn Olcott's recent call for more dialogue between new labor history and reproductive-labor studies (Olcott 2011)[3].

Rivera's mid-nineteenth century narrative identifies the workshop seamstress as "obrera," or female worker, and uses the word "obra"—work—to describe what she does: sewing sitting at her bench among other sewers, rushing to work only to earn a "miserable" wage. With the category of "skilled" work socially constructed, examining the work behind the making of clothing necessarily involves deconstructing naturalized classifications (Phillips and Taylor 1980; Weinstein 1999). In colonial Spanish society, sewing was recognized as skilled work when done outside the home and by men in tailor workshops, with guilds formally regulating the trade. Seamstresses, although often also in workshops, were not organized into guilds in colonial Latin America (Arrom 1985; Porter 2003, 8)[4]. Susan Socolow suggests that colonial tailors only sewed for men and seamstresses only for women, "although the actual work involved was virtually the same. A good seamstress needed to combine the skills of artist, geometrician, and engineer as well as showing imagination, stamina, and manual dexterity. Nonetheless seamstresses were paid far less for their work than tailors" (Socolow 2000, 120). Susie Porter argues that women were concentrated in sewing and tobacco work in the nineteenth century *because* they had been excluded from other productive sectors formally organized in guilds. Jose Moya insists that tailors' skills in the nineteenth century included design and fashioning of garments "instead of simply sewing." Tailors made outerwear such as suits and coats, while most seamstresses made undershirts, shirts, and, ties, as well as dresses and skirts (Moya 1998 and Porter 2003, 10) [5]. Anyone sewing for pay or for themselves was doing so by hand for most of the nineteenth century, with the sewing machine arriving in Mexico in the 1870s (O'Brien 1999, 18) [6].

In Mexican novels and short stories, who did one's sewing was a marker of class. Urban elites and those in small towns appearing in the pages written by José Joaquín Fernandez de Lizardi in the early nineteenth century through Rafael Delgado at century's end presented themselves in public in tailored and seamstress-made clothing, often made out of imported cloth, though those paid to stitch the clothes were usually invisible.

In Arnold Bauer's seminal history of Latin American material culture, the local production of cloth by women is featured but there is little attention to the construction of *clothing*. There is only brief mention that "the best tailors and dressmakers brought English and French fashions within reach of the Latin American elite" (Bauer 2001, 157) in the late nineteenth century. Yet despite their omission from the historical narrative, the women sewing for a living in the nineteenth century in Mexico came from a long tradition of seamstresses. Women identified themselves or were identified as seamstresses in census data, in newspaper ads, and in popular literature when they sewed for others for pay.

The census is one of few places to glimpse seamstresses as a group in historical documents. Yet, Mexican censuses undercounted working women: census takers only recorded economic activity for household heads (hence women were virtually absent in the 1790 enumeration), used narrow definitions of "job," did not count people with multiple part-time jobs, or acted on an ideology that defined women as not employed by definition. A sample of the 1753 census of Mexico City covering over 2,400 residents out of the population of over 125,000 included only 52 *costureras* living in 27 households.[7] Even fewer seamstresses were counted by 1811 census takers (Porter 2003, 46–47, 155). Despite low numbers reported in census, Lizardi describes a Mexico City in his 1818 novel *Quijotita y su prima* with a great many seamstresses, with competition keeping profits small for each (Arrom 1985, 190). We know that women regularly sought sewing positions in the *Diario de México* classified section in the first decade of the nineteenth century.[8]

Among 48 seamstresses in the 1753 sample identified by age, more than half were between the ages of 10 and 30; a third were 31–50 years old and four were between 51 and 70. The vast majority of seamstresses in the sample (N=40) were "españolas," whites born in the colony (i.e. not immigrants, also called Creoles). Among white women with marital status listed, 18 were widowed, 16 single, and only 3 married (though all 3 had absent husbands). None of the six *mulatta* (of black and white parentage) and six *mestiza* (of white and Indian heritage) seamstresses were married; three of each group were widows, and three single. A common pattern was for widowed seamstresses to live with daughters who also sewed. All sewing workers in the 1753 census sample lived in their own households, usually in a downstairs "asesoria" or street-facing room in a boarding house (17), occasionally in a shared upstairs apartment (10), and not as live-in seamstresses. Two widowed seamstresses living in upstairs rooms had a female servant each (one Indian, one *mulata*).

Nine seamstresses appear in the 1811 census sample. All nine were Spaniards born in Mexico, all but one single (the married one lived in her own home), and four were live-in servants in households headed by immigrant merchants from Spain.[9] At Bajos de San Agustín 3, a large merchant household headed by Don Gregorio Sinilia from Rioja, with his Mexican wife Doña Ana María Valiente, employed seamstress Juana Fernandez, a single Creole from Mexico City. Also on staff were four other Creole women (housekeeper, nanny, wet nurse, and chambermaid), two Indian chambermaids (one of them married), one widowed *mestiza* chambermaid, a female Indian cook, a married Indian doorman, and a married Indian coachman. The children and wives of the married male servants also lived in the 30-person household.[10] The social obligations of the women and men in this elite family would have created a steady demand for fashionable, expertly made clothing.

In her classic study of Mexico City, Silvia Arrom argues "it was a sign of status for women not to work. Sewing for one's own family was admirable, but *coser lo ajeno,* or 'sewing for a stranger,' was degrading." In an alimony suit cited by Arrom (1985, 157–158), Doña María del Carmen Andrade complained bitterly of having to work as a seamstress. And yet, some white women in need of money turned to sewing, as it was more respectable than other work. Three *costureras* in the 1811 sample lived in one household, all three with the title Doña (indicating they were likely white), two of them sisters, all three single Creoles in their fifties from Mexico City.[11]

For seamstresses working out of their homes, subsisting could be difficult. In Lizardi's 1832 novela *Noches Triste y Dia Alegre,* when they did not have enough work, seamstresses pawned a tunic or blouse "which they had made at the cost of a thousand million pin pricks, at the cost of illnesses and sleeplessness" (Lizardi 1984, 207), only to be in need and hungry again in two days time. Average earnings for sewing continued to be very low in the 1840s, although Fanny Calderón, the Scottish wife of the Spanish ambassador, apparently employed a more expensive one from time to time. Calderón also put her in-house chambermaid to work sewing for her, work that the maid enjoyed, according to her employer: "We found our house *in statu quo*—agreeable letters from Europe—, great preparations making for the English ball, to assist at which we had returned sooner than we otherwise should, and for which my *femme-de-chambre* has just completed a dress for me, very much to her own satisfaction" (Pérez Toledo 2004, 225–226; Calderón de la Barca 1952, 144). This "seamstress" would not have been counted as such in a census, but instead would have appeared as a maid.

In a sample of close to 1,500 residents in a downtown neighborhood of Mexico City in 1842, 45 women are identified as seamstresses. Sonia Pérez Toledo's statistical analysis of the census finds only 1,124 *costureras* recorded, out of nearly 115,000 residents counted (Pérez Toledo 2004, 220, 225; Arrom 1985, 162, 164, 189)[12]. If the same percentage of residents worked as seamstresses in the population at large as in the sample (3 percent), there would have been about 3,450 doing so. That the official count of seamstresses as reported by Pérez Toledo is less than a third of the extrapolation suggests a continued undercount of women who sewed for a living.

What can the census tell us about seamstress' identities in 1842? Echoing the pattern from a century earlier, none in the sample were married, with 23 widowed and 22 single (16 of them identified with the more honorable "doncella," 6 with the more generic "soltera"). The youngest *costurera* identified in the sample is 14 year old Doña Francesca Arce, a migrant from Otunaba. Her widowed mother served in the same household of Army Capitan Nicolas Dominguez as the *ama de llaves*, or housekeeper. The 34-year-old captain, native to the city and single, headed a household of 16 people at Tacuba no. 20, including a pensioner and his wife, and a widow, Doña Magdalena Lopez, with her two teen-age daughters. In addition to Francesca and her mother, the servants included the door man and his wife, daughter, and young son; a coachman and his wife; a valet; and a chambermaid. Did Francesca do the sewing for the peers of the captain living in the household, and perhaps also for the wives of the servants?

Sewing continued to be a family enterprise in the 1840s. The Caso sisters—Sebastiana, 39, Juana 35, Dominga 22—all identified as "doncellas" but neither doña nor soltera, lived together in room no. 9 in the casa de vecindad at no. 5 Callejon 1a de la Amargura. Neighboring families included that of a widowed candy maker and her four children, that of a married clerk and his wife, both from Aguascalientes, with their two Mexico City–born young children, and a married tailor, his wife, and three small children. These sisters might have sewn for any of these neighbors, forming intimate relationships around clothing production and consumption. Their situation is not unlike that of a widow and her three daughters in a short story entitled "Un Domingo" (One Sunday), purportedly written by Guillermo Prieto and published in 1838 in *Ensayo Literario*, who "maintain themselves by their needles" (Spell 1935, 291).

In contrast to the "doña" and white identity of seamstresses in eighteenth-century census data and notary documents, Rivera's 1855 seamstress is "very Mexican," "without doubt of the underground world." The 1842 census identified all of the 45 seamstresses in the sample as born in Mexico, with only 4 of them not from Mexico City. While the census does not have the "calidad" column of the 1753 census as proxy for ethnicity, five seamstresses in the 1842 data are identified as "doña." In his essay, Rivera suggests that the typical seamstress is perhaps the daughter of a retired captain or public school teacher but more likely of unknown parentage, taken as a young girl to a tailor's shop or an established seamstress to learn the trade. She is depicted as being at a peculiar intersection of production and consumption, very conscious of the difference between her attire (featuring ordinary *indianilla* fabric) and that of the luxury clothing she makes with linen and velvet. The seamstress in the story hopes to marry an artisan or a medical student, and the author notes, will likely sew all her life (Pérez Salas 1998, 51–55). Yet the shop seamstress had a better life than the "costurera domestica, privada, o ambulante." Closed up in the house, these women were vulnerable to unscrupulous designs of the men in the employing family. Indeed, the "ambulante" moniker refers to mobility, as turnover for private seamstresses was high, in part due to sexual harassment and assault.

Women sewing in workshops could also be sexually vulnerable. Historian Ana Lidia García Peña narrates the case of Dolores Pacheco, a 16-year-old migrant who secured work as a seamstress at the Casa de Tejidos Iglesias, owned by the Frenchman Andrés Lefall. Not long after she began work at Lefall's establishment in 1840, the business owner seduced the young Dolores, who gave in to his authority and persistence. The two maintained a sexual relationship until Dolores became pregnant, at which time Lefall ended the relationship. We know about this case because Dolores sued Lefall for the costs of her delivery and subsequent support for her and her baby. The court awarded her a one-time indemnity of 500 pesos (García Peña 2004).

Aside from domestic service, seamstress was the most common paid occupation for women in the middle of the nineteenth century in Mexico City, working "in countless small clothing businesses, for merchants who contracted outwork, as independent sewers, and as servants in convents" (Porter 2003, 10). For women of lesser means, Pérez Toledo suggests that "within textile production the clothing construction phase constitutes one requiring more skill, and therefore, more prestige" than spinning and weaving had, so for working-class women, sewing was "a mechanism of upward social mobility" (Pérez Toledo 2004, 224). This positive future is not evident in the popular literature of the nineteenth century surveyed, with no prosperous seamstresses found. A case from the notary archive suggests a positive example. It also attests to continued dependence of some white residents on live-in hired help to produce and care for their wardrobes and the identities tied up in them.

In her 1841 will, Doña Maria Alejandra Caso, a married Creole mother of two young children, left one hundred pesos to Doña Maria Gertrudis and another hundred to Doña Dolores Diaz, "both sisters my seamstresses." That the servant-employing housewife uses "doña" to refer to her employee-seamstresses reflects a social hierarchy among servants, and also suggests that these sisters might be from downwardly mobile white families. Some women moving down the ladder turned to live-in seamstress work, while others worked independently. Caso's will gives insight about social relationships surrounding clothing work, and the intimate relations between producers and consumers of clothing. The one hundred pesos each left to the Diaz seamstress sisters are in the same clause where Caso leaves three hundred pesos to her uncle. There are no other servants mentioned, though one would expect that if she could afford to keep two seamstresses in her residence she likely had other household help. When she married, her husband was worth four thousand pesos, a considerable sum, and she had shares in haciendas with her sisters.[13] That she only mentions the seamstresses, and that she has two of them, reflects the importance that clothing construction had in shaping the identities of those with means. Did Caso's apparent appreciation of the work of the Diaz sisters mean that their daily conditions were relatively favorable?

The 1838 story "One Sunday" pokes fun at clothing consumers' obsessions with fashion and presentation, dressing for going to the theater and to "in" restaurants (Spell 1935, 291). Rivera in "La Costurera" in 1855 also pokes fun at cajón clientele, with the sewing girls gossiping that an elegant customer buying ties in the shop has ripped pants below his frock coat, or that the student choosing a shirt really needs one badly as the sleeves of the one he is wearing is tattered under his jacket (Pérez Salas 1998, 53). This ridicule underlines the intimacy between producers and consumers, imbuing the young female sewers with the power to see behind the costuming of wealth and to reveal the vulnerability of identities built on thin wardrobes. This shallow material wealth in clothing is a common theme. When the boarding house manager in the same *costumbrista* collection removed the "degenerated ruffles" from her old jacket, its aristocratic traces were still evident, but so were the "comings-and-goings [*vaivenes*] of changing fortune" (Pérez Salas 1998, 241).

The sewing identity most prominent in late nineteenth century narrative sources but completely uncounted in the census records is the woman of scarce resources, sewing for herself or for her own family. A woman sewing at home could be a sign of gentility. One of the leading socialites in Mexico in the first decades of independence, La Güera Rodríguez, did at least some of her own sewing as a young mother, according to Fanny Calderón. Calderón reports La Güera's telling her about when she met Alexander Von Humboldt, renowned world traveler. She sat sewing in a corner unnoticed until she engaged the visiting baron in conversation about cochineal dye (Calderón 1952, 67). It is likely that the bulk of the sewing for the Rodríguez household was done by other women.

When women did sewing work for their families it was part of the "labor of love," unpaid reproductive work. Clothes represent a necessity at every level of society, of course, and those without the means to employ others to make them sewed for themselves in a combination of auto-production and auto-consumption "self-fashioning" (Giles 2007, 19). Calderón describes "common women" in the 1840s as dressed "chiefly in clear white, very stiffly starched muslins, some very richly embroidered, and the petticoat trimmed with lace, white satin shoes, and the dresses extremely short, which in them looks very well. A *reboso* is thrown over all" (Calderón 1952, 102). She does not identify the maker of the attire of women among the popular classes. Those who could afford to have their clothing made by professionals did, and those who could not made their consumer goods themselves—in both cases, using cloth they purchased.

The lower-class female protagonists in Delgado's stories in the late nineteenth century are shown doing their own sewing as well as that of those in their families. The laundress-turned-seamstress Carmen in *La Calandria*, orphaned by her laundress mother and kept at arm's length by her elite father, used fine satin funded by her father to fashion clothing using patterns of the latest fashions, in a vain attempt to hold up in a comparison with her half sister, her father's only legitimate daughter (Delgado 1997, 118, 135). Whether the one doing the work was paid or not, making, mending, and repurposing clothing was vital skilled work for consumption at both inconspicuous and conspicuous levels (Roche 1994, 264–268, 291–929; Vickery 1993, 279, 282). A piece of fabric could have many lives, witness many changes, be transformed by skilled sewing work. In Delgado's 1893 novel *Angelina*, the namesake works for and takes care of two downwardly mobile spinster sisters, spending her time making and adorning dress shirts and handkerchiefs for their nephew Rodolfo. In one episode, the aunts groom the aspiring clerk's appearance. Suggesting her nephew go out "so that you are seen," Aunt Pepa draws on both a trunk of formerly fine clothes and the stitching work of Angelina until she is satisfied with Rodolfo's appearance, exclaiming with "maternal satisfaction": "That's it, that way, like a decent person!" (Delgado 1964, 29, 31, 39–40, 75–76, 132). This story echoes concerns about being seen well dressed, as well as the intimate dependence on servant workers with sewing expertise and grooming skills of wives, mothers, and aunts. In republican Mexico, "persons on the top wrung presented themselves in public with every luxury and ornateness that is customary in more civilized countries," with being well turned out in public often due to the skilled eye and hand of a valet (Staples 2005, 313–314).

As vital as proper clothing was to shaping identities, social critiques surrounding consumption of clothing were common in postcolonial Mexico City, and not limited to fictional satirical representations. In her memoir of her stay in Mexico City in the 1840s, Calderón notes the "extravagant notions" of society women about what they should be seen in, and where, an extravagance that could have dire financial consequences: "Half the men in Mexico were ruined that year by the embroidered French and India muslins bought by their wives" (Calderón 1952, 113). Women took these fine fabrics home to live-in seamstresses, or to a self-employed seamstress or high-end dressmaker, to be worked up in the latest styles. Most laundresses in the 1842 census are not live-in domestics, only five in the total sample. Two of them, Rosario Olguen, 50 years old, and Maria Balcazar, 39 years old, both identified as "soltera," and both native to Mexico City, lived and worked at 1 Calle de San Francisco to meet the demand for clean clothing for Lucas Alamán's family of nine. The statesman and intellectual from Guanajuato lived with his wife Doña Narcisa Castillo, and seven children. Two 17-year-old girls are identified in the census, one with the last name of Castillo (perhaps Narcisa's sister or niece) listed first, and then Catalina Alamán listed as the oldest child of the marriage, with five younger brothers aged 16, 15, 6, 2, and 1. The stature of this family apparently warranted having two seamstresses. The Alamán house also employed two single laundresses and at least six servants (two wives of male servants are not identified themselves as servants, as well as four children of servants). Next door, Don Francisco Rubio, a businessman immigrant from Spain and his wife Doña Bernarda Arriaga lived with their four children under four years old, and a twenty-eight-year old sister of Doña Bernarda. Again, two seamstresses lived in—Guadalupe Marrolet, a 50-year old widow, and Eulalia Torres, 22 years old and single—along with Juana N., a 30-year-old widowed laundress. Doña Maria Alejandra Caso, the Alaman family and the Rubio family each had small children—may be one of the two seamstresses employed by each had specialized in children's clothing.

Calderón remarks on an heiress known to have "changed her dress four or five times a day." Having a live-in seamstress, or two, would facilitate this heavy consumption of clothing. When the occasions were formal such as a fancy ball in the Calle San Francisco, the same street that the Alamán's lived on, Calderón noted that "one or two girls. . .wore balldresses which could only have proceeded from the fingers of a Parisian *modiste*" (Calderón, 1952, 284). The ambassador's wife notes a proliferation of French *modistes*, who charged "exorbitant" prices. After mid-century, *modistas*, or dressmakers running stand-alone shops (i.e. not usually out of their homes), increasingly constructed the wardrobe-based images of those who could afford their services. While this sector could represent upward mobility for some seamstresses, Arrom argues that this was not the case for Mexican middle-class women for whom honor continued to be a concern. Instead, these professional clothing workers were often foreign in Mexico, just as they marketed foreign fashions. Indeed, most of the 22 dressmakers listed in a business guide from Mexico City in 1854 were French (Arrom 1985, 169). By the end of the century, British and French fashions were de rigueur among the city's elite. One visitor, Mrs. Alec Tweedie, remarked "The small boys are dressed in Jack Tar suits [and] many of the men get their clothes from London, as their wives do from Paris" (Tweedie 1901, 146). It is likely that it is the fabric for the clothing and the patterns with which to make them more than the clothing itself that crossed the Atlantic.

By the 1880s, the word "costurera" came to mean more often than not a woman sewing in a clothing factory, though as was true in Mexico and elsewhere in the Americas, women continued to sew for themselves and for others, a task made easier by the acquisition of sewing machines by those who could afford one (O'Brien 1999, 180–186; Moya 1998, 249–250)[14]. Even as consumption of fashionable clothing increased, paying for sewing remained beyond the means of many women. Visitors and residents to Mexico City at the end of the century noted that some society girls made their own dresses. In anticipation of her setting up house with the wealthy Eduardo (whose intentions she grossly misread), Carmen in *La Calandria* whips up with her sewing machine in a week's time "two percale *batas* (dresses with a train), six blouses, and half a dozen petticoats" (Delgado 1997, 169). Mexican periodicals such as *El Hogar* in 1902 highlighted the clothing work of relatively well-off women, as remembered by one: "In addition to the interesting articles, it included patterns for making diverse articles of clothing, figures and drawings to work up in cross-stitch, embroidery patterns in white, lace, and crochet and knitting."[15]

Concluding Threads

Work on consumption and identity alerts us to connections between people and goods—"A life built jointly on humans and objects" (Orlove 1994, 142). Census manuscripts, letters, notary documents, memoirs, and literature speak of differing degrees of relationships, both positive and negative, forged among the Mexican bourgeoisie, clothing workers, and material goods, as well as different levels of work involving clothing. With unreliable census data, we conjecture that the profiles of the women who were paid for the production of clothes by hand in Mexico likely included widowhood, and being under 40.[16] There was a range of socioeconomic circumstance for paid sewers. While paid sewing was done by many white women earlier in the century, most seamstresses were native-born, with a relative few European immigrant seamstresses working in Mexico at mid-century (Pérez Toledo 2004, 64; Francois 2006 , 118–121, 318; Moya 1998, 46). By 1910, when Mexico City had over 470,000 residents, females made up 64 percent of those counted in the "Clothing Manufacture and Toilette" category, with more than 7,000 seamstresses, 2,000 dressmakers, and nearly 6,000 laundresses (Francois 2006 , 333–336).

As depicted in Rivera's "La Costurera," other literature, and in archival documents, clothing-related work took place inside intimate and private homes, whether paid or unpaid, and in the public marketplace of sewing services, where relationships among workers and between producers and consumers could also be intimate. Lived experiences found in historical records defy easy demarcations in the clothing construction trade between skilled and unskilled work and gendered spheres marked by gendered garments: men shopped in seamstress shops for shirts and ties and not just with tailors; and live-in seamstresses sewed for men and women of the employer's household. Day to day living and the production and maintenance of constructed public identities of middling and elite individuals and families in Mexico depended on the sewing and grooming work of servants and family women as well as paid sewers. Seamstresses produced the "being served" identities of Fanny Calderón, the Alamán family, and emergent Creole *gente decente* such as Maria Alejandra Caso in nineteenth-century Mexico. In addition to the production of clothing, its maintenance and deployment also called for skill. Once made, caring for clothing was the charge of laundresses and those skilled at repair, while its deployment was the work of valets, *planchadoras* (ironers), chambermaids, mothers, daughters, and wives working to groom their charges for appearance in public with proper clothing both to protect against the elements and to perform their social status. The work of stitching clothing produced both garments and identities for those who wore them in Mexico, whatever their class.

Notes

1. On costumbrista authors and genealogy, see Segre 2007; and Perez Salas 1998.
2. See also Gonzalbo Aizpuru 2005; Gonzalbo Aizpuru 2006; Orlove 1997; Francois 2004; Earle 2001: 189; and Franco 1984.
3. See also Francois 2008.
4. The tailor guild was established in Mexico City in 1524, according to Dominguez Company 1987, 82. Guilds were abolished by the Cortes de Cadiz in 1813, though the structure of artisan workshops continued for the most part: male masters, journeymen, and apprentices.
5. See Porter 2003, 87–90 for industrial *costureras* organizing in 1880s.
6. See also Francois 2006, 180–184.
7. 2,441 residents sampled (1.9 percent of population of 126,477), includes 286 addresses and 564 separate households. Archivo General de la Nación [hereafter AGN], Padrones, vol. 52, 1753.
8. *Diario de México*, November 11, 1805, 1/32, p. 129; August 14, 1806, 3/318, 432; November 30, 1808, xx/10157, 632; February 28, 1811, 16/10975, 240.
9. AGN, Padrones vols. 53, 54, 55, and 57. For discussion of sample, see Francois 2008. Arrom's 1811 sample for different sections of the city yielded 11 seamstresses. Arrom 1985, 156–159, 163, 271–273.
10. AGN Padrones vol. 55, f. 80. See also vol. 55, f. 156; vol. 54, f. 51; vol. 53, f. 121.
11. AGN Padrones vol. 54, f. 241.
12. The 1842 census is located in AHDF, Vols. 3406 and 3407. The sample draws from downtown neighborhoods in Cuarteles Mayores 1 and 2, Manzanas 1 through 29. My sample of 45 laundresses accounts for 4 percent of laundresses *reported* in the 1842 municipal census.
13. Archivo General de Notariás del Distrito Federal, Mexico City, Notario José Lopez Guazo, vol. 2346, 1841, f. 197v-199
14. Porter notes the cost of the sewing machines was prohibitive. Porter 2003, 33.
15. Cited in Francois 2006, 181.
16. This is in contrast to Argentina, where seamstresses were more likely to be married.

References

Arrom, S. 1985. *The Women of Mexico City, 1790–1857.* Stanford: Stanford University Press.
Bauer, A. J. 2001. *Goods, Power, History: Latin America's Material Culture.* Cambridge: Cambridge University Press.

Delgado, R. 1890, 1997. *La Calandria*. México: Editores Mexicanos Unidos.

Delgado, R. 1893, 1964. *Angelina*. México: Editorial Porrua.

De Lizardi, F. 1832, 1984. *Don Catrín de la Fachenda y Noches Triste y Día Alegre*. México: Editorial Porrua.

Dobles Trejos, C. 1999. "Hilvando Historias: Una aproximación al conocimiento del oficio de la costura, 1900–1960." *Anuario de Estudios Centroamericanos, Universidad de Costa Rica*, 25 (1), 61–81.

Dominguez Company, F. 1987. "Regulación municipal del trabajo libre de los oficios mecánicos en hispanoamerica colonial." *Revista de Historia de América*, 103: 75–106.

Earle, R. 2001. "'Two Pairs of Pink Satin Shoes!!' Race, Clothing, and Identity in the Americas (17th–19th centuries)." *History Workshop Journal* 52: 175–195.

Madame Calderón de la Barca (Frances Erskine Inglis) 1983, 1952. *Life in Mexico: During a Residence of Two Years in that Country*. México: Ediciones Tolteca.

Franco, J. 1984. "Women, Fashion and the Moralists in Early Nineteenth-Century Mexico." In *Homenaje a Ana María Barenechea*. Edited by L. Schwartz Lerner and I. Lerner. Madrid: Editorial Castalia.

Francois, M. E. 2004. "Cloth and Silver: Pawning and Material Life in Mexico City at the Turn of the Nineteenth Century." *The Americas* 60(3): 325–362.

Francois, M. E. 2006. *A Culture of Everyday Credit Housekeeping, Pawnbroking, and Governance in Mexico City, 1750–1920 (Engendering Latin America)*. Lincoln, NE: University of Nebraska Press.

Francois, M. E. 2008. "The Products of Consumption: Housework in Latin American Political Economies and Cultures." *History Compass* 6(1), 207–242.

French, J. D. and Daniel James. eds. 1999. *The Gendered Worlds of Latin American Women Workers: From Household and Factory to the Union Hall and Ballot Box*. Durham, NC: Duke University Press.

García Peña, A. L. 2004. "Madres solteras, pobres, y abandonados: Ciudad de México, Siglo XIX." *Historia Mexicana* 53(3), 647–692.

Giles, J. 2007. "Class, Gender and Domestic Consumption in Britain 1920–1950." In *Gender and Consumption: Domestic Cultures and the Commercialization of Everyday Life*. Edited by E. Casey, and L. Martens, 15–31. Hampshire: Ashgate.

Gonzalbo Aizpuru, P. 2005 *Historia de la Vida Cotidiana en México*. México: El Colegio de México.

Gonzalbo Aizpuru, P. 2006. *Introducción de la historia de la vida cotidiana*. México: El Colegio de México.

Gonzalez Casanova, P. 1951. "La sátira popular en la Ilustración," *Historia Mexicana* 1(1), 78–95.

Hutcheson, E. 2001. *Labors Appropriate to their Sex: Gender, Labor, and Politics in Urban Chile, 1900–1930*. Durham, NC: Duke University Press.

Moya, J. C. 1998. *Cousins and Strangers: Spanish Immigrants in Buenos Aires, 1850–1930*. Berkeley: University of California Press.

O'Brien, T. 1999. *The Century of U.S. Capitalism in Latin America*. Albuquerque: University of New Mexico Press.

Olcott, J. 2011. "Introduction: Researching and Rethinking the Labors of Love." *Hispanic American Historical Review* 91(1), 1–28.

Orlove, B.S. 1994. "Beyond Consumption: Meat, Sociability,Vitality and Hierarchy in Nineteenth Century Chile." In *Consumption and Identity*. Edited by J. Friedman. Chur, Switzerland: Harwood.

Orlove, B. S. ed. 1997. *The Allure of the Foreign: Imported Goods in Postcolonial Latin America*. Ann Arbor: University of Michigan Press.

Perez Salas, M. E. .1998. "Genealogía de 'Los Mexicanos pintados por sí mismos." *Historia Mexicana* 48(2): 167–207.

Pérez Toledo, S. 2004. *Población y structural social de la Ciudad de México, 1790–1842*. México: Universidad Autónoma Metropolitana.

Phillips, A. and Taylor, P. 1980. "Sex and Skill: Notes toward a Feminist Economics," *Feminist Review* 6: 79–88.

Porter, S. S. 2003. *Working Women in Mexico City: Public Discourses and Material Conditions, 1879–1931*. Tucson: University of Arizona Press.

Rivera, J. M. 1855. *Los mexicanos pintados por si mismos*. México: Casa de M. Murguía.

Roche, D. 1994. *The Culture of Clothing: Dress and Fashion in the Ancien Regime*. Cambridge: Cambridge University Press.

Segre, E. 2007. *Intersected Identities: Strategies of Visualization in Nineteenth- and Twentieth-Century Mexican Culture*. New York: Bergahn Books.

Socolow, S. 2000. *The Women of Colonial Latin America*. Cambridge: Cambridge University Press. 120.

Spell, J. R. 1935. "The Costumbrista Movement in Mexico." *PMLA* 50(1), 290–315.

Staples, A. 2005. "Una sociedad *superior* para una nueva nación." In *Historia de la Vida Cotidiana en México. vol. IV. Bienes y vivencias. El Siglo xix*. México: El Colegio de México.

Tweedie, A. 1901. *Mexico as I Saw It*. London: Horst and Blacket.

Vickery, A. 1993. "Women and the World of Goods: A Lancashire Consumer and her Possessions, 1751–81." In *Consumption and the World of Goods*. Edited by J. Brewer and R. Porter. London: Routledge.

Weinstein, B. 1999. "Unskilled Worker, Skilled Housewife: Constructing the Working-Class Woman in São Paulo Brazil, 1900–1950." In *The Gendered Worlds of Latin American Women Workers: From Household and Factory to the Union Hall and Ballot Box*. Edited by J. D. French and D. James, 72–99. Durham, NC: Duke University Press.

8

Christmas Tamales in Costa Rica (1900–1930)

Patricia Vega Jiménez[1]
Translated by Fergus Grealy and Anna Cristina Pertierra

Introduction

The eating habits of any social group are deeply dependent upon the environment (what it can produce), methods and manners of distribution, the availability of technology (necessary for production), cultural and symbolic factors, and the cultivation of existing resources. In other words, culinary cultures stem from such factors as the nature of ingredients as much as from beliefs and practices (Pilcher 2006, 2). The meaning of food can differ according to socioeconomic group, age, and even gender, and eating habits help to define such aspects of self as ethnic identity or religious devotion. Religions in particular affect eating customs and regulate consumption through ideals of asceticism and conviviality. Meals, in addition to their nutritional value, have a cultural value, which indicates how they are understood by consumers; each society assigns a code of meaning that is shared by the community (Gonzalbo 2006, 217–218). This code typically includes not only the time when meals are eaten but also what is consumed for each of them, the method in which they are prepared, the rituals at the table, and the company of guests.

In each society or region, dishes regularly change or evolve over time. They acquire new products or combine flavors and colors in new ways, and they incorporate regional recipes adapting tastes to the palates of the area. The forms of food preparation also vary, arising equally in the selection of raw materials or the incorporation of condiments and the presentation of the plates. Correspondingly, losses and disappearance of ingredients also affect how food is eaten, as do imposed restrictions, medical concepts, aesthetics, or concepts of efficiency. "The fact is that a diet does not solely depend on the necessity to eat and the availability of food, but also the ideologies that impose a criterion of how, why and when it is reasonable to eat" (Gonzalbo, 2006, 217). Diet is a ritual and an identifier of grouping and is also a social construction of memory (Mintz and Bois 2002, 102).

Some foods acquire a symbolic value reserved for special occasions. In Costa Rica, for example, Christmas time, even in the contemporary era, calls for the presence of tamales. Like Thanksgiving in the United States, or the celebrations of patron saints in much of Latin America, Christmas—in the majority of the countries where Christianity is predominant—is a symbolic occasion during which food forms a fundamental part of the ritual as a "representation" of the celebration.

Tamales require considerable labor, which is directed by females but involves the whole family and other members of the community. Competitive attempts to give a particular flavor to the dish have led to the specialization and recomposition of tamale recipes, and some women can be famous for the taste that characterizes their tamales. Tamales containing pork, vegetables, and herbs, wrapped in lightly roasted[2] banana leaves, have been common since the 1910s, but when did the custom of preparing the tamales begin? What are the factors that drive the making of this dish that have remained practically unaltered for more than a century? What is the symbolic value of the tamale? Has this value varied in the last 100 years? The objective of this essay is to respond to these questions, and to trace the genesis of the tamale's presence on Costa Rican tables during the Christmas period, to better determine the symbolic value that they have had in the last century.

The Genesis of the Tamale

The name "tamale" originates from the Nahuatl language, meaning "wrapped." It does not refer to only one dish; rather it describes various foods in Latin American countries where maize is a highly utilized cereal in the community's diet, in combination with diverse ingredients. The tamale is maize dough, filled with combinations of meat, vegetables, fruits, or sauces. Tamales can be sweet or salty, and are wrapped in leaves from corncobs, banana trees, *bijao* and *maguey* plants, avocado trees and, recently, in aluminum and plastic wrap. The invention of the tamale is not attributed to any country in particular because in each region, even within the same country, the preparation varies. In Mexico, for example, in the years before conquest, wealthy men customarily celebrated their good fortune and showed off to the rest of the community by throwing a party for which they served at least six different types of tortillas, turkey stewed with pumpkin seeds, different wild birds carefully prepared, tomatoes, chilies, fish, and several tamales (Bauer 2002, 63).

This heterogeneity of tamales is also common in Costa Rica from the start of the twentieth century. Gonzalo Chacón Trejos, recalling Costa Rican traditions, notes that tamales have ranged "from those purely made of dough to those filled with red pigeon and *chiverre* seeds; there are [tamales] for every taste, for the different times of eating, in succulent and delectable variety" (Chacón 2006, 71). This plurality of tamales explains the abundance of recipes that Juana Ramírez de Aragón includes in the first cooking book published in Costa Rica in 1903. She presents seven different dishes named "tamale"; two of them are "rice tamales," both requiring the crushing of the grain until it becomes a powder, then moistened, kneaded and then filled, one with meat and the other with jam. The following five recipes are made with corn flour, to which dairy products and sugar are added in different ways. Interestingly, what we would think of as the "common" tamale, made of corn flour with meat and other greens or vegetables inside and wrapped in banana leaves, is not found in the wide array of recipes that Aragón compiles in her book (Aragón 2003).

Within such a diversity of variations, in the early twentieth century each celebration historically had one type tamale dish that characterized the occasion. In December, the pork tamale—dough filled with seasoned pork—was an essential dish, also sporadically made for Easter. It was custom in the first days of January to gather around a nativity scene, as families welcomed their neighbors into their house to recite the rosary and share a meal. This was a very expensive annual activity for the hosts as it involved a "priest or prayer leader, orchestra, choir, fireworks and traditional food gifts such as: lamb tamal, sponge cake, homemade bread, mashed papaya, *chayote*, etc. Everything washed down with black coffee, sweet water, *chicha de maíz* with ginger and *guaro*, and eggnog" (Zeledón 1999, 123). Tamales also became a useful snack for travelling. During trips that lasted several days, it was customary to take food that did not perish quickly; lamb tamales (González 1974, 27) and sweet corn tamales (Echeverría 2004, 206) were two such satisfying dishes, accompanied by coffee or sweet water prepared en route.

Tamales in Public Space

At the end of the nineteenth century, tamales of all types were offered in the marketplaces that took place every week. They were especially sold during religious celebrations. On January 15 every year, the *Fiesta del*

Cristo de Esquipulas was held in Alajuelita, a village close to the heart of the capital San José, at which "there were improvised sales of food and drinks; there was plentiful *chica brava*, ginger beer, tamales and *gallos*… " (Chacón 2006, 141). When the Berliner Helmuth Polakouski visited the capital in 1875 and recorded his observations of the daily life, he saw in the marketplace of San José that there also were "improvised restaurants" where women cooked, in view of the public, "an array of national dishes in large iron pans… The main dish was black beans, fried plantain and a mixture of rice, cayenne and *escalope*, whose pastry was colored bright red with *achiote*. Of course there was no lack of tortillas and other corn cakes which took the form of a bread roll and was filled inside with minced meat…" (Quesada 2001, 253). This last dish could refer to the "empanada," also made using corn flour, or the better known "tamales de carne." The consumers of these dishes were other vendors, soldiers, and "poor visitors" according to the German traveler's description.

Polakouski's account is consistent with other evidence that wealthy groups of the time had the option of visiting a variety of "restaurants" reserved for their demanding tastes. In 1908, for example, they could go to "*La Magnolia*, or in other words, the Rendezvous for the San José High Life." There they could enjoy "conserves, sweets, cakes, soft drinks, ice creams, raisins, olives" among other foreign delicacies (*La Luz* 1–10–1903, 4). Residents of Cartago could visit the *Hotel y Restaurante Siglo XX* if their palate desired French, American, or Spanish food, where they were attended to with great care (*La Lucha* 21–12–1908, 4). Meanwhile, Francisco Laporte offered in his "well stocked *cantina*, great wines. (And) a varied and constant selection of fine biscuits. (Furthermore, for the clients who preferred privacy, they had) a reserved salon (that was attended by a) good barman" (*La Lucha* 21–12–1908, 4). In 1912, Carlos Ventura advertised his hotel *La Europa*, where people were invited to a "restaurant of the highest order, excellent service, French food, an excellent and varied menu." The dinners, served until 11p.m., were prepared "for the taste of the most discerning clientele" (*La Información* 7-7-1912, 4).

In 1917, the American Hamilton Mercer Wright visited Costa Rica and complimented the cafés in the Atlantic zone. Different to the food that is served in San José, he received "a delicious first course of mountain turkey, and also some mouth-watering slices of wild pig killed the day before. Oranges, mandarins, bananas, eggplants, avocadoes, potatoes and cabbages from the highlands, and lettuce. Meanwhile, the travelling vendors located at train stations that serviced Puntarenas offered, besides oranges, bananas, and cactus fruit, cheese sandwiches, "tortillas rolled cylindrically and filled with minced meat, cheese and chillies… old ladies carrying hot potatoes and cups (of coffee)" (Quesada 2001, 665). These descriptions show the absence of tamales at least in the coastal regions of the nation at that time, showing how the local availability of products determined the dishes made. Fruit, for example, is abundant in these areas, as is the mountain turkey served in place of beef, or wild pigs serviced in place of pork reared in captivity.

Despite these regional differences, evidence of the tamales' historical importance is also demonstrated in the opportunities at which they are served. Tamales constituted a first course in the official activities of the nineteenth century; in 1833, for example, when the approval of the Law of the Press was celebrated in parliamentary chambers, an adjoining table was filled with special dishes to delight in the occasion:

> There were carafes of *mistela de leche* and pots of lemonade; *quesadillas*, *chiqueadores* and *suspiros, tanelas, manjar* and *tamal de olla*; *zopilotillos*, *rosquetes* and *encanelados*; nothing that Creole industry could offer was missing.
>
> (Jiménez 1964, 87)

Tamales were sold in local stores, stalls, and San José cafés. In 1913, Raquel Arias sold tamales on Thursdays and Saturdays in her guesthouse as part of the special dishes served on the premises (refer to photo 1). The owners of these businesses entrusted the preparation of tamales to women who made them to support themselves and their family. The Costa Rican writer Luisa González remembers the arduous work this meant for her mother, her aunts, and the children in her family to satisfy customer demand in 1915. Fridays and Saturdays were the most hectic days; Luisa and her father visited the market early to purchase what was required for at least 200 tamales, then organized the intrafamiliar sharing of the work:

> The youngest cleaned the banana leaves and cut the string that had been soaked since the night before to soften them; the older children peeled a mountain of potatoes and sweet chillies and took the orders to the guesthouses and cafés. The older family members cooked, soaked and grinded the corn, chopped up the pork meat, cooked the rice and assembled the tamales.
>
> (González 1994, 66)

Once the ingredients were prepared and the corn was ground by a manual machine, the women of the house applied themselves to the "work of filling hundreds of tamales that were then dropped one by one into pans of boiling water that covered the whole stovetop in the kitchen of my grandmother" (González, 1994, 66).

December Tamales

When travelers visited Costa Rica during the first half of the nineteenth century and they described the food they received during Christmas celebrations, there was no reference to tamales. In 1825, John Hale detailed a Christmas celebration in Heredia, calling attention to the sham fight:

> That involved the Indians of the conquest for their country against the Spanish (respectively represented by a chieftain and a priest, who conquered the Indians at the end of the presentation) then came bullfighting... the evening's diversions concluded with dances, artificial fires, etc.; and as in this occasion every person in the province that could gathered in the village, there was much hospitality, joviality and rejoicing for a number of days.
>
> (Fernández 1982, 26).

Referring to the customs to the four largest towns: San José, Alajuela, Cartago, and Heredia, Hale summed up Christmas in the following way:

> Christmas is a time of general joy in which they turn to theatrical performances, based on any domestic storyline adequate to the capacity of the Indian and Black actors. The stage generally formed outside a house, the seats in the street, and the open, starry sky. Neighbors contributed by lending benches and stools to accommodate the audience. No one paid anything to watch the performance and, in the intervals, in place of music they set off fireworks, etc.
>
> (Fernández 1982, 26)

While this tale describes a period during which communities gathered for an organized celebration, what the Englishman does not detail is the food that was consumed as part of the occasion. But by the beginning of the twentieth century, during the Christmas period, dough filled with pork and flavored with fat was already a traditional part of the festivities in Costa Rican kitchens. In the first decades of that century, Francisco María Núñez recalls how a landlady gave orders to her sisters before midnight when they celebrated the birth of Jesus: "Girl, did you remember to order the pork, lard and the *chicharrones* for the tamales and the sponge cake? You should hurry up, because you could be fired. There are always early orders. Ah, did you remember the *tamazón del tueste* to clean the oven?" (Zeledón 1999, 26). The preparation of tamales was clearly a team job where the female members of the family participated with help from the extended family. Getting sufficient quantities of meat and lard necessary for tamales required the killing and quartering of a pig in the home, acquiring one from a butcher's store, or even ordering one from a slaughterhouse in advance, as recollected by Francisco María Núñez. *Chicharrones* were prepared by marinating and cooking the pig meat with spices, whilst softening banana leaves over a flame entailed the additional labor of standing over a hot oven and carefully noting the exact point at which they could be used as wrapping for the dough. Some cooks substituted pork by chicken, which added a subtle change to the dish (Zeledón 1999, 41). Again, the resources within reach determined variations in the food; it was much cheaper to rear chicken than pigs in domestic gardens, and when there was not sufficient money even for this, the dough was filled with "simple beans" (Zeledón 1999, 73), although meat would not be missing at a Christmas dinner. The preparation of this special dish necessitated that "the oven and stovetop were turned on day and night. Tamales were essential, but they should have been homemade. In every case they were made in such a quantity that it was possible to send a *piña* (two tamales tied with flexible banana peel) to the neighbors. They were exchanged" (Zeledón 1999, 32). Thus, the dish became an identifier of the cooks involved in the preparation, since they had a taste that characterized them and showed their creator's culinary skill. The tamale's symbolic meaning was due to the specific taste attained as much as to the status of the women as housewives.

Such exchanges of tamales exemplify how exchange is a form of socialization with significant codes shared by members of the community. Besides displaying the generosity of the members, it also indicated camaraderie and community acceptance. The act of exchange gives value to the things that are involved in the exchange, upon which a previously established relationship is supposed. Unlike commercial circulation, with the exchange of gifts—in this case tamales—a spirit of reciprocity, sociability, and spontaneity develops. The gift, unlike a commercial transaction, contains a certain sensibility with respect to the giving and receiving, a higher codification in terms of etiquette and suitability and a tendency to follow socially established routes (Appadurai 1992, 42).

Before Christmas dinner at the beginning of the twentieth century, Joaquín Vargas Coto recalls that it was a custom to visit neighbors' houses and to receive a tamale with aromatic coffee in welcoming. Once the visit concluded, they returned home to prepare the Christmas dinner (Zeledón 1999, 119). In fact, the tamale accompanied with coffee, sweet water, *chica,* or *mistela* formed an eating pattern that remained unaltered for many decades. These annual visits suggest that the family home was not yet seen as an impenetrable and unknown space of private life, a perception that became more pronounced in the twentieth century. It seems very possible that, in the nineteenth century, family life more often transcended the household sphere and had manifestations in the public sphere. Open doors constituted a kind of flexible border between the public and the private; the "stickybeak" who watched over the street and neighboring houses played an important role in social control, as this constant observation of the lives of others fed gossip and rumors that put at risk those who dared to deviate from conventional conduct. It is possible that in Costa Rica, the idea of "the private" was not consolidated until the twentieth century, accompanied by processes of urbanization, industrialization, and the strengthening of a bourgeois and capitalist society.

San José residents with economic resources had the option, in 1910, to attend Christmas Eve or *Noche Buena* at the National Theatre, enjoying the evening in the fashion of the period. On December 24 of that year, they presented "The Divorce," a work of global reputation and by the authors of the "The Merry Widow" (*La Prensa Libre* 23–12–1910, 2). Upon leaving the theatre, spectators could delight in a Christmas dinner with tamales as the first course, in the Hotel Imperial where, according to the announcement, it was ensured that "the cook at this establishment has prepared some scrumptious (tamales)" (*La Prensa Libre* 24–12–1910, 3), prepared especially for the occasion. Evidently, by 1910, tamales had become a dish that characterized the celebration of Christmas in the private space and in some public spaces, since four years later the Grand Hotel Francais invited the San José clientele to visit on December 24, when they served "dinner á la Carte," and on January 1 to celebrate the start of the New Year. Guests enjoyed "exceptional food, a concert by DOS COLONES... (all accompanied by) FINE LIQUORS—FINE WINES" (*La Información* 24–12–1914, 2). The invitation does not mention tamales, which does not mean that they did not form part of the menu, however it is unlikely that they were served in a "French" restaurant whose charm was the French origin of their gastronomic offering.

Christmas and Consumption

Costa Ricans in the first two decades of the twentieth century did not take part only in the ritual exchange of tamales at Christmas. In 1914, the daily newspaper *La Información* reported on a variety of activities programmed for the days of December 24 and 25: following the nineteenth century traditions of Christmas charity (Fumero 1977, 72), the journalist referred to a "Matinee to benefit the poor who are helped by the Women's Society of St. Vincent de Paul." Gifts for poor children were distributed in San Pedro del Mojón, and the paper also announced the celebration of Christmas at private dances, hosted in private houses and attended by previous invitation, or in workers' clubs, open to the public in Cartago and in Limón; in this last instance, the party was carried out on board one of the docked boats in the port (*La Información* 24–12–1914, 3). Just as Christmas activities diversified, the range of and possibilities for gifts—already common since the 1870s (Fumero 1977, 82)— increased copiously. An example of this diversification is the advertisement that the store *La Fama* published in the weekly *El Derecho* in 1901. They offered "TOYS for Christmas Eve... all the most inexpensive, the most chic, the most polished... from the humble material for the village, to the exquisite fabric for the elegant, rich and of good taste (but they clarify) that silk manufacture is still the article of our particular attention" (*El Derecho* 22–12–1901,4 (see photo 2).

If, since the 1870s, Christmas Eve was promoted as an occasion to give toys to the children and to make December 24 a time for the infants, the gifts that promoted the trade were each time more creative, novel, and directed to diverse groups and distinct age groups. Advertisers suggested the gift of chocolate, "that constitutes the highest novelty... arriving exclusively for the parties for Christmas and the New Year" (*La Información* 24–12–1914,4), jewelry "for which your gifts will be duly appreciated" but they needed to be purchased in the jewelry shop *Ortiz* (*La Información* 24–12–1914,4), dressed for men and women, "postcards with inscriptions for Christmas Eve and New Year, an exclusive assortment in boxes of cards, paper and envelopes of fantasy or countless gifts" (*La Información* 24–12–1914,5), in the bookstore *Alsina*, imported foodstuffs, flowers, and imported liquors. Scarves made of Japanese silk, European and American ties, socks, perfumes, were all on permanent display during the Christmas of 1918 in the store of *Luis Aronne & Co.* (*La Información* 15–12–1918,3). In 1916, *Jardinería Española* promoted the sale of an unusual gift that would have been a creative, different, and exotic gift: "baskets adorned with a combination of flowers and fruits." Meanwhile the store *La Despensa*, a clear rival of *Jardinería Española*, added to their baskets "a bottle of Italian *Regina* champagne, a bottle of well aged wine (Muscatel, Sherry, Port, Angélica). A box of assorted foreign sweets. A box of fine chocolates... fresh pears... a basket of dried figs" all for the price of 10 colones. The sale was promoted with a drawing that reproduced some of the products contained in the basket (refer to photo 3).

Supplies of such imported foods as apples, pears, grapes, and dried fruits proliferated in Costa Rica, particularly after 1914. By 1916, one of the stores of the highest standing in the San José area sold "apples, grapes, walnuts, almonds, hazelnuts, coconuts from Brazil, figs, raisins, dates, plums, *gallegas*, fine sweets, nougats, cured hams, Italian sausage, herrings, mackerels, various types of cheeses, and an immense assortment of conserves and red and white wines, sweets, etc. Everything special for the Christmas period." (*La Información* 22-12-1916, 2). Imports, each time more frequent, of these goods created changes in patterns of consumption, inserting new products into the diet and into the celebration of Christmas. Imported merchandise, in the end, became increasingly associated with Christmas Eve and competed with tamales for this space.

Such advertisements appeared to be effective in 1914, when San José stores were filled to the brim with shoppers. This was despite the absence of products shipped from Europe, given the war that immersed the continent, for which reason shop windows displayed "a lack of the newest fads: toys, those remaining from the previous year...the store sells and sells a lot and almost everything is paid for in cash: the credit accounts had been almost totally suspended." According to a shopkeeper whose opinion was published in the newspaper *La Información*, although sales were constantly being made, they constituted "a bargain compared with what I have got in other years for this time" (*La Información* 23-12-1914, 3). We can conclude that well before 1914, Christmas was a time of shopping, which was necessary to carry out the exchange of gifts, extending the ways in which Christmas and consumption were intimately connected.

The Significance of Christmas Tamales

In general, the activities of December created opportunities for determined groups of individuals to come together in regular interaction and mutual understanding. There, sharing food around a table (or the front door, according to the disposition of the family), they constructed a surrounding world in which participants communicated within shared codes of significance through which they could interpret, exchange, create, and recreate symbols and meanings, connected to a shared heritage and a system of common beliefs. The kitchen, where the table around which they shared foodstuffs was located, was a blessed place of a sweet privacy. In these processes of social interaction, people shared their feelings, language and attitudes (Appadurai 1991, 41–42). As Douglas and Isherwood argued, individuals make a cognitive construction of the goods they consume. A social universe needed a perfectly demarcated temporal dimension; passing of time gave meaning to actions, for which reason the calendar needed to record annual, trimestral, monthly, weekly, and daily and even smaller periodicities. The calendar offered the possibility of establishing precedents, of revision, and renewal. Within such a context, then, tamales offered on December 24, with the family and community activity that they generated, represented the end of a working year and the commencement of another, differentiating calendar year from the life cycle. Costa Ricans have annually celebrated a specific diet associated with festive holidays and Christmas time; on these occasions, "the dishes are a means for the discrimination of values, and when the discrimination ranges are more abundant, more varieties of food will be necessary" (Douglas and Isherwood 1979, 81), which explains the diversity and quantity of dishes that are shared, besides tamales. The annual repetition of meals, including Christmas tamales, is also fundamental to the construction of memory. Community members can remember and maintain a sense of group identification, as their sense of belonging is activated through the ritual of eating, which starts with the process of preparation and finishes with its consumption in company. Food here not only symbolizes social limits and divisions, it participates in their creation and re-creation. In being a central part of such rituals, tamales that are prepared and consumed for Christmas, are official and expressive acts, carriers of a symbolic dimension. On the one hand, they remind of the birth of Jesus, while on the other hand, they indicate the end of an annual cycle and, furthermore, are reasons for family and communal reunions in an explicit ritual.

> The essence of the ritual is of the mixture of individual times and collective times and, in this sense, the ritual as a conjunction of relatively codified individual or collective conducts, causes a bodily state experienced through words, gesture, and through stance, and with a repetitive character, with a heavy symbolic load for the actors and witnesses.
>
> (Diaz 2007, XXVIII)

Conclusion

Food is culturally encoded in ways that enable the construction of a sense of belonging, shared between members of a particular community. In Costa Rica, tamales made in December, which possibly started as a tradition at the end of the nineteenth century, since there are no references before this time, favor reciprocal intercommunal relations. The shared table was the quintessential festive space where one combined the pleasures of eating and drinking with those whose company they enjoy.

Dishes and delicacies ordained as special in each region may differ, even within the same nation, in accordance with the detailed code of values, rules, and symbols around which the alimentary model is organized for a cultural area in a determined period. In that process, the availability of ingredients—available supplies, what is accessible because of its price, what is comparable through digestion, what is authorized by culture, what is valued by social organization—is fundamental. But eating serves not only the purpose of conserving the biological machinery of the body, but also of strengthening relations between the person and the world, and marking, in this way, space and time—through temporal cycles of food rituals.

The December tamales, those that wrap a variety of meats and vegetables, as well as grains or rice, in dough and are cooked covered in banana leaves, have at least three clearly established codes of meaning: first of all, they are the party food for the end of the year, when one life cycle finishes and another begins; also, in a fundamentally Catholic nation, they symbolize the time when God created man, a moment of jubilation for the Christian world. Third, tamales are exchanged every December, which converts them into an object fundamental to carry out the norm of obliged courtesy—that the receiver is equally prepared to give his tamales to the visitor. To not give tamales would be at odds with the heart of the community.

The objective of these gifts is the establishment of a bond between the giver and the receiver. Cordial relations are created and confirmed through the exchange of tamales. Relatedly, tamales represent, along with *chicha* and *mistela*, the essence of hospitality during Christmas time, as the common denominator of ritual and ceremonial relations. The customs of Christmas seem to have taken place both outside the home, in neighbors' houses, where local community identifications are created, and inside the home for the celebration of Christmas dinner. In both cases, the generosity of the hosts is measured by the volume of their offerings.

The cultural impact of this association between tamales and Costa Rican Christmas, which developed in the early twentieth century, remains clear. Despite fluctuations in the availability and price of maize, Costa Ricans continue to hold maize as an essential grain in their basic diet. Although tastes change over time (a dish appreciated at one time later will be considered as "too vulgar," "crude," or "heavy," since food, like clothing, is also subject to fashion), such historical trends have not stopped the presence of tamales on the Christmas table of Costa Ricans, but rather strengthens their continuing presence as an obligatory part of the national diet, one hundred years after their rise to prominence.

Notes

1. The author is grateful for the collaboration of her assistants Gloriana Rodríguez and Sofía Guerrero.
2. The leaves of the banana tree are held near a flame to soften them and they are then cleaned and used to wrap the mixture and the rest of the ingredients.

References

Acuña, José Basileo. 1965. "Mi vecindario." En Ramos, Lillia. *Júbilo y pena del recuerdo.* San José: Editorial Costa Rica.

Anuario Estadístico 1926. San José: Imprenta Nacional.

Appadurai, Arjun. ed. 1991. *La vida social de las cosas. Perspectiva cultural de las mercancías.* México: Grijalbo.

Barrantes, Emmanuel, Hilda Bonilla, y Olga Ramírez 2002. *Las susbsistencias en una coyuntura de crisis, Costa Rica 1914–1920.* Tesis de Licenciatura en Historia, Universidad de Costa Rica.

Bauer, Arnold. 2002. *Somos lo que compramos.* México: Taurus.

Chacón Trejos, Gonzalo. 2006. *Tradiciones costarricenses.* San José: Editorial Costa Rica.

Díaz Arias, David. 2007. *La fiesta de la independencia en Costa Rica, 1821–1921.* San José: Editorial de la Universidad de Costa Rica.

Douglas, Mary y Isherwood, Baron. 1979. *El mundo de los bienes. Hacia una antropología del consumo.* México: Grijalbo.

El Derecho, 12.22.1901.

El Derecho, 12.28.1903.

Fallas, Carlos Luis 1995. *Marcos Ramírez.* San José: Editorial Costa Rica.

Fernández Guardia, Ricardo 1982. *Costa Rica en el siglo XIX.* San José: EDUCA.

Fumero, Patricia 2997. "¡Viene Noel! La Navidad Moderna en San José (1850–1914)" En *La Sonora Libertad del Viento.* México: Instituto Panamericano de Geografía e historia. Comisión de Historia.

Gonzalbo Aizpuru, Pilar 2006. *Introducción a la historia de la Vida Cotidiana.* México: El Colegio de México.

González Feo, Mario 1974. Cuando no había ferrocarril [sic] a Limón. *La Nación* (San José) 16 de mayo.

González, Luisa 1994. *A ras del suelo.* San José: Editorial Costa Rica.

Hall, Carolyn 1976. *El café y el desarrollo histórico-geográfico de Costa Rica.* San José: Editorial Costa Rica.

Jiménez, Manuel de Jesús. 1964. *Selecciones.* San José: Editorial Costa Rica.

La Información, 07.07.1912.

La Información, 07.09.1912.

La Información, 07.13.1912.

La Información, 07.14.1913.

La Información, 12.23.1914.

La Información, 12.24.1914.

La Información, 12.22.1916.

La Información, 12.23.1916.

La Información, 04.05.1918.

La Información, 04.20.1918

La Información, 12.15.1918.

La Lucha, 12.21.1908.

La Luz, 10.01.1903.

La Prensa Libre, 12.23.1910.

La Prensa Libre, 12.24.1910.

La Prensa Libre, 02.21.1914.

La Prensa Libre, 01.24.1914.

Mintz, Sidney W. and Christine M. Du Bois. 2002. The Anthropology of Food and Eating. *Annu. Rev. Anthropol.* 31: 99–119.

Pilcher, Jeffrey. 2006. *Food in World History*. New York: Routledge.

Quesada Pacheco, Miguel Ángel. 2001. *Entre silladas y rejoyas. Viajeros por Costa Rica de 1850 a 1950*. San José: Instituto Tecnológico de Costa Rica.

Ross de Cerdas, Marjorie. 1986. Al calor del fogón. San José: Editorial Cultur Art.

Vargas Castro, Macabeo. 1952. *¡Oh tiempos aquellos!* San José: Imprenta Borrasé.

Wagner, Moritz y Sherzer, Carl. 1944. *La República de Costa Rica en Centro América*. San José: Biblioteca Yurusti.

Zeledón Cartín, Elías. 1999. *La navidad costarricense*. San José: Editorial de la Universidad de Costa Rica.

Zeledón, Elías. 1994. *Imágenes costarricenses*. Elías Zeledón, comp. San José: Editorial de la Universidad de Costa Rica.

Part 4

Images and Soundscapes

9

Quinceañera: Coming of Age through Digital Photography in Cuba

Anna Cristina Pertierra[1]

Taking a series of portrait photographs to mark a girl's fifteenth birthday is a common and highly celebrated practice in Cuba. The fifteenth birthday is considered in Cuba to be the marking point at which girls become women, and producing an album of printed photographs in which the fifteen-year-old, or *quinceañera,* wears special clothes, hairstyles, and makeup, constitutes the center of Cuban coming of age rituals. Girls' fifteenth birthday celebrations (commonly referred to as *quinces*) are widely celebrated in Latin America, especially in Mexico, Central America, the Hispanic Caribbean, and among Latino populations of the United States. In such rituals, which seem to be largely a twentieth century development, the centerpiece of the celebration typically includes a party at which the birthday girl (*quinceañera*) wears a long full-skirted gown and adornments such as flowers, jewelry, and a tiara. The aesthetics of the celebration are informed by a sense of "tradition" in which features such as candles, floral arrangements, pastel colors, and formal attire are understood to suggest an elegance and exclusivity that marks the celebration as apart from everyday life. But in this chapter, I consider *quinces* photography portraiture, and not the party, as a definitive moment in marking girls' fifteenth birthdays in contemporary Cuba. The chapter draws from ethnographic research and semi-structured interviews undertaken between 2004 and 2009 to understand how and why *quinceañera* photography has become increasingly popular in Cuba since the 1990s. My interest in *quinceañeras* first developed from

undertaking 13 months of participant observation in 2003–2004 studying women's domestic consumption practices in post-Soviet Cuba, where
the specter of economic crisis continued to affect consumers' percep-
tions of their lives as being defined by material scarcity (Pertierra 2011).
I was surprised that, despite an economic context in which shopping for
such basic items as toothpaste was felt to be an expensive ordeal, families
with young adolescent girls would go to extraordinary efforts to ensure
that their daughters commemorate their fifteenth birthday with a special
series of photographs. In contrast to the laments of shortage and struggle
that defined conversations about shopping for groceries with my (mostly
female) informants (Pertierra 2011, 75–106), conversations about planning a *quinces* offered the opportunity for women to associate consumption with such themes as beauty, hope, and dreams. But such contrasting
approaches to consumption—the shortages and struggles of expensive
grocery stores, and the possibilities for beauty and elegance in a photography studio—both seemed inherently tied to the very particular nature
of post-Soviet Cuban economy where market forces, foreign investments
and migrant remittances bolster a centralized system in which basic
welfare services continue to be provided and nonstate economic activity is limited to the level of very specific small businesses. As well as
these economic and political contexts in which Cuban *quinceañera* commemorations might be seen as doing something distinct to those of other
Latin American families, since the 1990s the parallel transformation of
digital media and other communications technologies has allowed many
Cubans—including the consumers and producers of photography—to
engage in new cultural practices that are intimately informed by global
and regional popular cultural forms.

While I have met more than 80 *quinceañeras*, attended several parties,
and collected more than 200 *quinces* photographs in recent years, for the
purposes of this chapter I draw specifically from two visits to Cuba—one
in 2008 and the other in 2009—in which I interviewed 30 girls between
14 and 18 years old, as well as 20 of their relatives (18 mothers, 1 grandmother, and 1 father). I engaged in participant observation with two photography studios in the city of Santiago de Cuba, as well as conducting
semistructured interviews with the studio owners. Although more than
twice the age of a *quinceañera,* I undertook my own photography session
amidst great amusement and curiosity from friends, in order to better
understand the physical process of grooming, dressing, and posing before
the camera.

The *quinceañera* phenomenon in Cuba specifically remains under-
studied (but see Härkönen 2011), although research on *quinceañera* practices and narratives elsewhere in the Americas suggest that the recent

burgeoning of *quinces* fashions and innovations build upon more long-standing conceptions of the female life cycle. The work of sociologists Mary Jo Deegan and Bert Watters (1998) on Mexican American rituals suggests that the *quinceañera* party in that context functions as a *rite de passage* of the sort classically described by Arnold Van Gennep and later by Victor Turner. Anthropologist Valentina Napolitano begs to differ, as the ritual is not obligatory; girls do become women even if they choose not to celebrate their *quinces*. Nevertheless, the parties as described in the Mexican (and Mexican American) setting can be argued to constitute phases of separation, liminality, and reincorporation outlined in Turner's classic analysis of rituals (Napolitano 1997, 282). The period of life in which a girl celebrates her *quinces* is often described in retrospect as "the time of illusion," or rather the time of "hope"—this section of a female life cycle, roughly from puberty until her first child, sits in contrast to an adult woman's life after having children, which one might presume is more likely to be the time of disillusion or hopelessness (Napolitano 1997, 286). The contemporary celebration of *quinces* in Cuba is particularly shaped by economic and cultural exchanges with the United States and especially with the Cuban community in Florida, and the party and fashion trends of *quinces* in Miami—a world center of *quinces* industries—are often the inspiration for girls in Cuba and their families when choosing dresses or other elements. Indeed, many of the dresses and other items required—from the jewelry to the photographic equipment—actually come from the United States, with relatives sending used or new goods. Women with *quinces* related businesses in Miami, such as party planners and dress shop owners, occasionally assist in informal or semiformal donations of used dresses and other goods sent to families in Cuba who are either planning their parties, or setting up businesses of their own (Alvarez 2007, 39–40)[2].

Within the ideals of desirable *quinces* images there are two distinct aesthetics, each of which is typically represented within a photo shoot. The first aesthetic represents the "traditional", "classic", and "innocent" image of a young lady in full gowns, with hair done up with adornments, and accessories such as formal jewelry, parasols, and full brimmed sun-hats known as "Pamelas." The second aesthetic represents the "modern", "sensual," and "knowing" image of a young woman in tight dresses, with hairstyles and poses that are copied from fashion magazines and music videos. Both aesthetics generally operate together to form the range of images in a *quinces* photo album. Unfortunately, it is outside the scope of this chapter to explore the contents and aesthetics of these wonderful images—the chapter instead considers the social practices that surround the production and consumption of the photographs. Extending

Napolitano's argument that in the case of Mexican *quinceañeras*, blessings and parties are rituals that embody "a process of self-becoming" (1997, 280), my research in Cuba suggests that the process of sitting for *quinceañera* portraits enables a girl to quite literally embody this transition, transforming her physical appearance, and perhaps also her behavior and comportment, through the organization, training, grooming, and eventual sitting for her *quinceañera* photographs. The practices of preparing for, taking, and subsequently displaying these photographs does not merely *represent* the transition of girls into women, but to some degree the photographic process in itself creates the transformation from childhood.

Such a transition is made possible through the material objects and technologies—ranging from dresses and makeup to the cameras themselves—which quite literally "work upon" a girl to make her a *quinceañera*. In doing so, the process invokes and reconfigures networks of relationships within and across families and friends. Digital technologies—specifically digital cameras, hard drives, and portable data devices such as compact discs and USB drives—have played an important role in expanding the reach and volume of *quinces* commemorations in Cuba in recent years; such digital technologies have actually been crucial facilitators of a *quinces* industry of small businesses in the very particular mixed economy that has characterized Cuba over the past 15 to 20 years. The properties of digital technology also allow this photographic ritual to be created and consumed across the transnational networks that sustain many Cuban households in a variety of ways, both economic and emotional. While photographic businesses allow the families who run them some financial resources in an otherwise difficult Cuban economy, the photographs they produce also enable a flourishing consumer culture—albeit within a post-Soviet socialist context—in which girls' participation in shopping, dressing, posing, and mediating oneself is an explicitly celebrated path into womanhood. Such photographs are then consumed many times over in their subsequent circulation through networks of friends and families at home and abroad.

Photographic Studios

In Santiago de Cuba (as in all cities and large towns in Cuba) many *quinceañeras* use small-scale photographic studios run out of people's homes that offer a more affordable and more flexible option for taking photos than the state-run "Foto-Servi" chain. Such studios (usually) operate under licenses issued by the Cuban government, which since the 1990s has allowed for specific kinds of small businesses to be established as part of a raft of economic reforms in which the role of the state as the only provider of goods and services has receded (Eckstein 2009, 207–228). Studios operate from a bedroom or spare room in the owner's home, and generally contain a series of curtains as backdrops, a number of props such as white pillars or chairs, one or two lighting umbrellas, and air conditioning. Even this basic setup requires considerable planning and investment as in Cuba acquiring these items is both difficult and expensive. Each studio has a single camera, and maintaining the camera is a major cost of the business since photographic parts and equipment are not sold in state shops. As a result, people rely on informal networks to buy or be gifted manufactured items necessary to the business that are brought into Cuba from abroad. Such items are not limited to photographic equipment but can also include artificial flowers for decoration, thread for repairing the rented gowns, sunhats, parasols, hair products, tweezers, and the gowns themselves.

In Cuba, photographers in home studios are rarely formally trained, and while they assert a pleasure in doing their job well or learning to take good pictures, most photographers freely admit that they came to photography as a business venture and not for artistic endeavor. Typically, they are amateurs in terms of training and equipment, but professionals in terms of intent, and their entry into the *quinceañera* business is more often prompted by opportunity than by a particular interest in photography. One studio photographer, Kelvin, went into the business because his grandmother, who lives in the United States, was a successful dressmaker. Once or twice a year, she would send *quinceañera* gowns to Cuba so that Kelvin's family could run a gown rental business from home, but they soon realized that adding a photography studio to their business would increase their income. *Quinces* photography therefore occupies a space between the amateur and the professional. As Susan Murray has noted in a study of photo sharing and social networking, affordable digital photography has transformed, if not conflated, this amateur-professional distinction in many contexts: "While theorists grapple with the meaning of photography without film, consumers have had to learn new practices and protocols and many have found new ways to use their cameras in their everyday lives" (Murray 2008, 152–153). New Cuban photography businesses such as Kelvin's depend upon the relative cheapness of digital cameras in order to exist; Kelvin's digital SLR camera and tripod were purchased by his relatives in Miami for around US $1000, and he would have neither the resources nor the expertise to use more complex professional equipment. However, *quinces* photography is specifically not an everyday digital photography of the sort Murray analyses in the United States (Murray 2008, 156). Far from valuing spontaneity, as in the genre of the snapshot, it is the artificiality of these portraits that makes them authentically *quinceañera;* natural beauty or relaxed appearances are not sought after and it is not only the dressing and make up of the girl, but also the studio props, the hotel locations, and the airbrushing and other effects that help to create the ritual of becoming a *quinceañera.* As Christopher Pinney has commented in the case of Indian portrait photography, such special effects upon the material image, far from seeming overdone, superficial, or inauthentic, actually enhance a revealing of the blossoming inner self (Pinney 1998, 137; see also Edwards and Hart 2004, 14).

The Ritual Practice of Taking *Quinces* Photographs

A few months before a girl turns 15, her mother takes her to one or more photo studios to start planning her *quinces* photographs so that an album is ready for display before any actual birthday celebration. In the preshoot meetings, the girl and her mother will discuss gowns, ideas for hair and makeup, and any particular requests for photographs (for example, some clothes sent as gifts from relatives may need to appear in photographs, with digital or hard copies sent to the gift-givers). A day or two before having her photographs taken, the *quinceañera* has her eyebrows plucked for the first time, usually by a stylist. On the day of the studio shoot, the girl comes, accompanied by her mother and one or two other relatives and friends, most often another woman of her mother's age such as an aunt or best friend. Photographers and studio owners limit the involvement of the mother and other visitors, insisting that they stay in the background or outside the studio, entering only to appreciate seeing their *quinceañera* dressed up. Usually the studio owner will act as the shoot coordinator, helping the stylist and photographer by arranging props or dressing the girl.

Often, a *quinceañera's* behavior is said to transform through the process of planning and then taking photos. Girls are said to dream of their *quinces* from when they are small. However as the time approaches, many teenage girls claim to be embarrassed about planning their *quinces*, and are resistant to many of their mother's choices or claim to dislike the process as a whole. On the day of the studio shoot, most girls start out as nervous and embarrassed. After a while, with encouragement and support from the studio team (who see helping the girl to enjoy her day as an important part of their job) the girl starts to relax and enjoy the process. Girls typically claim that they learned a lot from the shoot, about how to position their bodies or which type of makeup best suits them. All of the girls interviewed for this research agreed that despite any reservations beforehand, they were satisfied with their photos and glad to have taken them and were happy for everyone to see them.

Although fathers and extended families contribute money and other resources, often starting over a year beforehand to help make the photos possible, it is the mothers who take the daughters to choose a studio, who are the major influence beyond the girl's own preferences in choosing styles and locations, and who generally promote the quinces photos as an exciting and important event. Several mothers I worked with spoke at length of not being able to celebrate their own *quinces* properly, a regret that has made them want to ensure that their own daughters have a special commemoration. Many mothers have thought about their daughters' *quinces* since they were very small, and have actively planned parts of the celebration for at least two or three years before the daughter turns 15. The production and consumption of such photos is therefore especially important to female relatives, and in their hesitant early phase of preparation, girls often say that they do it to please their mothers and grandmothers. Härkönen (2009) links this ritual to broader matrifocal kinship structures in Cuba, arguing that celebrating *quinces* prepares girls as sexual beings to continue the family line. She suggests that the importance of this focus on women's self-becoming—as against the wedding, which focuses on conjugal relations—is in keeping with Cuban matrifocality. Certainly, in Cuba, the effort and expenditure of even a relatively humble *quinces* celebration is much more opulent than the average wedding, a ceremony entered into and withdrawn from with an ease and frequency commonly found in the Caribbean region.

While pornographic images are illegal and not freely available in Cuba, and the legal age of sexual consent between Cubans is 16, many *quinceañeras* photographs are undeniably sexually suggestive. The active role of mothers in pushing their daughters to undertake *quinces* photography that includes revealing clothing and/or "sexy" poses—not to mention the mothers' circulation of the subsequent photographs to a wide range of people—might be seen from an outside perspective as the promotion by mothers of their own daughters as sexual objects. One might easily assume that the imagined audience for consuming such images is men or boys. Yet from the perspectives of adult relatives of *quinceañeras*, the making of these photographs, subject as they are to both global influences and local sexual practices which commodify young women's sexuality in particular ways, is also—and, I argue, most importantly—about the creation of "women" by other women. Mothers are particularly proud of the photographs and the work undertaken to produce them, as they materialize the mothers' own care and success in guiding their daughters into the world of adulthood. That this key relationship through which *quinces* are made is between women, rather than between the girls and an imagined male audience, is confirmed by how the photos are distributed once they are produced. Looking at *quinces* photography is primarily enjoyed by women and girls; although men and boys are also shown the photos they usually take less time in looking at them and comment upon them in much less detail. Women gather around and talk about how beautiful the photos are, talking positively about the gowns and the makeup. Small girls from as young as three study the photos in great detail, already understanding that poring over *quinceañera* photographs is a pleasurable and important pastime. While there is clearly much scope for academics and others to critique the gender politics of such practices in teaching girls that femininity is best expressed through posing, dressing, and behaving within a very narrow range of aesthetics, the value of studying *quinces* images through ethnographic analyses of the practices that surround their production and consumption is precisely that it complicates, rather than simplifies, our understanding of how this transition to womanhood is more often mediated—through photographs among other things—among girls and women, rather than between women (or girls) and men (or boys).

The Digital Materiality of *Quinces* Photographs

Arguments well known in material culture studies help to explain this importance of *quinces* photographs as objects to be examined, admired and circulated; the material forms through which images are conveyed clearly embed photographs with distinct properties, possibilities, and histories. As Edwards and Hart note, "Albums in particular have performative qualities. Not only do they narrativise photographs...but their materiality dictates the embodied conditions of viewing" (2004, 10–11). Indeed, *quinces* photographs have long and public social lives. The photographs are public objects, to be shown to anyone and everyone on a regular basis, at least weekly, for up to three or four years after they are taken[3]. If the creation of these images produces feminine knowledge for the *quinceañera*, then after that their distribution also produces and circulates knowledge for other girls and women, and sustains relationships by providing opportunities for admiration and praise of the girl and, by extension, her family. In the relatively recent field of literature on the consequences of digital technology upon photography theory and practice, much concern has centered upon what might be lost in such a technological transformation (cf. Murray 2008). Joanna Sassoon considers how some of these ideas about the materiality of photographs may be challenged in the digital era, in which the "original" image no longer exists in material form, such that a digitized photograph in a museum collection, for example, will be missing crucial contextual information from the frames, or written on the back, of original photographs (Sassoon 2004, 191–192, see also Bruce 1994). Yet digital photography technologies in themselves offer new opportunities and practices, among them those of the *quinceañera*. Digital photography technologies, along with other technologies including computers, CDs, and hard drives, have been integral to the flourishing of *quinces* photography in the past decade. Email messages, CDs, USB drives, hard drives, and social networking sites offer new kinds of material references to the contexts and relationships that are the biography of the photograph to be found in the digital image. Indeed, *quinces* photos have much greater circulation in digital form, expanding the material contexts in which they may be found. Further, the key characteristics of digital technology—that it is reproducible, portable, and increasingly affordable—have allowed for the transnational flow between Cubans at home and abroad both of the *quinceañera* images, which are made to be circulated, and of the goods required to create such images in the first place.

Conclusion: Quinces Practices as a "Transnationalism of the Middle"

The process of taking *quinces* photos is a ritual that manifests and consolidates important relationships between Cuban girls and their families and friends, the undertaking of which gives girls new and celebrated ways of entering into adulthood. The practices that physically transform the Cuban *quinceañera* are based upon interactions with the material objects of cameras, lights, sets, makeup, costumes, and photo albums. The process of bringing together these material goods to create a photo session does not merely *represent* a moment of change, but is actually often the *cause* of the change into feeling adult. While it is too much to say that the *quinceañera* photo session creates a woman, the process of taking these photographs is certainly necessary to creating a *quinceañera*. Since the goods and money required to make the photo sessions possible are quite difficult to acquire in Cuba, there is a very conscious process of acquiring and caring for the objects involved. This is also true for the final product, which is the album of printed photos; the album is circulated extensively for years, and the photos are examined and commented upon by hundreds of people. In turn these people throughout their lifetime examine and comment upon thousands of photos. The *quinces* example therefore serves as a good discussion for the role of commemorative media in social life; photos, videos, and other visual records of events become significant objects that take on a life of their own.

The research material for this chapter was located in a very specific place, the city of Santiago de Cuba. But the photography studios, adolescent girls, and their families in that city form only one node in the transnational networks of people, goods, images, and remittances that sustain and expand the cultural practices of *quinces*. The production of these photographs both depend upon, and reinforce, an ever-growing flow of consumer goods, media, personal communications, and remittances that characterize family life across Cuba and the Cuban diaspora (Eckstein 2009, 178–206). As with many other aspects of popular culture and everyday practice in contemporary Cuba, what people do on the island often involves ongoing exchanges with friends and relatives who have emigrated elsewhere. Cubans who are doing relatively well in a difficult economic climate are largely able to do so by invoking and maintaining relationships—whether of friendship, romance, family, or business—with people overseas, and especially so for moments at which large amounts of money and specialist items are required. It is therefore important to acknowledge the interplay between transnational ties and local contexts through which the rise of the *quinceañera* in post-Soviet Cuba should be understood. The political economy of the *quinces* photography industry highlights changes that have taken place in Cuban society over the past 20 years, and reveals the expanded significance of transnational relationships and extended family networks, not only for the girls and families commemorating *quinces*, but also for the photography businesses that have flourished during this period. While these sorts of taken-for-granted transnational flows between migrants and their home communities have attracted much attention in Latin American and Caribbean research, their importance in the Cuban context, a context more commonly characterized by political hostilities and trade sanctions, has not been as fully examined. As Sarah Mahler and Katrin Hansing argue in a study of transnational religious practices between Cuba and Miami, "Vitriolic rhetoric has so dominated these relations that other ways of viewing them have been clouded if not completely obscured" (2005,122). They argue that when the actual practices of people in Cuba are studied, what emerges is a culture in which all sorts of practices invoke transnational networks for combinations of economic and noneconomic reasons. Looking at how Cuban cultural practices (in their case, religious ones) frequently cross national borders, Mahler and Hansing argue that such practices:

> constitute a communications bridge, a trans-national space, between the two Cubas...much of the literature compare only macro- against

micro- level cross-border phenomena and actors. We argue for a transnationalism of the middle that can bridge the global and the local and transnationalism from above with transnationalism from below.

(2005, 123)

The practices of *quinceañera* photography constitute a similarly clear
example of how Cuban cultural practices operate across transnational
communities, even while there remain radically different political and
economic contexts within which the *quinceañera* process is enacted.
Within this "transnationalism of the middle," as individuals and families constantly transact across borders, digital technologies allow
photographs to quite literally move between the island and migrant communities to sustain relationships. As the *quinces* photo initiates both a
literal and a metaphorical grooming for womanhood, the girl's transformation through portraiture both ties her into the networks of families
and friends who have supported and admired her, and also enables her to
encounter the world as an individual on newly adult terms. *Quinceañera*
photographs connect girls' intimate emotional and sexual development
to transnational cultural networks, allowing them to both participate in
a pan-Latino culture of consumption, and to play an important role in
maintaining family ties across borders in ways that have become much
more accessible with the arrival of digital photography.

Notes

1. Fieldwork for this chapter was funded by a University of Queensland New
   Staff Start-up Research Award. The chapter was written during a postdoctoral fellowship funded by an Australian Research Council Federation
   Fellowship awarded to Professor Graeme Turner. My thanks to the *quinceañeras* and their families whose experiences formed a part of this research.
2. My thanks also to Esther Pentón-Nodarse, for her extremely helpful conversations with me about *quinceañera* party planning in Miami.
3. In most cases, by the time a woman is in her twenties the photos are not
   shown very regularly, but an amplified photograph is permanently hung on
   the living room wall of her parents' house.

References

Alvarez, Julia. 2007. *Once Upon a Quinceañera: Coming of Age in the USA*.
New York: Viking.
Bruce, Roger. 1994. "Will the Digital Image Change Cultural Practice?" *Image*
37: 17–25.

Deegan, Mary Jo. 1998. "Weaving the American Ritual Tapestry." In *The American Ritual Tapestry*. Edited by Mary Jo Deegan, 3–18. Westport: Greenwood Press.

Eckstein, Susan E. 2009. *The Immigrant Divide: How Cuban Americans Changed the US and their Homeland*. New York: Routledge.

Edwards, Elizabeth, and Janice Hart 2004. "Introduction". In *Photographs, Objects, Histories: On the Materiality of Images*. Edited by Elizabeth Edwards and Janice Hart, 1–16. London: Routledge.

Härkönen, Heidi. 2009. *Matrifocality in Cuba: A Comparison*. Conference paper at Congress of Latin American Studies Association, Rio de Janeiro, Brazil. June 11–14, 2009.

Härkönen, Heidi. 2011. "Girls' 15-Year Birthday Celebration as Cuban Women's Space Outside of the Revolutionary State" *ASA Online Journal of the Association of Social Anthropologists* 01(4), 1–31.

Mahler, Sarah J., and Katrin Hansing. 2005. "Toward a Transnationalism of the Middle: How Transnational Religious Practices Help Bridge the Divides between Cuba and Miami". *Latin American Perspectives* 32: 121–146.

Murray, Susan. 2008. "Digital Images, Photo-Sharing, and Our Shifting Notions of Everyday Aesthetics. *Journal of Visual Culture* 7: 147–163.

Napolitano, Valentina. 1997. "Becoming a Mujercita: Rituals, Fiestas and Religious Discourses." *The Journal for the Royal Anthropological Institute* 3: 279–296.

Pertierra, Anna Cristina. 2011. *Cuba: The Struggle for Consumption*. Coconut Creek: Caribbean Studies Press.

Pinney, Christopher. 1998. *Camera Indica*. Chicago: University of Chicago Press.

Sassoon, Joanna. 2004. "Photographic Materiality in the Age of Digital Reproduction." In *Photographs, Objects, Histories: On the Materiality of Images*. Edited by Elizabeth Edwards and Janice Hart, 186–202. London: Routledge.

Watters, Bert. 1998. "Quinceañera: The Mexican-American Inititation Ritual of Young Women." In *The American Ritual Tapestry*. Edited by Mary Jo Deegan, 145–158. Westport: Greenwood Press.

10

Images of Work for Consumption: Factory's Representations in Ideological Propaganda and Advertising

Vander Casaqui
Translated by Marcela Ferreira da Silva and
Anna Cristina Pertierra

Publicizing the world of work has a long history. Especially since the twentieth century, images of workers have become complex ideological signs, driven by the culture of media, developed during this period. As Ciavatta argued: "Representations of the social world, though aiming at universality, are always determined by the interests of the groups who create them" (Ciavatta 2002, 22). Such representations thus are not just a reflection of reality. They are indeed produced, distributed, and symbolically consumed, while editing reality and constituting regimes of visibility. They spread, reinforce, and contrast worldviews and ideologies. This paper uses images of the world of work to explore discursive dynamics and ideological propaganda; such an object of analysis is not simple when taking into account the range of meanings that "work" can have for a human beings in the production of subjectivity, in their transformations of nature through work, and in their transformations of self:

The concept of world of work or worlds of work includes material and productive activities as well as processes of natural creation, which have been generated along with the reproduction of life. On that basis, we evoke the complex universe that has been significantly simplified to one of its apparent forms such as occupation, work product, work activities, regardless of the complexity of the social relations that underpin these actions.

(Ciavatta 2002, 126)

In Europe, the Industrial Revolution sustained the image of the factory as the embodiment of its economic strength, for the purpose of realizing a costly sense of progress to the modernity that both legitimated the bourgeois worldview and extended it to the Western society as a universal project. Smoke coming out of the chimney was a sign of human capacity to transform nature, to subdue it, and to build a new world made of iron and steel, heavy machinery, and large construction works that could be translated into power, ambition, and determination. Quoting Bauman:

The building site of the new—industrial—order was haughtily spattered with monuments to that power and ambition, cast in iron and carved in concrete; monuments which were not indestructible, but certainly made to look that way—such as gigantic factories filled to the brim with bulky machinery and crowds of machine operatives.

(Bauman 2001, 21)

Much imagery of the early twentieth century portrayed man-machine integration. Photographers like Margaret Bourke-White and Lewis Hine (Figure 10.1), among others, created scenarios drawn from a reality that considered the human being surrounded by factory equipment to sustain the sense of factory as identified with modernity and with the ideals of progress. Fascination with the machine reached its apex in this period, with the Futurist Manifesto signed by the Italian poet Marinetti and published in the newspaper *Le Figaro* in Paris on the February 22, 1909. The Manifesto turned the car into a symbol of a new era of speed and destruction, and the factory into a unit of mobilization of the modern man as well as a "beauty" to be admired:

The great crowds will sing excited by the work, by the pleasure and by the riot; we'll sing to the multicolored and polyphonic tide of revolutions in modern capitals; we'll sing to the vibrant nightly fervor of arsenals and shipyards blazed by violent electric moons; the transport stations insatiable, devouring smoking serpents; factories raised above the clouds by twisted strands of their smoke; bridges similar to giant gymnasts transposing the smoke and shining under the sun with a glow of knives; the adventurous steamships that sniff the horizon, the large chest locomotives that strut on the rails like huge steel horses restrained by tubes and the

Figure 10.1 Lewis Hine, "Power house mechanic working on steam pump" (1920), one among many images that represents a man as part of the gear of the economy in sharply growth. Available at: http://en.wikipedia.org/wiki/ File:Lewis_Hine_Power_house_mechanic_working_on_steam_pump.jpg. Accessed on August 9, 2012.

sliding flight of airplanes whose propellers agitate with the wind like flags and seem to cheer like an enthusiastic crowd.

(Extract of the Futurist Manifesto. Available at:
http://www.historiadaarte.com.br / futurismo.html Accessed on 8/9/12)

In such instances, the crowds, the factory, and other symbols of the Industrial Revolution and the modern spirit—such as steamships and locomotives, iron, and steel shaped to enhance human strength—are translated as new environment, one which is built by man and serves as an inspiration to artists, revolutionaries, and subjects of that time. In this environment, the past is established as something to be destroyed, and the future as a collective goal made possible by a system where man and machine work together. In differing ways, it was this spirit of modernity that motivated appropriations of work as an ideological sign by such movements as Nazism in Germany, Fascism in Italy, Stalin's Soviet regime, and even American capitalism in the Cold War period. During the Second World War, one of Disney studio's productions showed Donald Duck inserted on the symbolic battlefield. The short animation film called *Der Fuehrer's Face* presented a nightmare scenario: one day Donald wakes up in the context of the Nazi regime. From the sound of the morning alarm, he experiences a repressive and torturous routine, which presents itself even more intensely in the workplace: an arms factory that is the image of hell, having its background composed of a red atmosphere intensified by the uninterrupted smoke coming out of chimneys[1]. Donald's work is to adjust parts of bombs in a production line completely identified with Ford's method of division of labor and control of time: a continuously accelerating treadmill increasingly requires his efforts, leading him to exhaustion and madness. Reference to previous images of the classic Charlie Chaplin film *Modern Times* (1936) are clear; it is curious to see such a relationship between these negative meanings of work, and the ideological battle against the Nazi threat, by referencing a method of production that stemmed from American society in the first place.

In the case of Soviet socialism, the strength of the worker was a major element in the construction of the ideological propaganda, having its apotheosis in the anniversaries of the Russian Revolution, in commemorative dates to praise work, and through the incitement of mass participation in construction works. One example, from 1930, was a Soviet poster commemorating the "Working Women's International Day," in which women working in a factory for the textile industry were represented. Soviet propaganda is a classic example of the visibility regime strategically established for producing crowds of workers involved in sustaining the policy adopted by their leaders. Visual communication stimulates the consumption of the values and ideals associated with socialism, based on the call for individual action within a collective plan.

Lewis Hine, an American sociologist and photographer, was one of the persons who used images to denounce the inhuman conditions to which workers were subjected, mainly children, whom he portrayed working next to giant machinery in the textile industry (Figure 10.2), or during break time in coal mines. The eyes of these children constitute a visual grammar where the child's spontaneous expressions give way to disenchantment and to a forced maturity that denounces human enslavement to the gears of what Bauman would describe as the "heavy" capitalist

Figure 10.2 "Working girl" (1910), the image of a child worker in the textile industry in the early twentieth century: the photograph was a denunciation of the exploitation of child labor; the exposition of childhood is also found in other works by Hine. Available at: http://drx.typepad.com/psychotherapyblog/2007/11/photo-of-the-23.html. Accessed on August 9, 2012.

system. Bauman ascribes such heaviness to modernity in contrast to the "light" capitalism of the twenty-first century, in which the services sector is placed at the center of the economic system while praise to the machine—which represents industrial production—is left at the margin (Bauman 2000, 59). In this contemporary context, forms of publicity that continue to invoke the sign of the factory become especially interesting (França 2006; Casaqui 2009). What is the meaning of a manufacturing image at a time when the consumer is placed in the spotlight, often in opposition to industrial production? Communications strategies in marketing which invoke the world of work and industrial production as a link between consumer goods and the consumer's imagination, must translate the corporate environment of the factory and the image of the worker to fit into the symbolic universe of brands, values, and ideas that are mobilized to insert goods into individuals' daily lives (Casaqui and Riegel 2008; Casaqui 2008). Contemporary media representations of the world of work reveal much about the spirit of the consumer society in which we live. As Silverstone says:

> We consume media. We consume through the media. We learn how and what to consume through the media. We are persuaded to consume through the media. The media, it is not too far fetched to suggest, consumes us… consumption is itself a form of mediation, as the given values and meanings of objects and services are translated and transformed into the languages of the private, the personal and the particular. We consume objects. We consume goods. We consume information. But in that consumption, in its daily taken-for-grantedness, we make our own meanings, negotiate our own values, and in so doing we make our world meaningful.
>
> (Silverstone 1999, 79–80)

It is with this meaning of consumption in mind that this chapter discusses the world of work today, based upon an analysis of images and texts used for advertising, and more broadly on the strategies used for publicizing goods. In such advertising, the world of work is not only transformed by the presence of the consumer goods themselves, which change in response to the subjectivity and production of consumers but also by being edited to fit the universe of communication of brands. Within this universe, goods become mediators by offering "priceless" moments (MasterCard), or fragments of happiness (basically the entire communication campaign of the global brand Coca-Cola), among other life experiences that are fitted to offerings on the market. Pierre Bourdieu, in La Distinction (2007, 215–217), discusses this homology between production and consumption: the specter of consumer desire is to some extent permeated by the possibilities of the productive sphere, by the goods that are offered to society. In terms of material acquisition, despite the growing flexibility of production systems throughout the years—which increases the range of possible choices by allowing consumers to combine elements to compose "their" goods according to their individual preference (which is culturally filtered and expressed through the possibilities available to them)—this specter of consumer desire becomes increasingly disconnected from the "reality" of available offers, and increasingly connected to the imagery of *dream* consumption. While updating Marx's concept of fetishism of the commodity, Appadurai argues for the existence today of production fetishism and a related fetishism of the consumer (Appadurai 1990, 306–307). In this manner, the conjectural nature of conditions of production are masked in various ways so that—as in the example provided by the author—issues of locality become fetishized, erasing global factors that have stimulated production. Equally, global meanings may also mask local issues that arise as threats to the construction of the image through which corporations' desired meanings and brands are maintained. This is how we are able to consume the global spirit of brands such as Nike, without considering the conditions of production in Third World countries, such as the accusations of semislave labor undertaken by the sporting goods brand suppliers in Asian countries. Similarly, local issues make the operations of large global corporations that acquire shares and control companies round the world easier, without necessarily being exposed beyond balance sheets disclosed from time to time. For instance, the Telmex Group, a Mexican corporation, has controlled the Brazilian telephone company Embratel since 2004 without directly introducing itself to its consumers, in order to keep a sense of locality in its operations in the Brazilian market.

Just as the fetish of production transforms its conditions primarily in terms of communication, deletions, or visibility arrangements decided by corporate strategies supported by polls and market opportunities, the consumption fetish defines the consumer as an individual mobilized by media-landscapes, particularly by global advertising flows which influence his or her behavior, suggesting a spirit of freedom of choice that covers the options of goods made available by the market. These "images of agency" (Appadurai 1990, 307) are transmitted by flows of advertising communication in order to nurture the social imaginary and launch goods on the horizon of possible materialization of human needs and desires, contextualized in lifestyles packaged for consumption.

Returning to the homology between production and consumption as presented by Bourdieu, in the economy of symbolic exchanges the relationship between the two spheres becomes more complex: offers of consumption reach ever higher levels as communication processes broaden the meaning of goods, and consequently their promises. In fact, we are dealing with a language that is a kind of goods in itself. Quoting Quessada,

> Advertising has created and promoted a conception of language that is not
> only considered as means of describing the real, of relating to the world

or to social relations, but also presents itself as product, a consumer good which, in contrast to a tool or method, is there only to be bought and sold.
(Quessada 2003, 125).

The author suggests a mutually productive relationship between the language of advertising and the objects of advertising, since both are created according to a projected consumer, imagined on the basis of research and marketing analysis. It is thus the role of advertising to assimilate traits, values, and ideas that are identifiable by individuals, who in consuming advertising also consume these discursive strategies that are projected upon them. When consumption is connected to such advertising imagery it takes on sociocultural, behavioral, and identity-forming aspects that nurture consumer expectations of the value of goods far beyond the objective features of the products.

The Factory as a Sign in Contemporary Brazilian Advertising

The symbolic power of the factory when used in advertising is founded upon a brand strategy. What is hidden in the fetishist production process is brought back as a sign, embedded in narratives that support attributes associated with the goods being sold. The traffic between global and local meanings is, first and foremost, a way of narrowing language: it is the previously discussed specter of the fetish of consumption, as corporations and brands are translated according to calculations that expose, or hide, certain aspects depending on the target public and desired impact. Thus, the associative process has to be tributary of the social imaginary, being connected with the syntactic-semantic networks in which the brands are inserted and counting on permanent aesthetic upgrade. According to the study of Lipovetsky in *O império do efêmero* (1989), the logic of fashion governs this dynamic of the regimes of visibility of goods. The image of the factory is no exception to this condition as we may confirm in the images of the clothing catalog of the 2008 Fall-Winter Collection of the global brand Zara[2], in which the adult clothes are presented in an environment identified with heavy capitalism: an inoperative factory becomes the setting for presenting the new collection. The human body speaks to the hard lines of machinery resulting in a man-machine integration quite different from that of the photographic records of the early twentieth century discussed above. The factory is associated with this new context as an aesthetic element, through which an empty meaning of past and tradition is recovered. The world of work in the social lenses of the fashion field becomes an inspiration for new models as visual anchor of creative concepts. Representations of heavy capitalism and light capi-talism combine with the dominance of the ephemeral sign of fashion in order to organize the meaning of the image: the association is timely; the factory is presented as a background until launching the new collec-tion. As Ianni defines, "The meanings of modernity's signs, symbols, and emblems, including pictures and figurations, may be totally different if they are presented in post-modernity times and language" (2003, 239).

Developed in Brazil in 2008 for the beauty products brand O Boticário, the advertisement—Repression[3]—for the campaign "Believe in beauty," is set in a factory which employs only women; all of them are wearing identical clothes in grey and white and have the same haircut. One of the represented productive systems is based on the destruction of high heels—the task of women workers is to saw heels and burn them. The narrative calls to mind George Orwell's vision of the future in *1984*; or the work of Ray Bradbury brought to the screen by Truffaut in 1966 in *Fahrenheit 451*, which presented a time in which the books were forbid-den (the title is related to the temperature at which the books were burnt). It is a scenario of extreme control in which individualities are suppressed in favor of standardization. Such standardization is not limited to the sys-tems of work; it is used to control behavior, taste, way of thinking and liv-ing. The atmosphere is dark, cloudy, and grey; a truck passes through the streets repeatedly broadcasting the slogan "No Beauty!" Dehumanization is evidenced by the empty expressions of emotion; cold and distant looks with no hint of a smile. Everything is presented in a mass context: the movement of crowds, the haircuts, and the production of dolls (which replicate the appearance of the factory women workers). The female image of both women and girls is unified. According to Bauman, "the Fordist model was more than that [control of management on the work-ers], an epistemological site of construction on which the whole world-view was erected and from which it towered majestically over the totality of living experience" (2000, 56). This sense of total control related to the factory produced apocalyptic visions through artistic expression. Besides *1984* which was transported to the cinema, Fritz Lang's film *Metropolis* (1927) is a classic example of the imagery created around the factory and the delusion of the future considered on the basis of the structural pillars of the present. In the advertisement of the brand O Boticário, the exit or escape is offered though consumption as a way of individualization and of breaking with established standards. Off screen, a female voice asks: "Wouldn't it be good to live in a world without vanity, a world where image did not matter?" In the following scenes, high heels are thrown into a fire in allusion to the feminist movements of the 1970s. The voice continues "…where beauty was not considered valuable," while we see the mass production of dolls. The off screen question "Wouldn't it be good to live in such a world?" creates a suspense that is turned into breaking the rules of behavior. A woman suddenly runs down a street, and quickly up some stairs; she reaches the room of an abandoned hotel in which furniture is covered with bed linen, and finds an old box with an O Boticario branded lipstick. As she applies the red lipstick to her lips, a voice says in affirmative tone, "No, it wouldn't be," followed by the slogan "Believe in beauty" as the woman walks down the street, her hair swinging with the wind, a mysterious smile and shiny lips provoking amazement and wonder from those she passes on her path—a sense of beauty materialized through the use of the product. The factory is represented as the locus of order, a standard that is disseminated to all relationships, including to the behavior of consumption. The consumption of the promise of beauty is its antithesis, the way the woman makes herself up as if she were unique, expressing her individuality and experiencing the sense of freedom. It moves away from the sense of the mass production towards the production of oneself as a desirable good, based on the consumption of goods as Bauman argues in his book, *Consuming Life* (2007, 18).

The meanings of the factory are multiplied according to the proliferation of product segments and brand positioning, and the symbolic universe mobilized by them. In the advertising of beer, the brand Bohemia mobilizes meanings of tradition and craftsmanship related to its production, as in their 2006 film in which workers are conducted by the "Maestro of Beer,"[4] who leads the operation to produce beer, using his baton as if he was conducting an orchestra, to an accompanying symphonic track. The association with tradition is based on the myth of the brand's origins as the first beer produced in Brazil (in 1853). In another beverage advertisement, entitled "Secret" (2009) for the soda brand Guaraná Antarctica[5], the relationship with tradition is lined with signs of contemporaneity. The production of the soda, which has taken place for "almost one hundred years" according to the advertisement, is based on a formula "kept under lock and key." We see a factory within a city in the Amazon Forest region that is protected by technological security devices that remind us of old science fiction movies or bank safes. Doors are activated by cards or the laser identification of fingerprints and retinas, and are isolated from external contact by various levels of barriers and permission requirements. Inside the factory, the production line is seen in the background while a man—who identifies himself as a factory employee—talks about the secret of Guaraná Antarctica soda, a can of soda in hands. He says that only two people know the formula; the so-called "guardians," a designation that suggests an almost mystical, transcendental feature to the composition of the soda. The production line is free of employees as the bottles follow their way through the mechanical platforms. The man arrives at the "guardians' room" and addresses the camera, assuming the position of the interlocutor, and once his eyes are laser identified he is ejected from the factory, which is an underground structure in a place surrounded by guarana plantations. In the final scene the man reappears outside the factory saying: "If not even I, who work here can get close to the formula, imagine the competitors." Then he opens the can and drinks the soda; at the same time a voice says "Guaraná Antarctica. No one copies," and the advertisement ends.

Guaraná Antarctica's advertisement suggests a range of associations: the factory has local roots, and by choosing the Amazon Forest (for its visibility strategy) as the place to be identified with the fruit (guarana) from which the soda is produced—a fruit typical of the Amazon rainforest and one of the signs referring to the tropical Brazilian spirit—it assigns meanings of a natural product to the artificial drink. It is linked with attributes of tradition, since the formula remains the same for almost one hundred years—"always the same and impossible to be copied"—at the same time, it builds a spatial relation to high technology and automation of processes, establishing an aesthetic layer of contemporaneity, new machinery, and structures. In this allegorical way of portraying the personalization of production from the mysterious image of the two "guardians" of the formula (who are not shown in the film), it maintains implicit one of the most problematic issues in the workplace: the spectrum of uselessness. According to Sennett, the automation of processes is among the forces that constitute this contemporary spectrum picture, and that is not a new phenomenon: since the nineteenth century, with the first steam-powered looms, French and British weavers have rebelled against the risk of extinction of their functions (Sennett 2006, 90). Current figures show that industry progressively erases human jobs, never to be recovered, in favor of machines, "which is to say, modern workers are finally facing the specter of automated uselessness" (idem 92).

The dilemma of work in factories implicitly appears as an aesthetic sign in advertising language through the strategy of technological affirmation of goods designed to create the sense of their consumption. The production fetish is herein presented in an emblematic way: the contradictions and conflicts of labor activity are raised only by interdiscourse—other voices in the media which disseminate information about economic crises and technological adaptations that gradually eliminate jobs and positions.

Conclusion

The intention of this study was to discuss the meanings of the world of work through its imagery in different contexts, from the early twentieth century to the present times, from photography to publicity posters, in order to analyze the advertising language and its specificities by reflecting and refracting the realities of labor activity. Images of work operate as ideological signs in modern times (Bakhtin 1997), in discursive battles between social sectors and political regimes editing the world to compose messages in which work is valued or demonized according to the strategies designed to mobilize hearts and minds. In the contemporary context, the issue of work remains as a place of confrontation. Photographers—such as the internationally known Brazilian Sebastião Salgado—update the visibility of the inhuman conditions to which both formal and informal workers are subjected around the world. However, when we look at the language of advertising, we see the production systems and labor activity as signs at the service of the symbolic universe of brands. According to Martín-Barbero, this context is associated with the "*communication hegemony* of market in society: communication is converted into the most effective instrument for disengaging and inserting cultures—ethnical, national, or local—in market space/time and in global technologies" (Martín-Barbero 2001, 13). Thus, production is ennobled through the flavor of the beer, which is produced as a symphonic piece is conducted (Bohemia). It is involved by mystery and magic once the responsibility for its management is attributed to "guardians" of the formula (Guaraná Antarctica) in a clear allusion to the Taylorist division of labor. In such models, managers and supervisors have the knowledge to which workers have no access, and are left no options other than to perform specific tasks controlled by their superiors. The factory is also represented in its more rigidly Fordist character, immerged in the imagery and intertextual relationships with films and literacy pieces which characterize it as a place of control and absolute subjection in apocalyptic images of the future. It is implicit in speech, such as in the Dove brand's advertising, which defends "Real Beauty" and criticizes the cosmetic industry of which it is part, and the beauty standards disseminated by the media culture. In the case of O Boticário, this is the scenario of legitimation of its product's consumption and of the experience of vanity and femininity commercialized as a difference, as an exit or escape from the specter of standardization. Finally, the global brand Zara anchors its images in the scenario of a factory as aesthetic sign, as ambience to the ephemerality of fashion, as an image of man-machine integration though emptied of the meanings that have typically been identified with the imaginary of modernity. In the contemporary view, the fashion engine is generalized as a logic that supports both the obsolescence of images and their constant renewal.

This multifaceted characterization of the world of work, and particularly the representations of the factory environment, offer grounds for understanding the intrinsic relationship between human activity and communication processes, between production and consumption, between historical movements and the ideology of discourses, being such a relationship expressed by its choices and its omissions, and by its ethical and aesthetics function.

Notes

1. Images from this film are available at: http://www.flickr.com/photos /12436996 @ N00/773554646 /. Accessed August 4, 2009.
2. Some images of Zara 2007–2008 Fall-Winter Collection catalog are available at: http://www.pomegranita.com/2007/11/zara-fallwinter-2007/ and http:// static.lookbooks.com/campaigns/view/fashion/zara-man. Accessed March 24, 2012.
3 O Boticário—"Repression". Commercial available at: http://www.youtube. com/watch?v=3ZDT0_BVVso. Accessed March 3, 2012.
4. Bohemia—"Maestro of Beer." Commercial available at: http://www.youtube. com/watch?v=Wxrane9Zap8. Accessed March 3, 2012.
5. Guaraná Antarctica—"Secret." Commercial available at: http://www.youtube .com/watch?v=rCIQDFhf6Fc. Accessed March 3, 2012.

References

Antunes, R. 1999. *Os sentidos do trabalho: ensaio sobre a afirmação e a negação do trabalho*. São Paulo: Boitempo.
Appadurai, A. 1990. "Disjuncture and Difference in the Global Cultural Economy." *Theory, Culture and Society* 7(2), 295–310.
Bakhtin, M. 1997. *Marxismo e filosofia da linguagem*. São Paulo: Hucitec.
Bauman, Z. 2000. *Liquid Modernity*. Cambridge, UK: Polity.
Bauman, Z. 2001. *The Individualized Society*. Cambridge, UK: Polity.
Bauman, Z. 2007. *Consuming Life*. Cambridge, UK: Polity.
Bourdieu, P. 2007. *A distinção: crítica social do julgamento*. São Paulo: Edusp; Porto Alegre: Zouk.
Casaqui, V. 2008. *Do mundo do trabalho à retórica do consumo: um estudo das representações do trabalho na publicidade contemporânea*. In Baccega, M.A. (org.) Comunicação e culturas do consumo. São Paulo: Atlas: 203–215.
Casaqui, V. 2009. *A esfera simbólica da produção: estratégias de publicização do mundo do trabalho na mídia digital*. In Anais do XVIII Encontro da Compós. Belo Horizonte: PUC-MG.
Casaqui, V. and Viviane Riegel. 2008. *O mundo do trabalho na estética do consumo: representações da esfera produtiva na comunicação da marca Zara*. In Anales do IX Congreso de la Asociación Latinoamericana de Investigadores de Comunicación Social, México D.F.: ALAIC.

Ciavatta, M. 2002. *O mundo do trabalho em imagens: a fotografia como fonte histórica (Rio de Janeiro, 1900–1930)*. Rio de Janeiro: DP&A.

França, V. 2006. *Sujeito da comunicação, sujeitos em comunicação*. In César Guimarães and, Vera França (orgs.) Na mídia, na rua: narrativas do cotidiano. Belo Horizonte: Autêntica, pp. 61–88.

Ianni, O. 2003. *Enigmas da modernidade-mundo*. Rio de Janeiro: Civilização Brasileira.

Lipovetsky, G. 1989. *O império do efêmero*. São Paulo: Cia. das Letras.

Martín-Barbero, J. 2001. *Dos meios às mediações: comunicação, cultura e hegemonia*. Rio de Janeiro: Ed. UFRJ.

Quessada, D. 2003. *O poder da publicidade na sociedade consumida pelas marcas: como a globalização impõe produtos, sonhos e ilusões*. São Paulo: Futura.

Sennett, R. 2006. *The Culture of the New Capitalism*. New Haven: Yale University Press.

Silverstone, R. 1999. *Why Study the Media?* London: Sage.

11

Tango, Samba, and National Identities: Similarities and Differences in the Foundational Myths of "Mi Noche Triste" and "Pelo Telefone"

Ronaldo Helal and Hugo Rodolfo Lovisolo[1]
Translated by Marc Figuerola Delgado and Anna Cristina Pertierra

The goal of this essay is a comparative analysis between the symbolic dimensions of tango and samba as they are used in the construction of identity in Argentina and Brazil. We take as a starting point two so-called fundamental moments in the "official" history of these musical genres: the respective inaugurations of samba and tango styles that were the songs "Pelo Telefone" and "Mi Noche Triste."[2] Tango and samba are two musical genres that constructed, in Argentina and Brazil, a significant dimension of the respcctive national identities. Both share important characteristics since their birth; both came from the marginal or popular classes of society, emerging from the periphery to rise in status to become part of the so-called refined classes. Both genres emerged at almost the same historical period, and both are associated with former or current capital cities, which, in different ways, struggled at the beginning of the twentieth century with issues of unity and national identity[3]. In the case of tango, Buenos Aires and Montevideo are national capitals. From these cities tango spread to other places. In the case of samba, Rio de Janeiro is the capital of the Republic, recently established after the extinction of the Empire.

However, tango, like other genres of Argentinean folkloric music, has a regional character, meaning that the populations of two or more countries and several provinces were its makers, producers, and consumers. The *cueca* musical style, for instance, is from the Andean region, with a strong Chilean dominance and the *chamamé* tradition involves prominent participation from Paraguayans. Tango, in turn, is born in the Rio de la Plata region, in the *arrabales*, or suburbs, of the two cities—Buenos Aires and Montevideo. Tango music also makes reference to the city of Rosario, connected by waterway to Rio de la Plata and by railroad to Buenos Aires. In contrast, samba does not share its creation with other countries and the genre's historiography presents minimal influence from other parts of Brazil—such as Bahia and Sao Paulo—where this genre was also being produced. According to the storytellers of samba—in most cases, combinations of samba participants, samba lovers, journalists, and, more recently, academics—the geography of the genre is located on the streets and hills (*morros*) of Rio de Janeiro, as well as in the places of worship for Afro-Brazilian cults (*terreiro*)[4].

Although the shared characteristics of lower class origins, upward-social trajectories and historical timeframes are strong enough to find significant similarities between tango and samba, there remain notable differences between the two genres. Samba, for instance, appears intimately linked to the notion of racial miscegenation between Amerindian, African, and European populations as constituting the foundational mix of the Brazilian national identity[5]. In the case of tango, mixture is also regarded as an important feature; it is seen to arise from the mass arrival of migrants to Argentina in the second half of the nineteenth century and the first decades of the twentieth century, but is understood in reference to the *criollista* tradition (not to be confused with such terms as creole or *crioulo* elsewhere in Latin America), with only light reference to the role of black people in such local traditions as the *candombe*[6].

One strong connection that links the genres of tango and samba is a date: 1917[7]. The official dates of the creation of samba song and tango song always refer us to this year. Beyond this historical coincidence, which may be imprecise, the different meanings of these songs converge in our hypothesis. So, let us now turn to this foundational year of the samba and tango.

Samba was born as a seemingly indefinable genre. Although early comparisons were made with the *maxixe* and the (Brazilian, not Argentinian) *tango* that seemed to share similar features, as a specifically urban popular music samba represented a convergence of three racial groups: Amazonian Indians, whites, and blacks. In the National Library of Brazil, Ernesto do Santos, also known as Donga, registered the song

"Pelo Telefone," composed as a duet with Mauro de Almeida. The "car-navalesque samba" (as it was described by composers Donga and Mauro) entered history as a precursor to the samba song genre. The term "samba" subsequently achieved huge popularity, and within a few decades became identified as a "symbol of Brazilian musicality" (Diniz 2006, 34–35). Recorded in 1917 by Edison Records, "Pelo Telefone" became an instant success in the carnivals of the era, and historians frequently highlight the role of the song as the first recorded samba. Historical research indicates that the process of recording is the most important dimension in defining samba's constitution; Donga was accused of the misappropriation of songs that had already been circulating in the house or *terreiro* of Tia Ciata, a social space for musicians' gatherings of the time[8]. But more importantly, this recording registered samba in the popular imagination of Brazil and inspired a process of professionalization of musicians.

Lyrics of "Pelo Telefone":

O Chefe da Folia / Pelo telefone manda me avisar / Que com alegria / Não se questione para se brincar / Ai, ai, ai / É deixar mágoas para trás / Ó rapaz / Ai, ai, ai / Fica triste se és capaz e verás / Tomara que tu apanhe / Pra não tornar a fazer isso / Tirar amores dos outros / depois fazer teu feitiço / Ai, se a rolinha, Sinhô, Sinhô / Se embarçou, Sinhô, Sinhô / É que a avezinha, Sinhô, Sinhô / Nunca sambou, Sinhô, Sinhô / Porque este samba, Sinhô, Sinhô / De arrepiar, Sinhô, Sinhô / Põe perna bamba, Sinhô, Sinhô / Mas faz gozar, Sinhô, Sinhô / O "Peru" me disse / Se o "Morcego" visse / Não fazer tolice / Que eu então saísse / Dessa esquisitice / De disse-não-disse / Ah! Ah! Ah! / Aí está o canto ideal, triunfal / Ai, ai, ai / Viva o nosso Carnaval sem rival /Se quem tira o amor dos outros / Por Deus fosse castigado / O mundo estava vazio / e o inferno habitado / Queres ou não, Sinhô, Sinhô / Vir por cordão, Sinhô, Sinhô / É ser folião Sinhô, Sinhô / De coração, Sinhô, Sinhô / Porque este samba, Sinhô, Sinhô / De arrepiar, Sinhô, Sinhô / Põe perna bamba, Sinhô, Sinhô / Mas faz gozar, Sinhô, Sinhô / Quem for bom de gosto / Mostre-se disposto / Não procure encosto / Tenha o riso posto / Faça alegre o rosto / Nada de desgosto / Ai, ai, ai / Dança o samba / Com calor, meu amor / Ai, ai, ai / Pois quem dança / Não tem dor nem calor.

The term "samba" can refer to any number of musical variants; "*samba canção*," "*samba de breque*," "*samba de partido alto*," "*samba enredo*," and "*samba rock*," to name just a few. Sergio Cabral, a journalist recognized for his literary production about the genre and about samba schools, recorded an interview that took place in the late 1960s in which he asked Donga and Ismael Silva (another well-known Brazilian sambista) a question: "Which is the real samba?" (Cabral 1996, 37).

Donga: Ué, o samba é isso há muito tempo: "O chefe de polícia / Pelo tele-
fone/Mandou me avisar / Que na Carioca / Tem uma roleta para se
jogar."
Ismael Silva: Isto é maxixe.
Donga: Então, o que é o samba?
Ismael Silva: "Se você jurar / Que me tem amor / Eu posso me regenerar /
Mas se é / Para fingir, mulher / A orgia assim não vou deixar[9]."
Donga: Isso não é samba, é marcha.
(*Donga*: Hey, samba is from such a long time ago: "O chefe de polícia /
Pelo telefone / Mandou me avisar / Que na Carioca / Tem uma roleta
para se jogar."
Ismael Silva: That is *maxixe*.
Donga: So, what is samba?
Ismael Silva: "Se você jurar / Que me tem amor / Eu posso me regenerar /
Mas se é / Para fingir, mulher / A orgia assim não vou deixar"
Donga: That is not samba, it is *marcha*)

In discussing this difficulty of defining what samba "really" is, Cabral
points out that in this interview, Donga sings not the original version
written by Mauro Almeida, but a later parody of "Pelo Telefone," which
became the version of popular memory[10]. Cabral notes that debates about
the "exact form of true samba do not finish with the debate between two
generations," echoing the opinion of Hermínio Beto de Carvalho, who
argues that "true samba" could be found prior to the recording of "Pelo
Telefone."

Despite such differences in opinion over what defines the genre, there
is a consensus among many authors over the essential role of members of
the intelligentsia and government officials, in their use of media infrastructure and especially radio, in establishing samba as a Brazilian popular musical form (Viana 2004). It is important to note that "Pelo Telefone"
did not become a model or ideal form of samba, nor did it establish a
samba canon. It did not create a shadow for every composer who wanted to
invent a samba. Perhaps the frequent evocation of the role "Pelo Telefone"
by historians is rather due to the fact that that its recordings had a great
impact on the constitution of the popular musician as a recognized professional. It is very probable that the myth of samba celebrates not only
the creation of a profession, but also the invention of a market thanks to
modern technological resources.

The tango "Mi Noche Triste" was originally an instrumental piece
called "Lita" composed by Samuel Castriota in 1916. When lyrics were
subsequently added by Pascual Contursi, "Mi Noche Triste" consecrated
the existence of tango as an established form. In their biography of the
iconic tango singer Carlos Gardel, Barsky and Barsky (2004) emphasize

the evolutionary or incremental nature of tango's formation, alongside the evolution of the very character of Carlos Gardel as an entrepreneur of his own image. Perhaps due to this focus, they attribute little importance to the fact that, in 1917, Gardel sang the famous tango that became "Mi Noche Triste." Gardel recorded it in the same year, changing its original title from "Percanta que me amuraste" (cf. Benedetti 2007, 423–425). In fact, Barksy and Barsky do recognize that other accounts of the event highlight Gardel's ardent reception, and celebrate how the lyrics, music and interpretation of the song established tango. Interestingly, there is considerable conjecture about the day and venue of the song's premiere (Ostuni 2000; Del Priori and Amuchástegui 2003). At no time in the literature is reference made to the recording of tango as an important issue, and indeed "Mi Noche Triste" was not the first recorded tango. Among others, Angel Villoldo had already made a considerable number of recordings[11]. Perhaps the professionalization of musicians in Argentina was already underway in 1917; indeed, artists referred to in these accounts were professionals already. "Mi Noche Triste," then, holds a different meaning for tango than that of "Pelo Telefone" for samba. Del Priori and Amuchástegui (2003, 64) argue, for example, that:

> Both Gardel and those who have addressed the issue, giving *Mi Noche Triste* the honor of beginning the "tango song" do not realize the enormous quantity of lyrics accompanying tango music that existed from late in the previous century, with Angel Villoldo at the forefront of a large number of authors.

Lyrics, music, and recordings of tango were therefore produced before 1917. However, more than a few authors argue that such pieces—for example, the song "La Morocha" of 1905—did not reach the canonical status that tango would come to achieve. There is a consensus among specialists that "Mi Noche Triste" did inaugurate the tango song genre. The famous Uruguayan tango lyricist Horacio Ferrer, for example, affirmed that the tango "Mano a Mano" (lyrics by Celedonio Flores and music by Carlos Gardel and José Razzano) is certainly, with "Mi Noche Triste", by Contursi and Castriota, one of the pillars upon which historically all the singable varieties of tango are supported" (Benedetti, 2007, 431).

Thus, we ask: what is so important about "Mi Noche Triste"? Several authors, in different ways, emphasize the mythical value of "Mi Noche Triste" and seek explanations from universal to local points of view, and from psychological to sociological perspectives (Ostuni 2000). Nobody denies the enthusiasm of Gardel for this tango in the final moments of his departure from "criollista" music and his entry into the tango genre.

This transition occurred at the same time as his split with composer José Razzano, with whom he had formed the duo for which he was initially known. Ricardo Ostuni, a well-known Argentinian essayist, claims that Carlos Gardel wrote a letter to the son of "Mi Noche Triste" lyricist Contursi, in which he tells the story of a visit from Contursi during which Gardel was introduced to the art of tango, which he liked instantly.

Without downplaying the existential explanations for importance of the song "Mi Noche Triste" (Scalabrini Ortiz has called attention to the lyrical focus on the desperation of a man who is alone, perhaps waiting) or of sociological explanations (which consider the sociability of tango, the place of the city centre, the emergence of new lifestyles), we believe that the impact of this tango is to be found in the establishment of a corresponding relationship between lyrics and music that defined the genre, making it the model, the standard, and we would say the canon of tango, to take inspiration from Bloom (1995). From "Mi Noche Triste" onward, a composer was obliged to consider the model, standard, and canon of "Mi Noche Triste" when writing the lyrics or the music of a tango. It was from that point that a certain conjunction of music and lyrics could clearly be accepted as a tango, defined not so much by what was sung, nor by its themes, but rather in the mode by which the relationship between music, lyrics, and (to a certain point) interpretation was articulated[12].

In the case of samba, and especially of the samba song, the emergence of a canon would have to wait until the decade of the 1930s. Thus, 1917 is a mere coincidence between the two genres, at which point one genre reaches the canonical form for which the other genre must still wait. Our hypothesis is that it is the mode—*how* songs are played, sung and listened to—that forms a canon and the distinction of a genre. The canon is penetrated by "*how* something is said," and "*what* is said" becomes residual. Sociological interpretations of music are dominated by "what is said." This way, for instance, a comparative sociology of tango and samba could list the common themes, and the similar or different treatments of the characters and social categories present in their lyrics.

Caetano Veloso is distinguished in Brazil not only as a musician, but also for his reflections on music. In the opinion of many of his colleagues, and also in that of his audience, Veloso is an intellectual artist, or an artist- intellectual. In writings and interviews, Caetano underlines the power of the word, or groups of words in song. In response to a question by journalist Violeta Weinschelbaum (2006) about how he sees the relationship between music and text, Caetano answered: "What interests me most as a composer is that an idea appears in words that had already been sung; it is like a raw material that is distinct from melody and verses, which do cross over at the beginning, but this does not always happen" (2006, 24). If we think about what Veloso says, the sung words "Percanta que me amuraste / en lo mejor de mi vida…" (Woman who charmed me / in the best part of my life…) is an expressive raw material. As a result, the obsession of Tallón (1959) upon the word *percanta* (meaning woman, lover, concubine, possibly derived from *percal*, a word starting another famous tango) to identify the song as that of a procurer or pimp singing to the girl "ward" who abandoned him, may not have a lot of sense. Indeed, it would be a very special girl "ward" who adorned "the room with those cute little bottles garnished with laces, all of the same colour" (*bulín con aquellos lindos frasquitos adornados con moñitos, todos de un mismo color*). Beyond the question of this girl/ward, for which we may be accused of being anachronistic or guided by petty bourgeois interpretations, it is relevant that in the aforementioned other famous tango, "Mano a Mano," the first verse of the second stanza ends with the expression *pobre percanta* ("poor woman"), which, significantly, is directed straight to the listener (using the form *vos* to refer to "you"). Therefore, we invite the reader to merely try replacing the word *percanta*. The difficulty of such an exercise, and the power of this one word, exemplifies both the point made by Caetano Veloso, and the degree to which this song initiated the formation of the tango canon. Let us look, then, at this famous tango and see how most sung tangos are opened, or better, consider the words "already sung" with which they begin:

Lyrics of "Mi Noche Triste":

Percanta que me amuraste / en lo mejor de mi vida, / dejándome el alma herida / y espina en el corazón, / sabiendo que te quería, / que vos eras mi alegría / y mi sueño abrasador, / para mí ya no hay consuelo / y por eso me encurdelo / pa'olvidarme de tu amor. Cuando voy a mi cotorro / y lo veo desarreglado, / todo triste, abandonado, / me dan ganas de llorar; / me detengo largo rato / campaneando tu retrato / pa poderme consolar. Ya no hay en el bulín / aquellos lindos frasquitos / arreglados con moñitos / todos del mismo color. El espejo está empañado / y parece que ha llorado / por la ausencia de tu amor / De noche, cuando me acuesto / no puedo cerrar la puerta, / porque dejándola abierta / me hago ilusión que volvés. / Siempre llevo bizcochitos / pa tomar con matecitos / como si estuvieras vos, / y si vieras la catrera / cómo se pone cabrera / cuando no nos ve a los dos. La guitarra, en el ropero / todavía está colgada: / nadie en ella canta nada / ni hace sus cuerdas vibrar. / Y la lámpara del cuarto / también tu ausencia ha sentido / porque su luz no ha querido / mi noche triste alumbrar.

By Way of a Conclusion

The chronologic coincidence between these two songs is often misleading. The initial similarities between them are not sustainable after a more analytical view. But we suspect that there is little commonality in relation to the year 1917, between the tango "Mi Noche Triste" and the samba "Pelo Telefone" as founding songs of their genres. In the case of samba's "Pelo Telefone," accounts emphasize the composer's registration of the song, its recording, and its success in Carnaval. As a whole, samba does not develop a singular standard, model, or canon. Samba would continue to be diversified, becoming multifaceted and unfolding into different variations of samba.

In the case of "Mi Noche Triste," almost everything is inverted. The authors' registering of the song is not mentioned in histories, nobody talks about its recording, neither the date nor the site on which Carlos Gardel sang it is disputed. What matters much more in this case is that after "Mi Noche Triste," tango developed a model, standard, and canon. Tango became one identifiable thing. There are no variations of tango, at least until much later, when Astor Piazzola generated debates about authenticity and ruptures. Alongside "Mano a Mano," the opening lines *Percanta que me amuraste* cast a shadow over all of tango's poets and musicians for almost half a century. Has it ever ceased being so?

Notes

1. Ronaldo Helal dedicates this essay to Alicia Díaz Farina, who first provoked his passion for tango. Hugo Lovisolo dedicates this essay to Héctor Palomino, with whom he sang many tangos out of tune, but with enthusiasm and respect, and to his son, Pablo Palomino, for his good critiques, including giving him the title of "petty bourgeois."
2. Our interest here is predominantly in musical genre; we are not studying the sociological dimension of each dance, although we consider that very important. This essay is part of a wider research project that makes a comparative analysis between tango and samba, recognized as fundamental dimensions of respective national identities in their home countries and also internationally. In that project we consider the sociological study of the dancing.
3. Such stories about movement from the lowest classes to the most refined social strata, from the suburbs to the city centre, seem to characterize distinct cultural products—music, dances, food, and sports, inter alia—as they become dimensions of national identity.
4. In Brazil, a *terreiro* is the temple where practices of "*candomblé*," "*umbanda*" take place. The term comes from the fact that most of these places had an earthy floor, as *terra* in Portuguese means earth. Although today's *terreiros* do not have earth floors, they retain this name.
5. On the subject cf. DaMatta (1987), and the classical piece of Gilberto Freyre *Casa Grande e Senzala* (1933).

6. About the immigration flood see, for instance, Varela (2008) and Vásquez-Rial (1996). About the controversy on the origin of tango and the participation of black people see the first chapter of Savigliano book *Tango and the Political Economy of Passion*. Note as well that in Argentina "criollo" is the son of the land, no matter whether man, culture, or animal. In Brazil "crioulo" mainly means black or mulatto. It is said that Gardel only "spoke Creole," although his mother was French. A good interpretation of the speech of Gardel and its implications can be found in Barsky and Barsky (2008).

7. Cf. Garramuño (2007).

8. The house of Tia Ciata, in "Praça Onze" was a traditional venue of people from carioca samba. It is said that in the first years of "samba schools parades" it was "mandatory" to pass in front of her house.

9. "Se Você Jurar" was recorded in 1931, and is authored by Ismael Silva, Nílton Bastos, and Francisco Alves.

10. The later version begins as follows: "O Chefe da polícia / Pelo Telefone / Mandou me avisar / Que na Carioca / Há uma roleta/ Para se jogar." On October 20, 1916, Aureliano Leal, the police chief of Rio de Janeiro, then capital of the Republic, ordered his subordinates by letter to inform criminals about to be arrested for illegal gambling "before by telephone." Immediately, "carioca humor" made a joking reference to the episode and improvised verses were sung in Tia Ciata's house. This story has been recounted by several authors.

11. See, as an example, "El Porteñito" (1903), "Cuidado con los 50" (1907), "La Morocha" (1909), among others. This material is available in the first class of the course *"Tango: genealogía política e historia"* from FLACSO, coordinated by Gustavo Varela.

12. According to Tatit (2004), the Brazilian song would develop over several decades, taking, in our language, its canonical form of relationship between lyrics and music in the decade of the 1930s.

References

Barboza, Marília e Oliveira Filho. 2003. *Arthur Cartola, os tempos idos*. Rio de Janeiro: Gryphus.

Barsky, Osvaldo and Julian Barsky. . 2004. *Gardel, la biografia*, Buenos Aires: Taurus.

Barsky, Osvaldo and Julian Barsky.*La Buenos Aires de Gardel*. 2008. Buenos Aires: Sudamerica.

Benedetti, Héctor Ángel. 2007. *Las mejores letras de tango*. Buenos Aires: Booket.

Bloom, Harold. 1995. *Cânone Ocidental: os livros e a escola do tempo*. Rio de Janeiro: Editora Objetiva.

Cabral, Sérgio. 1996. *As Escolas de Samba no Rio de Janeiro*. Rio de Janeiro: Lumiar.

Cadicamo, Enrique. 1975. *La História Del Tango en Paris*. Buenos Aires: Ediciones Corregidor.

Caldeira, Jorge. 2007. *A Construção do Samba*. São Paulo: Mameluco.

Carretero, Andrés M. 1999. *Tango, Testigo Social*. Buenos Aires: Ediciones Continente.

Coutinho, Eduardo Granja. 2002. Velhas histórias, memórias futuras: o sentido da tradição na obra de Paulinho da Viola. Rio de Janeiro: EdUERJ.

Damatta, Roberto. 1987. Relativizando: uma introdução à antropologia social. Rio de Janeiro: Rocco.

Del Priori, Oscar and Irene Amuchástegui. . 2003. *Cien Tangos Fundamentales*. Buenos Aires: Aguilar.

Diniz, André. 2006. Almanaque do Samba: A História do Samba, o que Ouvir, o que Ler, onde Curtir. Rio de Janeiro: Jorge Zahar Editor.

Elias, Cosme. 2005. O samba de Irajá e de outros subúrbios: Um estudo da obra de Nei Lopes. Rio de Janeiro: Pallas.

Flores, Rafael. 2000. *El Tango desde el umbral hacia dentro*. Madrid: Catriel.

Freyre, Gilberto. 1933. *Casa Grande e Senzala*. Rio de Janeiro: José Olympio Editora.

Garramuño, Florência. 2007. *Modernidades primitivas: tango, samba y nación*. Argentina: Fondo de Cultura Económica de Argentina.

Gasió, Guillermo. 1999. *Jean Richepin y el tango argentino en Paris em 1913*. Buenos Aires: Ediciones Corregidor.

Kaz, Leonel et al. *Brasil, Rito e Ritmo*. Rio de Janeiro: Aprazível Edições.

Lovisolo, Hugo R. 2000. Vizinhos Distantes: Universidade e ciência na Argentina e no Brasil. Rio de Janeiro: EdUERJ.

Marras, Sergio. 1992. *América Latina—marca registrada*. Barcelona: Grupo Editorial Zeta.

Martinez, Roberto L., Natalio P. Etchegaray, , and Alejandro Molinari. 2000. *De La Vigüela Al Fueye: Las Expresiones Culturales Argentinas que Conducen Al Tango*. Buenos Aires: Ediciones Corregidor.

Matos, Claudia Neiva de. 1994. A Poesia Popular na República das Letras: Sílvio Romero Folclorista. Rio de Janeiro: FUNARTE, UFRJ.

Mina, Carlo. 2007. *Tango: La Mezcla Milagrosa (1917–1956)*. Buenos Aires: Sudamerica.

Ochoa, O. Pedro. 2003. *Tango y el cine mundial*, Buenos Aires: Ediciones del Jilguero..

Ortega y Gasset, J. 1981. *Meditación del pueblo joven y otros ensayos sobre América*. Madrid: Revista de Occidente and Alianza Editorial.

Ostuni, Ricardo. 2000. *Viaje Al Corazón Del Tango*. Argentina: Ediciones Lumiere.

Palomino, Pablo. 2007. "Tango, samba y amor." *Apuntes de Investigación Del CECYP*, Year XI, Number 2, 71–101.

Pedroso, Osvaldo (org.) 2007. *Debates en la Cultura Argentina 2*. Buenos Aires: Emecé Editores.

Porto, Sérgio. 1996. *As escolas de samba do Rio de Janeiro*. Rio de Janeiro, Lumiar editora.

Prieto, A. .1989. *El discurso criollista en la Argentina*. Buenos Aires: Sudamericana.

Ribeiro, Bruno. 2005. *A Suprema Elegância do Samba*. Campinas, SP: Pontes Editores.

Sandroni, Carlos. 2001. Feitiço Decente: Transformações do samba no Rio de Janeiro (1917–1933). Rio de Janeiro: Jorge Zahar/UFRJ.

Savigliano, Marta. 1995. *Tango and the Political Economy of Passion*. Colorado: Westview Press.

Tallón, José Sebastián. 1959. *El Tango en su etapa de música prohibida*. Buenos Aires: Cuadernos Del Instituto de Amigos Del Libro Argentino.

Tatit, Luiz. 2008. *O século da canção*. São Paulo: Ateliê Editorial.

Tinhorão, José Ramos. 1998. *História Social da Música Popular Brasileira*. São Paulo: Editoria, 34.

Varela, Gustavo. 2005. Mal de Tango: historia y genealogía moral de la música ciudadana. Buenos Aires: Paidós.

Varela, Gustavo. 2008. *Tango: genealogía política e historia*. Buenos Aires: Curso FLACSO.

Vazques-Rial, Horacio. 1996. *Buenos Aires: 1880–1930*. Madrid: Alianza Editorial.

Vazques-Rial, Horacio. 1996. *La capital de un Imperio Imaginado*. Madrid: Alianza Editorial.

Vianna, Hermano. 1995. *O Mistério do Samba*. Rio de Janeiro: Jorge Zahar.

Weinschelbaum, Violeta. 2006. *Estação Brasil, conversas com músicos brasileiros*. São Paulo: Editora 34.

Part 5

Spaces and Places

12

Spaces of Consumerism and the Consumption of Space: Tourism and Social Exclusion in the "Mayan Riviera"

David Manuel-Navarrete and Michael Redclift

Introduction

This chapter discusses the commoditization and enclosure of space by the tourist industry. It is argued that commoditization takes place through the production of spaces destined to promote consumerism while at the same time strategies of enclosure are developed to intensify the private consumption of space. Spaces of consumerism are expansions from rational self-contained shopping spaces, such as malls and markets, toward urban space, and, through tourism, also to far-flung nonurban space. In contrast, consumption of space refers to the private appropriation and use of space, and the emptying, physically and symbolically, of public/collective uses and local meanings[1]. The chapter examines the development of the Mexican Caribbean south of Cancun, a coastline that has come to be known as the "Mayan Riviera." On the one hand, it describes how tourist-based economies create spaces of consumerism such as all-inclusive resorts or tourist promenades in order to attract capital and monetary flows. At the same time, it considers the consequences of this process: the ways in which specific patterns of access and exclusion are promoted in order to intensify the private consumption of space. For instance, the ways in which certain ethnic groups and their social practices are segregated from places, such as "public" beaches, which are appropriated for exclusive tourist use.

In the Mayan Riviera, both processes—the creation of spaces of consumerism for tourists and the privatization of space—are legitimized by claims and discourses equating human progress and development with the growth of tourism (Manuel-Navarrete 2011). This legitimacy is crucial to gain local people's consent to restrictions over access to tourist spaces. Our discussion takes as its point of departure the ways in which primary claims were made for "pioneer" tourism in this region, claims which assisted commercial interests in gaining control of the development discourse, and disseminating the idea that tourism growth is both sustainable and "natural." Building on this characterization of the effect of discourses, both past and present, on the process of space appropriation, the paper unveils the patterns of space consumption in the Mexican Caribbean, through the case of Playa del Carmen[2], one of the fastest growing towns in Latin America. Today Playa exhibits shopping malls selling designer clothes and global brands. International gourmet restaurants compete for the lucrative tourist business; almost three million tourists visited the Mayan Riviera, not including Cancun, in 2007. The beaches of Playa draw migrants from all over Mexico, particularly from the poorer states such as Chiapas, and the town's hinterland contains large residential areas for tourist sector workers. These areas have names that sometimes suggest wider political struggles: like "Donaldo Colosio," the "squatter" area named after a prominent politician in the PRI (Party of the Institutional Revolution), who was murdered in 1994 in Tijuana by a crime syndicate.

Patterns of tourist space consumption in Playa are largely consistent with the global process of accumulation by dispossession described by David Harvey (2010). In this Caribbean town of more than 200,000 inhabitants and about 12,000 hotel rooms, international corporations, real estate agencies and global economic elites compete to amass and speculate with beachfront property. At the same time, passageways of consumerism are produced in the immediacies of the beach for the entertainment of tourists, while marginal living spaces sprawl inland, away from the tourist's gaze, but ensuring the supply of cheap labor. This chapter provides a nuanced characterization of the genesis of three patterns of tourist space consumption in Playa. These three patterns manifest today in: (1) tourist/residential hybrid spaces of downtown Playa, (2) utterly enclosed spaces such as Playacar gated resort, and (3) spaces shaped by the resistance of tourist service workers to commoditization as illustrated by the Colosio colony. These patterns were progressively developed as commoditizing pressures from global mass tourism expansion increased in the region (Redclift et al. 2011). In order to facilitate such expansion, global capital and the Mexican State imposed a sociospatial regime that promotes the functional separation between spaces of tourist consumerism and public/ living space for workers. However, this segregationist regime has to negotiate with spatial outcomes from previous regimes and the strategies of resistance articulated by tourism workers. Our characterization of three patterns provides elements for the discussion of politically and culturally contested processes of spatial consumption, which are however largely determined by globalization (Jessop et al. 2008).

The Global Consumption of Tropical Paradises

Today a myth has developed around Cancun that probably explains why so much of its history is unwritten. One of the foremost tourist guides to the area says:

> Cancun, until very recently, was an unknown area. Formerly it was a fishing town but over a period of thirty years it evolved into a place that has become famous worldwide. It is located in the south-east of Mexico with no more "body" to it than the living spirit of the Mayas, a race that mysteriously disappeared and who were one of the great pre-Columbian cultures in Mexico. The only thing that remained was the land transformed into a paradise on earth.[3]

This extract reveals all the major myths about the area: Cancun was uninhabited when it was "discovered"; it embodied the spirit of the ancient Maya (who had mysteriously disappeared); and the few remaining mortals who survived had the good fortune to be in possession of "paradise." These three myths guide much of the "Maya World" tourist discourse today. That is: space was devoid of culture, Indians were devoid of ancestors, and paradise was waiting to be "discovered." However, if we examine these claims closely it is possible to distinguish ways in which the metaphorical grounding of tourist growth borrows from earlier travel writing, such as the use of pioneer "succession" as an organic process, the preference for the natural sublime over human landscapes, and the utilization of "virgin" resources (Salvatore 1996; Martins 2000; Jones 2003).

This "active," transitive conceptualization of space carries implications for the way in which we view resource peripheries, particularly within the context of "globalization" (Hayter 2003). Geographical frontiers are ascribed, figuratively, temporally, and spatially, in ways that serve to influence succeeding events. Their "discovery" and "invention" are acknowledged as part of powerful myths, which are worked and reworked by human agents, serving to create environmental histories as important as the material worlds that they describe. The creation of existential spaces, as part of the fabric of environmental history, is seen clearly in the accounts of the Caribbean coast of Mexico, today's state of Quintana Roo. Over time we view a "wilderness," discovered by archaeologists, an abandoned space utilized by capitalist hoteliers and, today, a "tropical paradise" promising escape to international tourists[4].

The development of Cancun, beginning in the 1970s, made earlier tourist incursions seem very modest indeed. In the view of some observers, Cancun was chosen because the Mexican Caribbean was like a political tinderbox, liable to explode at any time (Cesar-Dachary and Arnaiz Burne 1998). Cancun was not simply a gigantic tourist playground; in this view, it was an "abandoned space" on the frontier, which needed to be settled, employed, occupied, and commercialized.

Before work even started on the vast physical infrastructure of Cancun, the Mexican Fund for Tourist Infrastructure (Infratur) and the "Banco de México" completed an unusually comprehensive feasibility study of the tourist potential of the region. The study reported that the withdrawal of Cuba from the tourist scene had left a vacuum that Mexico was in a weak position to exploit, since so much of its Caribbean coast was undeveloped. The danger was that other places such as the Bahamas, Puerto Rico, Jamaica, and the Virgin Islands would fill the vacuum. The study suggested that two sites should be given priority for Mexican investment: Cancun in the Caribbean, and Ixtapa-Zihuatanejo on the Pacific. The early development of Cozumel gave the development of Cancun an advantage, and the reasons why the Yucatan peninsula should be favored were spelled out in the document. It possessed an army of underemployed or irregularly employed workers since the demise of henequen and chicle, and these workers lived in the centre of the the peninsula and therefore relatively close to some of the most beautiful marine environments in the Caribbean. Rapid tourist development would attract the Maya workers to the coastal fringes.

The development of Cancun provided a global dimension to tourism on the Mexican Caribbean, while the aesthetic, ecological, and political problems which Cancun revealed led the way to an "alternative" model to that of Cancun in the coast to the south. Playa del Carmen became the locus of this development and involved a contradiction. The pursuit of "Green" tourism meant that tourist promotion emphasized the congruence between "nature" and new forms of sustainable or "eco" tourism. Much of the development of Mexico's Caribbean coast has been at the expense of conservation objectives—whether of marine turtles, mangroves, or coral reefs. The natural environment is fragile and needs protection. Nevertheless, the economy of the region is highly dependent on tourism and any suggestion that the environment is under threat rebounds against tourism. The response has been to provide a new "eco-tourist" discourse that appears to pay attention to the concerns of the environmentalist and concerned tourist. Coastal development has been "rebranded" as "eco-friendly," "natural," and sustainable. However, these new ways of repackaging development pay scant attention to the history of the area, which shows every sign of social and political conflict, and little consideration for long-term sustainable development.

The "Discovery" of Playa by Tourist Pioneers

The coastal resort of Playa, today one of the most rapidly growing urban centers in Latin America, was "discovered" in the summer of 1966, according to one account in a tourist magazine:

> Playa was discovered by a sixteen year old boy, in the summer of 1966. A momentous event, which changed forever the face of history for this small fishing village…In 1966 Fernando Barbachano Herrero, born of a family of pioneers, arrived there and found it inhabited by about eighty people, with a single pier made of local (chico) zapote wood. Fernando befriended the local landowner, Roman Xian Lopez, and spent the next two years trying to talk him into relinquishing some of his land[5]

Two years later, in 1968, Fernando Barbachano bought 27 hectares of this land adjacent to the beach for just over US$13,000, or six cents a square meter. In 2003 it was worth about US$400 a square meter, an increase of over six thousand percent.

Today this piece of real estate constitutes less than half of Playa's prime tourist development. As Playa developed, piers were built for the increasing number of tourist craft, and game fishers, hotels, and bars were constructed fronting the "virgin" beach, and clubs were opened a short way from the shoreline. The first hotel to be constructed was Hotel Molcas, in the 1970s, next to the little ferry terminal to Cozumel. Gradually, more people were attracted to the tourist potential of Playa, and the list of celebrated "pioneers" grew longer.[6]

Tourist "pioneers" had taken an interest in the Mexican Caribbean coast even before Fernando Barbachano stumbled upon the resort potential of Playa. In the longer view, tourist expansion on the coast of Quintana Roo can be compared with the trade in dyewood three hundred years ago, or of mahogany, and chicle, the raw material for chewing gum, during the last century. All three were milestones in the development of the region, and linked it with global markets and consumers (Cesar-Dachary and Arnaiz Burne 1998). Each possessed their own "pioneers," like Fernando

Barbachano, who "discovered" a land of rich natural resources, apparently untouched by human hand. To some extent, however, these timber and gum pioneers not only paved the way for tourism; they reentered the story at a later date as pioneers of tourism themselves. It is worth recalling that the account of Playa's "discovery" in the passage above refers to a "single pier made of local *zapote* wood…" Chicozapote was the tree from which *chicle* (chewing gum resin) was tapped. The chicle industry occupied what had become an "abandoned space."

Patterns of Tourist Space in Playa

The negotiation between the spatial needs of the tourism industry and competing needs of locals has, we argue, drawn in Playa a mosaic of three patterns of space consumption (Figure 12.1), which differ in the degree to which spaces of consumption can be extricated and de-contextualized from local traits.

Downtown Playa: Tourist/Residential Hybrid Pattern of Space Consumption

The first pattern is manifested in downtown Playa and it is characterized by a relatively successful hybridization between tourist spaces and

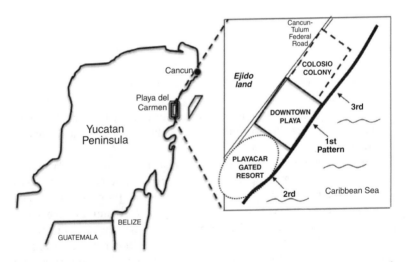

Figure 12.1   Schematic distribution of Playa del Carmen three patterns of tourist space

living spaces for locals. Before the early 1990s, space mythmaking in Playa was heralded by tourism pioneers. During this period the consumption of space was relatively affordable. Newcomers were able to find available lots to build a *palapa*[7] and establish their residence or business. Some even assert that in the 1970s there were public programs to provide free lots on proof of having a job. Mexicans, Europeans, and Americans were attracted by early myths portraying Playa as a space hidden from the circuits of mass tourist consumerism. When asked about why they decided to move to Playa, it is common to hear claims such as: "It was very casual. One could walk barefoot around the whole town. All the streets were sandy and there was vegetation everywhere. It was very quiet and the sea is so beautiful here." The myth of Playa as a space free from mass consumption is still alive and has been used, and abused, to promote the town as a centre for different sorts of holistic and "natural" experiences. Hotels such as "Las Palapas" and "Shangri-La," and restaurants such as "La Tarraya" are remnants of pioneer developments. They still include *palapa*-like constructions in close contact with the sea and surrounded by exuberant vegetation. The Fifth Avenue, which runs parallel to the beach, was originally flanked with rustic bars and hotels, which were integrated with the surrounding vegetation; some, like the "Maya Brique," still operate. There were also houses for tourism workers allocated along the streets contiguous with the Fifth Avenue ("La Quinta"). Initially, therefore, unlike neighboring tourism centers such as Cancun or Puerto Aventuras, Playa displayed relatively low levels of spatial segregation.

In the early 1990s, pressures for spatial segregation mounted in Playa as global tourist capital increasingly claimed exclusivity over beachfront space and amassed property around the Fifth Avenue. Land became progressively scarcer and the consumption of space more affordable for tourists and international capital than for immigrant workers. However, the original pattern of space consumption established by tourism pioneers hindered the development of pure spaces of tourist consumerism in downtown Playa. For instance, restricting beach access to local people was highly problematic in Playa. In fact, unlike Cancun, streets in downtown Playa are still public pathways leading to a two-kilometer long shoreline, which anyone can, in principle, enjoy[8]. Thus, a new pattern emerged, characterized by the strict separation between residential space for workers and space for tourist use.

Playacar: Gated Spaces of Consumerism

Limitations on the establishment of pure spaces of tourist consumerism downtown were effectively overcome by concentrating the development efforts of global capital in Playacar, a large estate to the south of Playa that, as explained above, had been acquired a few decades earlier by Fernando Barbachano. This strategy brought about a second pattern of space consumption characterized by social exclusion and a more commercial tourism. Playacar is today a gated community containing an 18-hole golf course, 16 large all-inclusive hotels, and hundreds of private condos. Consumption of space in Playacar is reserved for the few who can afford to buy or rent condominiums, or to spend a night in one of the many "all-inclusive" hotel rooms.

All-inclusive gated resorts like Playacar are not uncommon across the Caribbean (see Pattullo 1996, for a brilliant and comprehensive critique of their ecological and sociopolitical impacts in the Caribbean Islands). Sheller (2009, 196–197), comments on the respatialization provoked by the tourism industry:

> The creation of the "all-inclusive resort" throughout the Caribbean has created spatial enclaves that carved off tourists territories from the surrounding locality and their inhabitants [...]. The gated security guarded, even fortified, private enclave of the all-inclusive resort is exemplary of a development strategy that makes Caribbean space more accessible to foreign visitors than to local inhabitants.

Access to Playacar is strictly restricted for local people, who are kept "outside the fence" through private surveillance services. In our experience, people who look like European or American tourists are allowed to enter and wander along Playacar, but people who appear, to security guards, as belonging to minority ethnic groups or the "lower-classes" have to provide proof of being employed within the condominium to enter. Tourism developers and government officials justify strict surveillance on the premise that a space of "safe" tourist consumption needs to be created. This premise is often invoked as a "global market requirement." However, beyond any arguments for safety, surveillance also contributes to commercialize Playacar as a place for elitism, luxury, relaxation, and intimate contact with nature. In a sense, these themes sought to recreate some of Playa's pioneer myths, which, ironically, were partly erased from downtown Playa with the massive arrival of immigrants attracted by jobs in Playacar. Thus, tourism and population pressures, partly driven by the construction and operation of Playacar's hotels, intensified the consumption of space in Playa and exhausted pioneers' myths representing the town as a place hidden from the mass tourism circuits. In fact, shopping on the Fifth Avenue was progressively incorporated into international retail strategies, through the marketing of stores and products under global brands. This prompted the exodus of many pioneers who left in search of more peaceful locations. For some of them, the very construction of Playacar's all-inclusive hotels was the reason to leave; for some it was the first traffic lights; and for others the arrival of Wal-Mart.

Colosio: A Contested Segregating Pattern

Between 1990 and 1993, population numbers in Playa jumped from 3,098 to 16,901 (Solidaridad Municipal Government 2007). The housing situation of workers in tourism had become critical. As one person expressed it: "People were desperate. There was no way of finding housing. They were renting little shacks for 1,000 pesos. One could feel the outbreak; I could feel the eagerness for *invasión* [taking of land to create a shantytown]."

In interviews with planning authorities we found that by the early 1990s the government had outlined a plan for, "ensuring the rational growth of Playa." The spirit of the plan was to reproduce Playacar's pattern of space consumption in the north, and then accommodate local population towards the west (away from the coast) in lands owned by Playa del Carmen's *Ejido*[9] (Figure 12.1). However, the implementation of this plan encountered two major obstacles. First, the development of *Ejido* lands involved a complicated legal process requiring the consensual approval of Playa's *Ejido* members. Second, the lands to the North were a 273 hectare forest owned by the government of Quintana Roo, but claimed by the Rangel Castelazo family. The state government held a title granted by Federal President Luis Echeverria in 1973, which designated the area as a land reserve with the purpose of enabling the urban growth of Playa. However, Francisco Rangel Castelazo[10] alleged that a family of *chicleros* (Velázquez Catzím) had acquired the right of possession from the Agrarian Reform Agency and had sold it to another *chiclero* (Francisco Amaro), which in turn sold it in 1962 for 32 pesos to Castelazo's wife Ofelia González Whitt. Intriguingly, all these hypothetical transactions would have been carried out in the absence of titles or even affidavits. However, there was proof that in 1980 Castelazo had paid almost two million old pesos to the Agrarian Reform Secretary in exchange for a receipt. Based on this frail and shady evidence of ownership, Castelazo proceeded to fence in the claimed land.

The government's inaction and the mounting sociospatial tensions in downtown Playa sparked off an outburst of spatial consumption through which tourist workers sought to appropriate the forest, limiting the expansion of Playa towards the North. This gave rise to Playa's third pattern of space consumption, a pattern characterized by conflict and division between residential and consumerist uses of space. In April 1994, hundreds of people invaded 40 hectares in the estate under dispute[11]. This land would become the colony Luis Donaldo Colosio Murrieta. Street grids were mapped out in less than two days, as squatters cleared out vegetation and assembled precarious sheds in predesignated plots. Despite obvious organizational challenges, there was enough coordination to trace precise blocks of 20 lots each in perfect alignment with the already existing streets and avenues of downtown Playa. Most of the squatters were immigrants who had recently arrived to work in Playa from different parts of Mexico.

There are multiple versions to explain how and why this episode of urban squatting took place. A key actor was the Playa del Carmen Union of Settlers (*Unión de Colonos*) led by Gildardo Sosa and Julio Cano. According to testimonies, the members of this and other associations had reached the conclusion that the only option to alleviate the scarcity of living space in Playa was "consuming" the lands claimed by Castelazo. However, the role of Mario Villanueva, Quintana Roo's governor (1993–1999), in the squatter movement remains unclear. Some leaders claim that he arrived just a few days later and declared that he was unable to reverse the situation, thus implicitly acknowledging the squatters' right to stay. However, many people believe that Villanueva played a stronger role. A very popular expression used to describe this role is: "It was the first ordered invasion;" implying that it was both organized (in order), and instructed (ordered) by the government. Another popular expression to describe the operation is: "Villanueva threw a piece of meat and the hungry ran to catch it." Some people even argue that the idea of naming the new colony after the assassinated candidate Luis Donaldo Colosio was Villanueva's idea, given that he was a close friend and political ally of the murdered politician.

Mario Villanueva is well known in Quintana Roo for his authoritarian and paternalistic style, as well as his political boldness. As an outcome of his provocative actions, he gained as many loyal followers as bitter enemies. He is often regarded as the only governor who actually did something to defend the interests of the poor, but his actions and decisions were highly controversial, and he ended his office term running away from the federal justice, accused of encouraging drug-trafficking. A few months after leaving office, he was captured, convicted, and has remained since then imprisoned for money-laundering offences.

From the point of view of the consumption of space, the pattern in Colosio differed from downtown Playa and Playacar. Colosio's coastal strip, extending along three kilometers of coastline and about 250 meters wide, was mysteriously "saved" from the squatter invasion and left to be exclusively consumed by tourists. It is hard to find a definitive explanation for this strange contingency. A common suspicion is that Villanueva somehow arranged to leave this space intact for subsequent

Figure 12.2 The fence separating the colony Donaldo Colosio from its beachfront (2008, photography by David Manuel Navarrete).

tourism development. In any case, these over 60 hectares of "saved" beachfront land remained untouched for more than a decade. In fact, a dividing wire fence was erected that prevented access to the beach from the Colosio (Figure 12.2). This fence created a curious pattern of space consumption in which a valuable strip of coastal land remained "protected" while people inhabiting land barely 300 meters away from the beach were forced to walk several kilometers in order to bathe in the sea. However, beach access was probably not among the priorities of Colosio's new settlers. For more than five years, anyone inhabiting Colosio had to endure a life without any basic urban services due to the prevailing legal dispute with Castelazo, which presumably prevented the government from undertaking any public works in the colony.

Despite the unofficial support from Villanueva, it soon became clear that the authorities would not allow Colosio to set the precedent to guide future space consumption. Villanueva's government offered property titles to the squatters in exchange for a monthly payment, but this regularization program was suddenly cancelled after 15 months of payments, alleging that Castelazo had appealed to the courts for legal protection against the program. As a result, squatters neither had their payments returned, nor did they get the promised titles. One of the squatters commented:

They did a perfect business. They settled 1,500 people in one shot and started to charge [both taxes and titling rights] for their lots from day one, but nobody provided water or paved the streets until recently. They are still charging poor people big amounts of money. For them it was a sound business.

Castelazo and the government were not the only actors seeking to benefit from Colosio's "liberated land." The colony continued to grow as new immigrants arrived searching for cheap land. According to our informants, immigrants were brought from Chiapas and Tabasco by *coyotes* who used to sell the same property twice or three times to different people. One of the first squatters relates the ordeal of the early years in Colosio as follows:

> I was amongst the first squatters. The first to invade were people from Playa. Here everywhere was jungle and mangroves. Some squatters built small cabanas and put someone to take care of the property. We could not live here because there were no services. Sometimes the families that were put to watch over the land ended up staying. That is why I always left single construction workers watching out my lot. I am the only one from my group of invasion who still keeps her land. At some point violent people from Tabasco and Chiapas came with machetes and settled in lands that had been already invaded and cleared. There were many coyotes that took advantage of this.

In addition to *coyotes*, there were also squatter leaders who sought to take advantage of their position and negotiated with the government for their own benefit. According to the testimony of yet another squatter: "At the beginning everything was done through leaders. Some were honest and believed in what they were doing. However, the majority started to buy big houses."

The election of a new governor, Joaquin Hendricks, in 1999, brought about some significant changes, but not to the benefit of Colosio's inhabitants. Hendricks declared his intention to settle the conflict by reaching a definitive agreement with Castelazo. His solution consisted of splitting in half the 273-hectare estate under dispute, which was already inhabited by around 5,000 families. Ofelia González Whitt would hold half of the property, and the other half would be held by Quintana Roo's housing agency (INFOVIR). Then, INFOVIR and the Castelazo family created the Desarrolladora de la Riviera Maya, a corporation in charge of both commercializing Colosio's 60 hectares of still untouched beachfront land, and extracting some profit from the families settled in Colosio. The Desarrolladora unilaterally decided to charge between 66,000 and 775,000 pesos (about US$6,000 to 77,500), according to different sources, for each lot in Colosio. The amount was to be paid monthly in advance by settlers over ten years. Many inhabitants decided to join the scheme in order to avoid further problems, but some chose to resist on the basis that the Supreme

Court had acknowledged the public ownership of the lands claimed by Castelazo. One of the settlers who chose to pay explains her decision as follows: "I am paying because it is not much money and I prefer to do things well, but there are people who cannot pay 600 pesos every month and are then forced to sell." Eventually a civil association, *Tierra y Libertad* was formed by the four hundred families that still refused to pay.

Today, Colosio is the largest human settlement in Playa with around 40,000 inhabitants. It is fully served with electricity, water, drainage, paved streets, schools, market, library, and health centers. In 2005, Colosio's beachfront started to be cleared of its original vegetation, including mangroves. The 60-hectare coastal strip was sold to international and Mexican corporations under the umbrella of the so-called Turquoise Coast development. This project includes all-inclusive resorts, hotels, "ecological" villas, "eco"-parks, condominiums, residential areas, and commercial areas. It is not clear yet whether new passageways or street accesses to the beach will be opened for the inhabitants of Colosio.

The effective commoditization of Colosio's coastal strip consolidated a pattern of tourist space consumption resembling Playacar's segregation. However, the proximity of Colosio to the beach provides a different topography that, perhaps in combination with Colosio's distinctive culture of resistance, problematizes social exclusion. It is not yet clear whether new passageways or street accesses to the beach will be opened for the inhabitants of Colosio once the all-inclusive and residential resorts are completed. One of the first corporations to start construction was the Spanish "Sol Meliá" in 2008. Interestingly, "Sol Meliá" included in its projected hotel a public beach facility (to be named *Balneario Público Municipal Luis Donaldo Colosio*). However, the Federal Environmental Agency (SEMARNAT) rejected the project arguing that it was inconsistent with environmental planning legislation. From a social perspective, it is difficult to explain why permission was denied for a small beach area, to be enjoyed by local inhabitants, while at the same time the same company obtained all environmental permits to develop an adjacent massive complex, including restaurants, beach clubs, pools, and spas. This apparent absurdity attests to the complexities involved in the consumption of space in Playa. It also shows that the explanation of space consumption patterns requires a close look at complex governance processes (for a discussion of the region's governance see Manuel-Navarrete et al. [2011]).

Conclusion

Tourism in the Mexican Caribbean has had a powerful impact on the consumption of space. The analysis of these patterns in Playa shows the overwhelming influence of globalized forms of consumption that prioritize the creation of secluded spaces for tourist consumerism. Despite instances of resistance by local groups, public and collective spaces are increasingly under siege from commercial strategies to privatize space.

Theoretical exploration of the consumption of space and place has built on the work of Henri Lefebvre (1991), who argued that space is not a neutral, passive geometry but characterized by a dialectical structure that is embedded in a societal politic. Hegemonic spatial practices, such as those promoting spaces of consumerism, can be contested by space users through explicit political resistance as well as "veiled criticism of established orders re-codings and decodings of dominant spatializations" (Lefebvre 1991, 39). In the case of Playa, the patterns of consumption of space, overtly dominated by tourist commercialization, have been resisted locally, but with little success in terms of shifting these politicized spatializations. The users of space have indeed tended to conform to dominant discursive constructions of space. By so doing, they have engaged in the (re)production of spaces of consumerism, such as shopping avenues and malls, while at the same time silently withdrawing from those spaces whose consumption is "reserved" for the wealthier foreign tourist.

As we have seen in the case of the Colosio, the government's role in the consumption of space has often been ambiguous, but it has generally prioritized the interests of tourist capital over those of local inhabitants, and tended to enforce a pattern of segregation. The three patterns of space consumption identified in Playa differ in the degree of separation between tourist space and local living space and the restrictions imposed on the use of the beach by local people. An interesting facet in the genesis of Colosio's pattern is the way it was marked by dynamics of conflict and resistance, in which corrupt local governance structures were determinant. The ubiquitous "fence," the existence of the Desarrolladora, and the failure to establish a public beach for local people are all evidence of the role of political pressures promoting Playacar's pattern.

Local people are often vocal in their rejection of the consumption of space patterns entailed by Playacar and Colosio's Turquoise Coast:

> They have knocked down all the mangroves that were protecting us from the hurricanes to put up a couple of ridiculous buildings [in reference to the hotel that the Spanish company Sol Meliá is building]. The most ridiculous of all is that they advertise it as the "last virgin land of Playa," and look what they are doing with the last virgin land: screwing it up.... This is a problem that goes 500 years back. It is a problem of poverty and malnutrition; not only physically but also culturally and intellectually. The destructive capacity and power of money are too strong. Nothing can be done against the powerful. It is like hitting one's head against a wall.

The patterns of space consumption in Playa suggest that political resistance is not entirely futile, but it nevertheless has limited impact in terms of putting the needs of locals before those of global tourism, or restricting the commoditization of public space. In the case of the Mexican Caribbean, the paradoxes offered by an increasingly unequal consumption of space suggest the weakening of local control as entire locales are subjected to politically corrupt, and personalistic, planning arrangements and the execution of corporate power by global players. Thus, the trajectory of the tourist "gaze" (Urry 1995) casts a long shadow over the Mexican Caribbean, stirring the phantoms of the colonial "past" and sustaining the nightmare of the total commoditization of the entire planet.

Notes

1. This theorization of space consumption holds some parallelisms with John Urry's theory of consuming places. Our notion of spaces of consumerism coincides with Urry's (1995,1) claim that places are increasingly restructured as centers for consumption. However, our notion of consumption of space emphasizes patterns of social exclusion rather than Urry's (1995,1–2) emphasis on visual consumption, the depletion/exhaustion of emblematic elements of places, or the consumption of localities' identities.
2. Subsequently abbreviated as "Playa."
3. Everest Tourist Guide to Cancun and the Riviera Maya 2002.
4. See Torres and Momsen (2005) for an account of the thematization of Cancun's space by large-scale mass tourism.
5. Quoted in the glossy *Playa!* Magazine, August 1999 published in Playa Del Carmen.
6. The search for a history of its own has recently intensified in Playa. The newspaper *Por Esto!* carried a report on November 16, 2003 that a commemorative plaque, carrying the names of "the founding families" of Playa had been unveiled in the centre. The report noted that most of the one hundred thousand people living in Playa today had no idea that the town had such a long history. It had been a fishing village only "a few decades ago." However, Playa had been mentioned on November 14, 1902, when a local chicle contractor had sought permission for a road to the coast, and it was agreed that this was now the date on which it was "founded."
7. Thatched roof Caribbean-style wooden huts.
8. Although, in practice we heard complaints and witnessed cases of discrimination by local police against construction workers seeking to use the beach.
9. A characteristic Mexican legal and economic regime of organization based on the communal ownership of land. The 1920 "*Ejido* Act" granted land rights to farmer communities, many of indigenous origin, and was made part of the constitution in 1932. In 1992 the "New Agriculture Act" established that *ejidatarios* can sell their individual land rights to other Mexicans, if 75 percent of the *ejido* members agree as a community.

10. Castelazo is a retired military man, sadly known for his struggle to force-fully extend his 25 years concession of *Puerto de Abrigo* marina in Cozumel that had been granted by President Echevarria. This struggle resulted in the bankruptcy of the marina and the ending of its operations.
11. According to squatter leaders, about two thousand people were congregated at the northern edge of Playa to start this popular operation of rapid urbanization.

References

Antochiw, M. & A. Cesar-Dachary. 1991. *Historia de Cozumel*. México: Consejo Nacional para la Cultura y las Artes.

Blomley, N. 2003. "Law, Property, and the Geography of Violence: the Frontier, the Survey, and the Grid," *Annals of the Association of American Geographers*, 93: 121–141.

Cesar-Dachary, A., & S.M. Arnaiz Burne. 1998. *El Caribe mexicano. Una frontera olvidada*. México: Universidad de Quintana Roo.

Harvey, D. 2010. *The Enigma of Capital*, London: Profile.

Hayter, R., T. Barnes & M. Bradshaw. 2003. "Relocating Resource Peripheries to the Core of Economic Geography's Theorizing: Rationales and Agenda." *Area* 35: 15–23.

Jessop, B., N. Brenner & M. Jones. 2008. "Theorizing Sociospatial Relations." *Environment and Planning D: Society and Space* 26(3), 389–401.

Jones, G. 2003. "Imaginative Geographies of Latin America." In *The Companion to Latin American Studies*. Edited by P. Swanson, 5–25. London: Edward Arnold.

Jones, M. 2009. "Phase space: Geography, Relational Thinking, and Beyond." *Progress in Human Geography*, 33(4), 487–506.

Lefebvre, H. 1991. *The Production of Space*. Translated by D. Nicholson-Smith. Oxford: Blackwell.

Manuel-Navarrete, D. 2011. "The Ideology of Growth, Tourism and Alienation in Akumal, Mexico." In *Climate Change and the Crisis of Capitalism: A Chance to Reclaim Self, Society and Nature*. Edited by M.Pelling, D. Manuel-Navarrete, and M. Redclift, 143-156. London: Routledge..

Manuel-Navarrete, D., M. Pelling & M. Redclift. 2011. "Critical Adaptation to Hurricanes in the Mexican Caribbean: Development Visions, Governance Structures, and Coping Strategies." *Global Environmental Change*, 21: 249–258.

Martins, L. 2000. "A Naturalist's Vision of the Tropics: Charles Darwin and the Brazilian Landscape," *Singapore Journal of Tropical Geography*, 21(I), 19–33.

Pattullo, P. 1996. *Last resorts: The Cost of Tourism in the Caribbean*. Kingston: Ian Randle.

Salvatore, R. D. 1996. "North American Travel Narratives and the Ordering/Othering of South America (c.1810–1860)," *Journal of Historical Sociology* 9(1), 85–110.

Sheller, M. 2009. "The New Caribbean Complexity: Mobility Systems, Tourism and Spatial Rescaling." *Singapore Journal of Tropical Geography*, 30: 189–203.

Solidaridad Municipal Government. 2007. "Actualización del programa de desarrollo urbano del centro de población de Tulum, 2006–2030." Servicios Urbanos Municipales y Estatales.

Torres, R. M., and J. D. Momsen. 2005. "Gringolandia: The Construction of a New Tourist Space in Mexico." *Annals of the Association of American Geographers*, 95 (2), 314–335.

Redclift, M., D. Manuel-Navarrete & M. Pelling . 2011. *Climate Change and Human Security: The Challenge to Local Governance under Rapid Coastal Urbanization*. Cheltenham, UK: Edward Elgar.

Urry, J. 1995. *Consuming Places*. London: Routledge.

13

Singing for Shaved Ice: Glacial Loss and *Raspadilla* in the Peruvian Andes

Katherine W. Dunbar and Katy Damacia Medina Marcos

Introduction

In the mountain valleys of north-central Peru, people often seek out a sweet treat with local flair: *raspadilla*, or shaved glacial ice. Though very old, *raspadilla* is changing. Different ingredients are used to sweeten the treat, the blocks of glacial ice are more difficult to obtain and often of a lesser quality than in previous years, it is more widely sold throughout the valley, and is in competition with much-sought-after imported sweets. Transformed by economic expansion, cultural preferences, and environmental pressures, this treat reflects the tensions of change. While it appears fragile in many ways, it has been adaptable. However, some of the sweetness is lost for the people who have long consumed it, and even for those who only encountered it recently as tourists, due to the knowledge that it may soon be gone. This chapter discusses the ways in which community members, *raspadilla* vendors, and the individuals contracted to gather glacial ice are adjusting to the reality of the receding glaciers and market pressures.

Within the north-central Peruvian Andes, this study focuses on the Callejón de Huaylas, a valley running north-south bordered by the heavily glaciated Cordillera Blanca on the east and the significantly drier Cordillera Negra on the west. The valley is further defined by the Rio Santa, which flows between the two ridges before cutting through the Cordillera Negra at the north end of the valley and flowing west towards the Pacific Ocean. Many of the peaks along these ranges rise above 6,000 meters, sitting roughly 3,000 meters above the valley. The valley itself is relatively narrow, in some areas only as wide as the river itself, but in other sites small cities swell or citrus plantations thrive on the river banks. The valley gives way to impressively sloped hills where there is a mix of agriculture, eucalyptus and pine plantations, and small clusters of houses. Climbing higher, villages appear with plazas, fields, pastures, and extensive canal networks. Above these villages, in the Cordillera Blanca, lies more pasture and native, high-altitude trees and shrubs, which fade away to bare rock walls and eventually to the glaciers themselves. Some of the glaciers are relatively smooth fields of ice, while others are steep peaks that seem to almost hang from the sky. This research is based on field-work undertaken from 2008 through 2010 in the Callejón de Huaylas, using a combination of participant observation in households, communities, and city centers; semistructured interviews with *raspadilla* vendors, consumers, and those who travel to the glacier to collect glacial ice; and focus groups with communities living in the foothills of the glaciers themselves.

Raspadilla Culture

Coming from the Spanish verb *raspar* which means to scrape, the treat is also known by its Quechua name, *shikashika*, onomatopoeia for the scraping sound of the wood plane across the ice. Today, these treats are sold by street vendors with tricycle carts, typically in the major plazas along the valley. A traditional *raspadilla* consists of shavings from a large block of glacial ice combined with several thick syrup flavorings, honey, and sometimes milk. *Raspadilla* is enjoyed either in a pint glass with a spoon if you plan to sit and eat nearby, or with a straw in a plastic cup if it will be eaten on the go. Most people choose the glass, taking the time to sit and enjoy the refreshing treat while seeking shade from the hot midday sun. Though practice of using glacial ice or mountain snow for desserts has been largely elaborated throughout the world into myriad cool treats from sophisticated sorbet to simple snow cones, the ice itself has been replaced by manufactured ice in most parts of the world. In the Callejón de Huaylas, however, where communities live in close proximity to glaciered peaks, using glacial ice in the consumption of cool treats persists.

Collecting glacial ice and snow has been in practice for thousands of years across the globe. It is unclear when the practice may have begun in the Andes; however, we do know that there is a long tradition of contact with glacial ice. Pre-Columbian peoples frequently traveled through the mountains onto the glaciers for various ritual practices (see, for example, Bolin 1998 and Reinhard 2006). In the Callejón de Huaylas, there is evidence that prior to Incan expansion into the valley, certain groups established themselves at the edge of the ice fields as this was highly defensible territory (see Lau 2010). Ritual activities that persist today continue to revolve around traveling to the glaciated areas of the Andes. The most popular in the Callejón de Huaylas is the *Fiesta de San Juan* on June 24, which celebrates both the birth of Saint John the Baptist and summer solstice. Traditionally, communities observe *San Juan* by trekking to the glacier and burning offerings for the continued fertility of their livestock.

Members of communities established higher in the hills just under the glaciers recall often visiting the ice in their youth, when glaciers came lower into the foothills and were much easier to access. While pasturing animals in grazing land high above the community, significant time was spent in areas that were once near the ice. In the often echoed memories of one woman, "We went looking for flowers; we played in the snow, and pursued rainbows." In addition to the festival of *San Juan*, New Year's Day was often marked by families or groups of friends hiking up to the glacier edge and spending the day playing and communing with the glacier and the mountain. Young women often visited areas just below the glacier to gather special flowers which only grow there. Some are said to have medicinal benefits, or are particularly valued when placed in the band of the ubiquitous wool hat worn by local women, and said to induce attraction from men.

During these visits, people often made *raspadillas* at the glacier edge. To do so, they collected ice that had fallen from the glacier, or they scrambled up to the ice field itself and chopped off a block of the more solid ice. In either case, the ice was placed in a *lliklla,* or carrying cloth which is another element of the traditional dress in the region, and slammed against the ground to break it up into more manageable pieces. People often speak of being taught by their parents and grandparents to "*silbar antes de entrar,*" or whistle a few notes to the glacier before entering the ice field. This practice was meant to encourage any large pieces of ice at the entrance on the verge of falling off to do so before people entered the ice field. Whistling to the glacier avoided people suffering injury when small avalanches occurred. If ice did fall when they whistled, it made harvesting the ice much less work as they could gather the pieces that fell instead of climbing further and having to work at extracting blocks of ice. Since those gathering ice for these impromptu *raspadillas* were not overly concerned with whether the ice would last longer than a few days, they preferred the crumbling ice as it was easy to turn into *raspadilla*. If they planned to bring the ice down to their family, the more solid ice was sought out, kept intact and immediately wrapped for protection.

In the past, flavoring was added using special native flowers that were gathered along the paths on the way to collect glacier ice. These beautiful and fragrant flowers are said to have made the sweetest *raspadilla*, though even when the practice of using these flowers was at its height, they were scarce and only certain people knew where to find them. Using native flowers for flavoring is no longer practiced, even among those families making *raspadillas* while visiting the glacier. There are now large quantities of colorants and essences offered in the markets which are much easier to obtain and very inexpensive. When we accompanied families collecting glacial ice for their own use, native flowers used in the past were not sought out, or even mentioned, and instead packets of artificial drink flavorings were used.

While those interviewed for this study trace the commercialization of *raspadilla* in the region to the 1970s when their parents or grandparents taught them the trade, other accounts describe *raspadilla* sales as a well-established practice in the valley dating to before the 1950s (Stein 1961). Stein goes on to describe the practice of individuals extracting blocks of glacial ice to sell in town when in need of money, again differing from the memories elicited in this study, which recall those who sold *raspadillas* along the valley also extracting their own ice in previous generations. *Raspadilla* vendors approached for this study remember the tradition of *raspadilla* in these times as revolving largely around the first *fiestas patronales*, which are celebrations of the day a particular town or community was established following the Agrarian Reform of 1969.

In contrast, this research concluded that most, if not all, ice used for commercial *raspadillas* in 2009 was collected by a specific group of about 20 people living in communities above Yungay, who traveled to the Huandoy glacier to extract ice blocks. In a typical week they trekked to the glacier twice, on the nights before the two main market days for the region. They would also make special trips before festival days, or if there was a particularly large order from their more regular customers. In order to extract ice, people used picks, axes, machetes, and other handmade tools. These were the same technologies used in previous generations of ice extraction. Those contracted for the job climbed onto the glacier to extract the ice blocks and carry them down to the point where the donkeys were tethered at the start of the ice fields. Then they loaded the ice blocks onto the donkeys and led them back to small storage facilities in their respective villages. When harvested for sale, ice was extracted in blocks of about 50 kilos and paired to travel down the mountain. Once loaded onto the donkeys, ice blocks were typically covered by a native grass that grows in high altitudes, known as *ichu* in Quechua. This natural covering was later layered with large white plastic bags, previously used to store rice, which further protected the ice. Early the next morning trucks moved through the communities picking up the ice blocks, marking them to distinguish among those of each *nievero* and carrying them down to the market.

Glacial Loss Develops the Trade

Glaciers have been receding rather dramatically in the last few decades. From a 1970 baseline developed using aerial photographs, the national inventory of Peruvian glaciers shows that glaciers in the Cordillera Blanca have shrunk by 27 percent in the last 30 years (UGRH 2010). This recession is most visible at the edges of the glacier, which directly affects the accessibility of quality glacial ice. Previously, carrying glacial ice down the mountain was undertaken by the same families that sold the ice at festivals or in city plazas and by those who lived close enough to the ice edge to occasionally extract and sell blocks of ice for supplemental income. As glaciers receded further up the mountain, there was simultaneously more and less opportunity for supplementing agricultural livelihoods. As the glacier receded, the task of traveling to the glacier became much more onerous as one needed to climb further, over increasingly difficult paths, to reach the desired ice. Farmers who infrequently made the journey for supplemental income turned to other activities, like working for a neighbor or working on paid municipal projects. This left open the opportunity for specialization in glacial extraction, which is what followed.

In contrast, as the glaciers became more difficult to reach for opportunistic glacial extractors, specialized groups established a business out of extracting ice to sell in the markets. Referred to throughout the valley as *nieveros* (people of the snow), these are the only people extracting glacial ice commercially today. A monopoly has been created through environmental changes that limited access to glacial ice. In the Callejón, the proliferation of small-scale marketers is evidence of the increasing need for families to supplement farm production as they are further incorporated into cash-based economies. *Raspadilla* vendors and *nieveros* are part of a long tradition of petty commerce in Peru (Babb 1987). This type of work allows for under-educated or illiterate individuals to sustain themselves, but also allows people to supplement their income in a depressed economy. The majority of vendors are either illiterate, or have only partially completed primary school.

Since glacial ice was easier to obtain once *nieveros* were dedicated to the task, *raspadilla* vendors multiplied leading to an increase in competition for customers. However, tourism had steadily increased in the valley as well. Tourists began to travel from all over the world to climb the glaciers, scale the rock walls, and visit the numerous cultural sites in the valley. Vendors and tour companies tout Huaylas *raspadilla* as a treat that cannot be found in other parts of Peru, or even in most of the world. Although there are *raspadilla* vendors on the coast and in the rainforest, these are made with manufactured ice from potable water systems or river water. There are few places in the Andes where you can purchase a *raspadilla* from natural glacial ice; most Andean cities are too far from glacial zones to sell natural ice *raspadillas* because the cost to transport the glacial ice is too high. In the Callejón, international tourists, along with local populations and Peruvian tourists, help to maintain the *raspadilla* trade, supporting the additional vendors.

In the Callejón de Huaylas region, as with much of the Andes, there has been long-term devaluation of indigenous culture and practices since colonial times. The value of *raspadillas* as a local treat is now being undermined by the increase in the availability of and value placed on national and international confections that are widely available throughout the valley. The continual improvement of roads and the spread of electricity allow national and international goods to be easily obtained and able to be served cold, which creates direct competition with locally made cold treats. Typically local products are less valued than those from

Figure 13.1   Raspadilla vendor in Marcará. Photograph by author.

Lima or imported from other countries. In contrast, *raspadilla* is more expensive than these mass-produced treats. A *raspadilla* is typically sold for one Nuevo Sol (~US$0.15) while a packet of gum or other sugary treat is usually sold for half that, or even sometimes a tenth of the price. While treats based on glacial ice retain significant value for the part they play in local tradition and identity, rises in price will make them unaffordable for local families. If the practice of using glacial ice is discontinued due to changing glacial conditions, it will no longer hold the traditional appeal as manufactured ice is felt to be less authentic and holds no value for locals.

Market and Climate Pressures

Raspadilla sales have been a significant source of, or supplement to, income for the families interviewed in this study for many years. However, individual sales are dropping now due to increased competition, higher living expenses, and the rising cost of glacial ice and other supplies. Vendors claim that individual sales were greater in previous years because there were only a handful of known vendors who were typically well dispersed throughout the valley. Families had particular locations where they worked and there was little overlap. Since obtaining ice to sell *raspadillas* can be purchased through the market and is no longer such time-consuming work requiring specialized knowledge, there are many more opportunistic vendors changing the map of vendor territory.

Prices have increased also due to a small tax that vendors pay to the municipalities where they work, which goes towards street cleaning and other city maintenance activities. Vendors pay the municipality for each day they set up to sell. Recently the tax climbed to one Nuevo Sol per day. Vendor prices also have gone up as a result of the rising cost of supplies. The price of sugar, used in the making of home-made flavorings, is climbing as well as the price of the glacial ice itself. *Nieveros* have had to increase the prices of glacial blocks as they meet additional expenses of paying the necessary outside help to load the blocks of ice (blocks are reported to be cut larger than in previous years), the taxis or trucks that carry the ice down to market, and the third party that receives and sells the glacial blocks in the market.

The price of glacial ice has also risen because of the change in path accessibility and deterioration of the glaciers. As the glaciers continue to recede, ice extraction becomes a significantly longer undertaking and those extracting ice are putting themselves in danger by being in close proximity to sites of small but dangerous avalanches. Those who are contracted to extract ice report having to climb continually higher for the "good quality" ice that does not have rocks or impurities and is more consistent. Previously, ice at the glacial edge was relatively sturdy and predictable. The ice was still strong, clear, and shining; still safe for extraction with donkeys and able to last the journeys down the mountain. Now, most ice is extracted from Huandoy as other glaciers have receded to the point where the ice is no longer viable for *raspadilla*, the access points are either no longer accessible, or are too dangerous. These paths are risky because the glacier is very unstable and landslides are often reported. Several glaciers that are easily accessible and were previously used as tourist destinations have since been closed due to increasing instability due to recession. For example, the Broggi glacier, which has been monitored since 1932, disappeared entirely in 2005 and Pastoruri, a popular tourist destination for glacial adventures, has now been declassified as a glacier and closed due to its extreme recession and fragmentation.

For years, the transport of ice from remote areas has been on the backs of donkeys. Even now the paths to the glacier are not suitable for any other type of transport and *nieveros* report that with increasing frequency, the rock walls left behind by the most recent recession are not even suitable for the donkeys to climb, so they must be tethered farther and farther away from the point of extraction. Beyond the spatial recession of the glacier, those who have built an occupation on extracting ice, as well as locals living near the glaciers who visit on a more casual basis, have observed many changes in the consistency of glacial ice over the last several decades. There are two main categories of ice discussed with regard to the glacier: porous and granulated. Porous natural ice has more consistency, is more compact, is stronger, has a blue crystal color, lasts longer, and is said to shine. This ice is used more when vendors work with a machine to shave ice. Granulated natural ice is weaker, whiter, it is "very soft and has a bad consistency, it is like sugar," and breaks apart easily when you work with it, "it disintegrates like sand," and is not appropriate for making *raspadillas* (Hyde 2008).

Now the glacier has "deteriorated" so that there are no longer solid fields of ice greeting you when you approach the edge. It is more often described as a crumbling slope of slush. Some of the earlier entry points have retreated to a steep rock wall and are no longer passable. Not only does this unstable ice cause a problem for those eventually purchasing the blocks of ice, but it is also extremely dangerous for the *nieveros* themselves, who have to climb further into the glacier to extract acceptable blocks of ice, increasing the possibility of accidents. Several years ago, there was a small avalanche from Hualcan while *nieveros* were extracting ice. Of the 22 people working on the glacier that day, 11 were buried but were able to dig themselves out, but 9 died. Those who were farther off the ice, shaping or loading blocks, were able to run to safety and escaped unharmed. Though glaciers in the Callejón are known to be increasingly unstable, unfortunately, the demand for glacial ice has not waned. *Nieveros* report that the blocks they bring to market are sometimes gone in under two hours. The accounts of *nieveros* show that 60 or 70 blocks of ice go solely to the city of Yungay, which is only one of the main cities in the valley requesting ice (Hyde 2008).

Raspadilla culture is also experiencing pressure from those concerned with the conservation of the glaciers and related ecosystems. Huascarán National Park was established in 1975 at the 4,000 meter line around the Cordillera Blanca to protect the native vegetation and species of the region. It is widely recognized that the extraction of ice occurred long before the establishment of the park boundaries, and because of this, the park cannot flatly prohibit ice extraction. When the park was initially created, it was managed in Lima and did not monitor ice extraction activities within its borders. Under the government of Fujimori (1990–2000), the park began to issue permits to those who wanted to extract ice, in order to estimate the amount of ice being utilized. Following his administration, the headquarters moved to Huaráz as the decentralization process unfolded throughout the country. No registration lists or permits were transferred and people were again extracting ice without any monitoring on the part of the park. In May 2009, the park prohibited the extraction of ice for several weeks, in order to encourage those extracting ice to form a committee and negotiate agreements with the park to help monitor the movement of ice. *Nieveros* report increasing pressure from the park regarding their extraction activities, which could pose further problems for the trade.

Conclusion

While the *raspadilla* itself is iconic, the shifts in *raspadilla* culture lie at the center of several ongoing changes for the Callejón de Huaylas. The region is witnessing unprecedented environmental change alongside significant economic shifts, accompanied by deep-seated historical and cultural tensions. Each of these dimensions exert pressure both on the ice itself and on the people who consume it, or whose livelihoods depend upon its consumption. By approaching changes to the *raspadilla* culture and trade through an examination of these factors, this chapter provides a more holistic approach to understanding how consumption practices change, and what consequences such change has on the social and natural worlds.

The rapid recession of glaciers in the Cordillera Blanca is cause for widespread concern throughout the region and indeed the country. This recession has made the glaciers less accessible physically to both casual and commercially motivated visits. Concern surrounding the deteriorating glaciers and the ecosystems in which these glaciers exist led to the establishment of a national park which has created restrictions in use and access for highland communities who have traditionally depended on resources within the park for myriad livelihood practices. *Nieveros* are not only facing more difficult and dangerous conditions to harvest ice, but also increasing oversight and management on the part of park staff. These environmental and cultural shifts affect the economic scenario of *raspadilla* culture. Prices climb due to the difficulties involved for *nieveros* in obtaining glacial ice, the further incorporation of informal street vendors into municipal tax structures, and the paradoxical ease with which glacial ice can be purchased in the markets.

Raspadilla production in the Callejón de Huaylas affirms local identities: locals refer to *raspadilla* as made from "our ice." The sale of *raspadilla* is still most popular during the months of *fiestas* and other traditional activities, and the curative power of glacial ice still brings national tourists from coastal cities. However, as prices climb on the traditional treat, it may dissuade families from purchasing the iconic treat in lieu of much less expensive nameless confections from national and international manufacturers. This would be yet another move toward replacing local, indigenous customs and values with globalized miscellany, an ongoing tension between highland populations and their urban counterparts. As *raspadilla* becomes more commercialized, and the number of vendors increase, so too do the places, times, and people to whom vendors sell *raspadilla*. While the ingredients for its creation have and continue to shift, from native flowers to homemade syrups to even store-bought essences and flavors, this does not seem to affect the responsiveness of customers. Shifting from the use of glacial ice, however, as its use becomes prohibitively costly could be the factor which causes the practice to become unrecognizable, blending into the sea of other nameless sugary treats. The increasing commercialization of the trade, rising prices of supplies, competition for customers with processed confections, and potential loss of access to glacial ice due to glacial recession and more strict conservation measures, could completely sever the connection people of the Callejón feel with regard to these sweet treats.

With all the other changes that *raspadilla* has undergone, why does glacial ice still retain such importance for the treat? Glacier-made *raspadillas* are symbolic of a larger loss. As residents of the Callejón mournfully watch their glaciers recede, they view it as a harbinger of impending shifts in subsistence that will have dramatic effects on highland peasant populations. The threats to *raspadilla* reflect the larger tensions of change occurring in the agropastoral livelihoods of highland communities in the valley and such rapid environmental changes trigger deep-seated uncertainties for the future, leaving locals longing for the days when they were singing for shaved ice.

References

Allen, Catherine J. 1988. *The Hold Life Has: Coca and Cultural Identity in an Andean Context.* Washington, DC: Smithsonian Institute Press.

Babb, Florence. 1987. "From the Field to the Cooking Pot: Economic Crisis and the Threat to Marketers in Peru." *Ethnology* 26:137–149.

Bolin, Inge. 1998. *Rituals of Respect: The Secret of Survival in the High Peruvian Andes.* Austin: University of Texas Press.

Carey, Mark. 2010. *In the Shadow of Melting Glaciers: Climate Change and Andean Society.* New York: Oxford University Press.

Hyde, Stephen. 2008. *Shikashika: A Documentary Short.*

Keatinge, Richard W. 1999. *Peruvian Prehistory: An Overview of Inca and Pre-Inca Society.* Cambridge: Cambridge University Press.

Lau, George F. 2010. "House Forms and Recuay Culture: Residential Compounds at Yayno (Ancash, Peru), a Fortified Hilltop Town, AD 400–800." *Journal of Anthropological Archaeology* 29: 327–351.

Lynch, Thomas F., R. Gillespie, John A. Gowlett, and R. E. Hedges. 1985. "Chronology of Guitarrero Cave, Peru." *Science* 229: 864–867.

Reinhard, Johan. 2006. *The Ice Maiden: Inca Mummies, Mountain Gods, and Sacred Sites in the Andes.* Washington, DC: National Geographic Society.

Stein, William M. 1961. *Hualcan: Life in the Highlands of Peru.* Ithaca: Cornell University Press.

Tacsi, Arnaldo, Marco Zapata, Yves Arnaud. 2010. *Inventario de Glaciares, Cordillera Blanca.* Unidad de Glaciologia y Recursos Hidricos (UGRH), Autoridad Nacional del Agua (ANA).

14

Becoming Middle Class? Consumption, Respectability, and Place in Sex Tourism

Megan Rivers-Moore

Introduction

Recent work has demonstrated the growing importance of the sex industry in a wide variety of settings, suggesting that participation in the industry is expanding and that it can no longer be considered in isolation from
other sectors, especially tourism. As Brents and Hausbeck argue, "sex
businesses as forms of commerce must be situated in local institutional
fields of consumption as they intersect with global late capitalist culture
and economy" (2007, 426). Similarly, Bernstein (2007) suggests that sexual consumption has become increasingly acceptable, and respectable, in
recent decades and that there is a marked increased in the participation
of middle-class people, both as clients and as sex workers. The sex industry thus is intricately linked to late capitalist consumption and, in many
places, to mainstream tourism. Yet how have these trends played out in
Latin America? What are the specific manifestations of the connections
between tourism, consumption, and the sex industry?

The role of consumption in tourism encounters has been fruitfully
explored, particularly in the context of the Caribbean, both in terms
of historical narratives and of contemporary tourism advertising and
practices (Ballerino Cohen 1995; Mullings 2000; Patullo 2005; Sheller
2003). While there has been comparatively less academic work on Latin
American tourism, scholars have demonstrated how the region is packaged and sold to Northern consumers and the resulting impact on Latin

American economies and communities (Cabezas 2008; Kirtsoglou and Theodossopoulos 2004; Mowforth et al. 2008; Rivers-Moore 2007; Streicker 1997; Wilson, 2008). Discussions of sex tourism in particular have demonstrated profound inequalities of gender, nation, and race, highlighting the misogynist and racist attitudes of sex tourists and the ways in which the bodies of women of color in the global south are treated as commodities by Northern consumers (see for example O'Connell Davidson and Sánchez Taylor 1999). While this perspective is useful, relevant, and highly revealing of the dynamics of sex tourism, there are, of course, many other important questions that have been addressed much less frequently in the literature. In this chapter, rather than focusing on the ways in which Latin America and Latin American women's bodies are consumed through sex tourism, I suggest that social mobility is of primary importance in how both sex tourists and sex workers make meaning out of their participation in the sex tourism industry; and that social mobility is understood mainly through particular kinds of consumption practices. I argue that sex tourists and sex workers are engaged in surprisingly similar processes of seeking out social ascension and respectability through consumption, facilitated by their participation in the sex industry. However, I also conclude that place and mobility play a crucial role in determining the extent to which respectability can be successfully and publicly claimed.[1]

My claim here is not that some sort of linear movement is actually occurring, an observable shift from easily definable working-class status to easily definable middle-class status. Furthermore, the search for mobility is not only contingent and incomplete, but any attempt to concretely define class identities in Latin America or in North America is potentially rife with all manner of conceptual and historical difficulties. It seems more useful to follow Skeggs' suggestion that rather than trying to define or redefine class, we need to step back from classifications and ask how and why they have been established: "Analysis of class should...aim to capture the ambiguity produced through struggle and fuzzy boundaries, rather than to fix it in place in order to measure and know it. Class formation is dynamic, produced through conflict and fought out at the level of the symbolic" (2004, 5). It is also important to note that though I am looking at class and consumption amongst both sex tourists and sex workers, I am not arguing that sex tourism encounters are "an interaction between two sets of liminal people" (Ryan and Hall 2001, 1). As Kempadoo (2004) has asserted in the Caribbean, liminality is at best a questionable concept in spaces where tourists are dominant and given preferential treatment. Theorizing sex tourism as liminal erases the materiality of the encounters as well as the effects of geopolitics on who can move, for how long, and at what cost. Instead, I suggest that while both sex tourists and sex workers understand the sex industry as providing the possibility of becoming (more or partially or temporarily) middle class, social mobility is ultimately curtailed by place in ways that are significantly more limiting for sex workers than for sex tourists.

Costa Rica is best known (and extensively marketed) as an ecotourism destination, but sex tourism emerged visibly alongside other types of tourism development in the 1990s. The largest concentration of male sex tourists is in the capital city of San José, and particularly in one neighborhood, now known colloquially as Gringo Gulch due to the omnipresence of North American men. Sex tourists and sex workers meet in the neighborhood's bars and hotels where they negotiate the terms and cost of their exchanges without intermediaries. Because sex work is currently neither a criminal offence nor is it regulated in Costa Rica, it is impossible to provide reliable data on the size or extent of the industry. What is evident from online sex tourism websites and from spending time in Gringo Gulch is that the sale of sex is booming in San José.

Sex Work, Consumption and Economic Mobility

Sex work is a source of income that allows increased consumption and status. Sex workers described making strategic choices about participating in the sex industry based on an assessment of how much money they could earn compared to other types of employment available to them. Though sex workers did not necessarily identify themselves in class terms, all came from families that could best be described as working class, low income, or poor. Most sex workers' mothers were housewives or domestic workers. Their fathers were involved in a wider variety of occupations, including agriculture, policing, and mechanics, but the highest concentrations by far were vendors and bus and taxi drivers. It was most common for sex workers to have started but not completed high school, and a sizeable minority had only primary school education (often incomplete). Like their mothers, most sex workers had employment experience as domestic workers and also in factories, but their limited levels of formal education severely constrained the possibility of finding other kinds of work that paid anywhere near as well as sex work. Because sex work is often referred to derisively in Costa Rica as "*la vida fácil*" (the easy life), many of the women interviewed emphasized that while sex work certainly pays significantly more than their previous occupations, it is not easy. Ruby, 27, explained: "[Sex work is] easy in comparison to any other job in the sense that I can make in one day or in one night what someone could earn in a month or even a year. But that's not to say that it's easy. But maybe it's not as difficult as some other jobs."[2]

Simply choosing to participate in sex work required a certain level of investment in consumer goods not considered necessary in other employment. For example Ana, a 37-year-old Costa Rican mother of three said:

> You become completely another person. From when you get dressed for work, you become another person. Because you wear different kinds of clothes. I'm one who likes to look different than everyone else, I like to wear different clothes and really transform myself. I wear really high heels. And really short shorts. Things like that.

Ronda, a 28-year-old immigrant from Nicaragua, said that investing in "exotic clothing and make-up" was a necessity for the job, but stressed "We don't really get dressed up for the men, we get dressed up for the competition amongst the women so that the others will see that I make more money than they do and that I can invest more in myself than they can."

Indeed, the informal sale of make-up, clothing, and jewelry occurred constantly at the various bars where I spent time with sex workers. The arrival of regular vendors was always greeted with excitement, especially when business was slow and women were bored. Items would be spread out carefully on the bar and a great deal of time was spent trying things on, comparing options, and making decisions about what to buy. The ability to spend was extremely significant for women who had, until very recently, experienced deprivation. Claudia, a 26-year-old who had temporarily left the sex industry following her third daughter's birth, told of growing up without shoes and rarely having enough to eat. Once she entered the sex industry,

> We went out dancing, drinking, taking drugs, all those things. I worked to pay my rent, to buy food, and I liked to dress well... I always went to the doctor, I used the finest brands of clothes, perfume, everything. I earned well. Not because I liked gringos, no. But if a man I don't know is going to touch any part of my body, he has to pay. [3]

For some, this ability to consume relatively easily was the impetus for entering sex work in the first place. Valentina, a very popular 19-year-old, had been working in the industry for a year. She started because she saw that her older sister was working with sex tourists and making a lot of money, enough to be able to afford to buy expensive clothing. Through her work, Valentina supported her mother and daughter, paid off her debts, and bought a multitude of home appliances, as well as a car. In addition, Valentina underwent liposuction and breast augmentation surgery following the birth of her daughter. While acknowledging that her changed body might increase her attractiveness to clients, she insisted that "I did it for me, because I was getting lots of work before I had the surgery. I did it for me, not for the gringos."

As Skeggs has argued, physical attractiveness is a form of corporeal capital, as well as a marker of class privilege (1997, 102). Valentina's plastic surgery and the money spent by many young women on hair weaves, brand name clothing, and elaborate lingerie all can be read as attempts to look sophisticated and to demonstrate their income and ultimately their economic success and shifting social position. Furthermore, investing in beauty means investing in femininity, and therefore middle-class respectability, which in itself has the potential to generate value (Skeggs 1997, 110–111). Yet while the consumption practices of sex workers were often used primarily as demonstrations of success to one another, the ways they spent their money were policed: women who were seen as spending "too much" on the wrong things were particularly criticized. As such, sex workers demonstrated an uncomfortable relationship with consumption, carefully treading the line between not wanting to confirm widely held notions that women in the sex tourism industry are frivolous and immoral, but also wanting to display pride at being able to get ahead, through access to consumer goods otherwise unavailable to them. This tension was especially clear when sex workers' analyses of the economic benefits of sex work and the consumption that sex work allows centered on stories about their families: "I got used to making a lot of money. I spent it on my kids and on my mom too. I bought a house for my mom. When you work in this [sex work], I don't know, you want to give so much to your kids, give them the best, and so you spend, spend, spend on them" (Ana). In fact, interviews suggest that providing consumer goods generally associated with the middle classes (such as video games, DVD players, and bicycles) for their children provided many women with emotional compensation for the stigma associated with sex work.[4] Angie, a 34-year-old Costa Rican mother of five whose partner was in jail on drug trafficking charges, said, "I support my kids, I pay for my house, I pay a domestic worker. I replaced everything in my house, the washing machine, the refrigerator, everything, everything new. I gave everything to [my kids], anything they wanted, and I dedicated time to them too." This ability to consume is, to some extent, what sets sex workers apart from other working-class and poor women in the other kinds of employment that sex workers themselves have had and who share a similar experience of structural disempowerment. Factory work and domestic work, however, are not stigmatized the way that sex work is. Finding themselves in a position to purchase middle class goods for themselves and their children for the first time is both an important measure of success as well as a way of mitigating some of the stigma of working in the sex industry.

However, the possibility of fully claiming social respectability to go along with middle class consumption patterns is impossible for most women, who go to great lengths to hide the source of their financial success from their families and communities. Consumption allows access to important corporeal and other kinds of symbolic capital, but the method of attainment must be hidden.

The limits to the social mobility that might accompany increased consumption are similar to Mills' study of migrant women in Thailand, where the display of commodities was deemed crucial for modern identity and status among peers, without receiving wider recognition in the broader urban context (1997, 47). Consumption is, of course, not just about economic opportunities but is also potentially linked to social and political strategies (Colloredo-Mansfeld 2000, 131). However, the stigma surrounding participation in sex work has a significant impact on the extent to which advancement through consumption can be anything other than economic, particularly given that sex workers do not have the same distance that sex tourists do from their homes and communities. For female sex workers participating in the sex industry in the same city in which they live, which was the case for virtually all of the sex workers interviewed, sex work provides enough income to allow them and their families to consume in new, and middle class, ways, yet this economic mobility is rarely accompanied by social mobility because of the need to hide the details of where their money comes from. While their ability to consume is recognized by their peers, sex workers must carefully contain the knowledge of their activities much more tightly than sex tourists. Political strategies are even less likely to emerge in this context, as sex workers are unwilling to speak publicly or run the risk of being identified by their families and communities.[5]

Sex Tourism, Consumption and Social Mobility

Processes and practices of class formation become even more complicated when they are transnational, yet most work on transnationality has focused on the two extremes: "transnationalism from above" (that of wealthy cosmopolitans) and "transnationalism from below" (that of counterhegemonic subalterns) (see for example Mahler 1999; Guarnizo and Smith 1999). While tourism and travel virtually always involve issues of racial and ethnic differences and colonial and imperial histories (Enloe 1989; Kincaid 1988; Mowforth and Munt 2003), my research challenges the idea that mobile North Americans are always necessarily wealthy cosmopolitans. Many of the men interviewed were not seasoned or "hard core" sex tourists (O'Connell Davidson 2001). Only two had travelled regularly for sex to Thailand, and seven had paid for sex in Tijuana or Las Vegas years before as young men. According to the only existing study of sex tourism in Costa Rica, tourist website postings reveal "psychological insights and awareness of international politics and culture" that imply that sex tourists to Costa Rica must be "professional men with high incomes" or middle class rather than "typical American working class guys" (Schifter 2007).

Leaving aside the problematic implication that working class people cannot be insightful or aware, interviews (and extensive reading of sex tourism websites on Costa Rica) suggest that the class background of sex tourists in Costa Rica is less securely upper and middle class than Schifter's study concludes. On Costa Rica Ticas, the most popular sex tourism site for the country, a huge variety of occupations are represented, from university professors and IT professionals to truck drivers and janitors. Of the men interviewed, 17 could be considered working class according to their job descriptions (for example, postal work, construction) and level of education (only secondary school completed). Seven identified as middle class (in jobs such as teaching and engineering) and/or were university educated. Six more refused to discuss their jobs and education altogether. Here it should be noted that class is a notoriously difficult category to discuss, particularly with North Americans. For example, in Frank's (2002) study of strip club regulars in the United States, all of her interviewees described themselves as middle class, despite a wide range in incomes, educational attainment, and occupations. Class is, however, constantly at play in the production of sexuality, as studies such as McClintock's (1995) and Skeggs' (1997) have shown. Thus, while occupation and educational attainment are certainly only two of many possible identifiers of class, they are useful, if partial and clearly fraught, indicators of the backgrounds of sex tourists.

Despite the difficulties in getting men to talk about class and income directly, economic power emerged constantly as a theme during interviews, pointing to the status enhancement that comes with transnational travel to Costa Rica. For example, after his friend Moe said that as a 55-year-old man, he has trouble attracting the attention of 20-year-old women at home, Bobby stated "in the US, we don't have that value. You purchase anything, you look for a value proposition. And the value in Costa Rica is sensational. Women are just one of the values. It's an economy." Some men complained about the high prices:

> Now it's getting more Americanized, and when it's Americanized you really pay the price. The best girls in 1990 were 35 bucks, now they're 120.

That's Americanized. Now it's 100, 120 [dollars], and it's the same pussy, really. It's out of reach for me.

(Funny Face, Canadian, late 1960s)

What should be evident here is that previous analyses of the ways in which sex tourists produce sex workers' bodies as consumable commodities remain apt. As Sheller has argued, "The Northern consumer's desire to get close to exotic others…and to seek out the pleasure of excess consumption, operates to reconstitute boundaries of difference between dominant and subordinate positions" (2003, 173). Indeed, my research confirms the findings of many others that sex tourists travel in part to seek out particular racialized constructions of Latin American sexuality that echo colonial representations of women of color as hypersexual. However, what I am suggesting is that there is more going on than the simple racist and misogynist commodification of Latin American women. Instead, I argue that the obsession with the economics of sex tourism indicate both sex tourists' anxieties about money and their search for increased social and economic status while on holiday. For example, though Rod, a US citizen in his 50s, claimed to pay $100 consistently (the going rate that most women start out demanding), he too expressed anxiety about payments:

They think we're millionaires. Not that they really know what a millionaire is, but they think we have an endless supply of money, every one of us, no matter what we tell them. They don't believe it. They think "no, no, you have mucho dinero." And the majority of these guys who come down here are not necessarily rich, they're down here trying to talk the girls down. Most of the guys will try to negotiate a low price.

Despite these anxieties about being able to afford the prices women demand, sex tourists were able to use their relative economic power to construct themselves as generous. This economic empowerment impacts sex tourists' analyses of their interactions with sex workers. For example, Jeff, a 55-year-old from the United States, recently separated from his wife, described an on going relationship with a Colombian sex worker:

I give her money every…essentially…not just for sex, but you know what? They're very poor here. Average income, possibly $300, $400 a month on the high side. One night she asked me if she could borrow a couple hundred dollars. And I said "no problem." Every dime that I gave her…was sent home to her mother [and] two brothers…So there's a good feeling about that.

Jeff suggested that his generosity was not unique, but a national trait: "I think as Americans [sic], we're very generous people. Maybe Canadians too. We are. [Costa Ricans] are so grateful for things like that, they don't take it for granted." Jeff and his friend Darryl gave many examples of their own generosity and Costa Rican gratitude, even beyond the sex industry, including tipping taxi drivers and waiters. They clearly enjoyed feeling appreciated, and Jeff noted "if you leave a dollar tip here, they are as grateful as if it was a $10 or a $20 or a $50 tip." The ability to seem generous, while spending little money, allowed sex tourists to claim a kind of economic empowerment that is unavailable to them at home.

Poverty in Costa Rica is used in order to demonstrate the relative economic power of North American men on holiday. Sex tourists are amazed that "if I moved here, I could have a maid, I could have a yard man, and still live well off of my pension… There's no unhappiness here, they're poor but they don't seem to know it" (Edward, 69 years old, from Tennessee). Similarly, Mark, a US citizen in his early 30s, said that "you see that people here are poor. But they're happy. That's the amazing thing. They're so poor but they're a lot happier than people in the States." The poverty that sex tourists observe in Costa Rica provides them with a sense of economic power, particularly given that they believe that their generosity is met with genuine appreciation. For men who are not especially economically privileged, their ability to contribute to the financial well being of women in particular and Costa Rican families more generally gives them access to a set of traditional masculine expectations about protecting and providing for others. Most crucially, their ability to fit into this role in Costa Rica requires relatively little of them in terms of actual expenditures.

Bishop and Robinson (2002) argue that the obsessive recounting of economic transactions that can be found in sex tourists' narratives on websites demonstrates that sex tourism is a quintessential example of total capitalist alienation, as every experience is tied to cost and value, with women described as consumable products. While I found that sex tourists interviewed in San José could easily provide a full break down of the costs of their holidays, including the money spent on sex, this was often in fact because they had saved for months to be able to travel. For example, Barry, a 51-year-old primary school teacher from Ohio, had taken a second job as a hospital orderly in order to be able to pay for his sex tourism vacations. Part of the attraction was that money saved carefully at home goes much further in Costa Rica, buying the opportunity to consume like wealthier men, both within and beyond the sex industry. Access to particular commodities, including the commodified bodies of Costa Rican women, demonstrates participation in consumption practices that play a role in defining social position. Though spatially and temporally limited, participation in sex tourism in Costa Rica allows this group of North American men to access respectability, primarily through generosity, as well as economic power through their ability to spend money on sex and leisure, usually associated with the middle classes (see Bernstein 2007 on the rise of participation in sex work amongst middle class men and women in the United States).

While it is ultimately impossible to definitively establish the class background of the sex tourists interviewed or of those who make posts on the Internet, the observed variations challenge the notion that those travelling from the global north are necessarily wealthy, cosmopolitan elites. This demonstrates the importance of considering the specifics about sex tourists, rather than simply assuming that we already know who they are and where they come from. That said, geopolitics plays a major role in determining who can move, where they can go, for which reasons, and for how long, including in the case of sex tourists. Sex tourists hide their activities from their families and communities, but because they take part in sex tourism thousands of miles away from home, they are able to enjoy themselves and their economic power, even if it is temporary, without fear of being discovered. Distance from home, then, is key for sex tourists, allowing mobility to be accompanied by respectability, at least while in Costa Rica. Sex tourists' relative economic power provides social status when compared to their own lives at home and to the lives of the Costa Ricans with whom they interact. In addition, members of sex tourist websites often meet up in Costa Rica, allowing for instant community and friendship that can be enjoyed publicly while away from home. Indeed, as Frank (2002) has demonstrated in the context of strip clubs, spending time with beautiful women, and being seen with beautiful women by other men, can maintain, and I argue temporarily improve, men's respectability and class status. While the social mobility that sex tourists achieve through consumption in sex tourism is temporally and spatially limited, that it is witnessed by other men who are also far from home but involved in similar activities is crucial for its recognition.

Conclusions

Sex tourists' and sex workers' narratives demonstrate surprisingly similar discourses about consumption, respectability, and class mobility through participation in the sex industry. What is key here is that consumption does not simply reflect material interests and economic needs, but also a cultural process that engages with powerful but conflicting discourses about gender and modernity (Mills 1997, 54). The extent to which consumption can move beyond marking an economic achievement to gaining social recognition and respectability varies significantly according to gender and nationality, and especially place and proximity or distance from home. Particular kinds of consumption help facilitate enhanced class status for both sex tourists and sex workers in Costa Rica, but the ability to fully adopt middle-class respectability is impacted by mobility in that US and Canadian citizens are able to move around the world with much more ease than Costa Rican citizens. While respectability cannot be fully claimed when at home by either group, sex tourists' mobility allows them to make these claims in Costa Rica, while sex workers must be much more careful in ensuring that their working lives and successes remain separate from their nearby communities. As such, how successful consumption is in guaranteeing economic and social transformation depends significantly on place. Both sex tourists and sex workers negotiate a certain amount of stigma associated with their participation in the sex industry, but place plays a crucial role in determining how effectively that stigma can be negotiated. As such, sex tourism in Costa Rica demonstrates the importance of continuing to explore who gets to move and who does not, how different bodies move and what that mobility allows. Participation in the sex industry is more than the simple commodification of Latin American bodies by North American travelers, it rather involves the pursuit of respectability and changing class status, specifically through shifting consumption practices by both tourists and workers.

Notes

1. This chapter is based on 14 months of ethnographic fieldwork in San José, Costa Rica that involved participant observation, informal conversations and in-depth, semistructured interviews with sex tourists, sex workers, and public and private sector employees.
2. The names and any identifying characteristics of all interviewees have been changed.
3. The Costa Rican state runs a free HIV/AIDS prevention and treatment clinic that is primarily used by female sex workers. Women who are earning well prefer to pay to see a private doctor as a matter of pride and a demonstration of success.
4. I develop this argument in much more detail in Rivers-Moore (2010).
5. There are, of course, many examples of sex worker organizing around the world. In Costa Rica, there has been a sex workers' rights organization called La Sala since 1994. However, few women working exclusively in the sex tourism industry had even heard of La Sala, which is located in San José's red light district and tends to attract the women who work with local clients in the brothels and streets in that area.

References

Ballerino Cohen, C. 1995. "Marketing Paradise, Making Nation." *Annals of Tourism Research* 22: 404–421.

Bernstein, E. 2007. "Sex Work for the Middle Classes." *Sexualities* 10: 473–488.

Bishop, R., and L. Robinson. 2002. "Travellers' Tails: Sex Diaries of Tourists Returning from Thailand." In *Transnational Prostitution: Changing Global Patterns.* Edited by S. Thorbek and B. Pattanaik, 13–23. London: Zed.

Brents, B. G., and K. Hausbeck. 2007. "Marketing Sex: US Legal Brothels and Late Capitalist Consumption." *Sexualities* 10: 425–439.

Cabezas, A. L. 2008. "Tropical Blues: Tourism and Social Exclusion in the Dominican Republic." *Latin American Perspectives* 35: 21–36.

Colloredo-Mansfeld, R. 2000. "Modernity, Nation, and Material Culture in Post-Colonial Latin America." *Identities* 7: 127–137.

Enloe, C. 1989. *Bananas, Beaches and Bases: Making Feminist Sense of International Politics.* Berkeley: University of California Press.

Frank, K. 2002. *G-strings and Sympathy: Strip Club Regulars and Male Desire.* Durham, NC: Duke University Press.

Guarnizo, L. E., and M. P. Smith. 1999. "The Locations of Transnationalism." In *Transnationalism From Below.* Edited by M. P. Smith and L. E. Guarnizo, 3–34. New Brunswick: Transaction.

Kempadoo, K. 2004. *Sexing the Caribbean: Gender, Race, and Sexual Labor.* New York: Routledge.

Kincaid, J. 1988. *A Small Place.* New York: Farrar, Straus, Giroux.

Kirtsoglou, E., and D. Theodossopoulos. 2004. "'They are Taking our Culture Away': Tourism and Culture Commodification in the Garifuna Community of Roatan." *Critique of Anthropology* 24:135–157.

Mahler, S. J. 1999. "Theoretical and Empirical Contributions Toward a Research Agenda for Transnationalism." In *Transnationalism From Below.* Edited by M. P. Smith and L. E. Guarnizo, 64–100. New Brunswick: Transaction.

McClintock, A. 1995. *Imperial Leather: Race, Gender and Sexuality in the Colonial Contest.* London: Routledge.

Mowforth, M., C. Charlton, and I. Munt. 2008. *Tourism and Responsibility: Perspectives from Latin America and the Caribbbean.* London: Routledge.

Mowforth, M., and I. Munt. 2003. *Tourism and Sustainability: Development and New Tourism in the Third World.* London: Routledge.

Mullings, B. 2000. "Fantasy Tours: Exploring the Global Consumption of Caribbean Sex Tourism." In *New Forms of Consumption: Consumers, Culture and Commodification.* Edited by M. Gottdiener, 227–250. Lanham: Rowman and Littlefield.

O'Connell Davidson, J. 2001 "The Sex Tourist, The Expatriate, His Ex-Wife and Her 'Other': The Politics of Loss, Difference and Desire." *Sexualities* 41: 5–24.

O'Connell Davidson, J., and J. Sánchez Taylor. 1999 "Fantasy Islands: Exploring the Demand for Sex Tourism." In *Sun, Sex and Gold: Tourism and Sex Work in the Caribbean.* Edited by K. Kempadoo, 37–54. Boulder: Rowman and Littlefield.

Patullo, P. 2005. *Last Resorts: The Cost of Tourism in the Caribbean*. London: Latin American Bureau.

Rivers-Moore, M. 2007. "No Artificial Ingredients?: Gender, Race and Nation in Costa Rica's International Tourism Campaign," *Journal of Latin American Cultural Studies* 16: 341–357.

Rivers-Moore, M. 2010. "But the Kids Are Okay: Motherhood, Consumption and Sex Work in Neo-Liberal Latin America", *British Journal of Sociology* 61: 716–736.

Ryan, C., and C. M. Hall. 2001. *Sex Tourism: Marginal People and Liminalities*. London: Routledge.

Schifter, J. 2007. *Mongers in Heaven: Sexual Tourism and HIV Risk in Costa Rica and in the United States*. Lanham: University Press of America.

Sheller, M. 2003. *Consuming the Caribbean: From Arawaks to Zombies*. New York: Routledge.

Skeggs, B. 1997. *Formations of Class & Gender*. London: Sage.

Skeggs, B. 2004. *Class, Self, Culture*. London: Routledge.

Streicker, J. 1997. "Remaking Race, Class, and Region in a Tourist Town." *Identities* 3(4), 523–555.

Wilson, T. D. 2008. "Introduction: The Impacts of Tourism in Latin America." *Latin American Perspectives* 35(3), 3–20.

Contributors

Jason Antrosio is associate professor of Anthropology at Hartwick College, and his work was supported by a Hartwick College Faculty Research Grant. Antrosio's research is on artisan and agrarian economies in the Andean highlands of northern Ecuador and southwestern Colombia. Since 2005, he has collaborated with Rudi Colloredo-Mansfeld on a project comparing family businesses in the Kichwa economy of Otavalo with apparel businesses in the old factory town of Atuntaqui, Ecuador. This project also explores linkages between Ecuador and Colombia in the northern Andes.

Tomas Ariztia is assistant professor at the Sociology department of Diego Portales University, Chile. He holds a PhD in Sociology from the London School of Economics and a MA in Sociology from the Universidad Católica de Chile. He is interested in cultural economy and consumption studies, particularly consumer markets professionals, consumer cultures, and ethical consumption.

Vander Casaqui is a Communication and Consumption researcher, with a PhD from the University of São Paulo (ECA/USP). He is currently professor of the postgraduate program in Communication and Consumption Practices of the Escola Superior de Propaganda e Marketing—ESPM, São Paulo, Brazil. He's been developing research from a thematic project that deals with representations of the world of work in media communication. His works have been presented regularly in the leading Brazilian congresses of communication and other major international events, besides being published in collective books related to issues of communication, consumption and advertising.

Katy Damacia Medina Marcos studied at "Santiago Antunez de Mayolo" National University (Perú). She holds a bachelor's degree in Environmental Engineering and is currently working as a project assistant in environmental issues at "Santiago Antunez de Mayolo" National University. She is interested in improving the quality of life of people through the development of sustainable alternatives to monitoring and remediation for water and soil.

Katherine W. Dunbar holds a PhD in Environmental Anthropology from the University of Georgia and is currently a postdoctoral researcher with the Center for Integrative Conservation Research. Her research interests focus on the social dimensions of climate change and variation.

Marcela Ferreira da Silva is a studying for masters in Governance and Public Policy at the University of Queensland and has a bachelor degree in International Relations from the Pontifical Catholic University of Minas Gerais State. She has worked for the State Secretariat for Economic Development of Minas Gerais as a project coordinator on initiatives to improve small companies' competitiveness and for the alignment between public and private stakeholders involved in such initiatives. In the private sector, she has assisted the projects team of a mining company in developing governance tools. This is Marcela's first contribution to the editing of a book.

Marc Figuerola Delgado holds a masters in International Studies from the University of Queensland, although his main background is in Media Studies: he holds a degree in Journalism from the Universitat Ramon Llull in Barcelona. He has worked as a freelance photojournalist for several Spanish and Catalan newspapers, like *El País, La Vanguardia, El Periódico de Catalunya, Avui* and *20 Minutos*. Beyond traditional media, Marc has collaborated in the internet-streamed show *Vist i No Vist* and has been head press officer of the civic platform *Plataforma per l'Autodeterminació a Sabadell*. Marc has also done internships in the TV network *Televisió de Catalunya*, and in the radio stations *Onda Cero Barcelona* and in the most popular radio show of Catalonia, *El Matí de Catalunya Ràdio amb Antoni Bassas*. This has been the first time that Marc has contributed to the editing of a book.

Marie Francois, professor of History at California State University Channel Islands, is author of *A Culture of Everyday Credit: Housekeeping, Pawnbroking, and Governance in Mexico City, 1750–1920* published by the University of Nebraska Press (2006). Her chapter "Vivir de prestado. El empeño en la ciudad de México" appears in Vol. IV of *Historia de la vida cotidiana en México* (El Colegio de México / Fondo de Cultura Económica, 2005). She published "Products of Consumption: Housework in Latin American Political Economies and Cultures" in *History Compass* (January 2008). Her research continues to explore connections between economics and culture, currently focusing on laundry.

Fergus Grealy is a staff member at the Centre for Critical and Cultural Studies at the University of Queensland. He completed a bachelor of arts (honors) in Spanish Language and Cultural Studies with a thesis on cinematic coproductions between Latin American and Western nations. Fergus has previously assisted Anna Cristina Pertierra with a number of translations related to her research projects.

Ronaldo Helal is professor of the Graduate and Undergraduate Program in Social Communication at the State University of Rio de Janeiro; Researcher of the CNPq (Brazilian Research Council); he holds a masters and PhD in Sociology from New York University and a postdoctoral degree in Social Sciences from the University of Buenos Aires. His interests are about the relationship among media, sport, national identity, and idolatry. He coordinates with Hugo Lovisolo, the research group Sport and Culture (http://comunicacaoeesporte.com/) and has published several books on the field. Among these are: (a) *Futebol, Jornalismo e Ciências Sociais: interações,* (b) *A Invenção do País do Futebol: mídia, raça e idolatria,* and (c) *Passes e Impasses: futebol e cultura de massa no Brasil.*

Hugo Rodolfo Lovisolo holds a BA in Sociology from the Universidad de Buenos Aires and a PhD in Anthropology from the Federal University of Rio de Janeiro. He has a postdoctoral degree in Sports Science from the University of Porto and another one in Social Communication from Universidad de Buenos Aires. He was once a researcher of CNPq and professor of the University of Campinas and the State University of Rio de Janeiro. Currently, he is a professor and a researcher at the Graduate School in Local Development at UNISUAM (Rio de Janeiro). He has published many books and articles in the field of anthropology, education, physical education, social communication, and sociology of sports. He coordinates with Ronaldo Helal the research group Sport and Culture (http://comunicacaoeesporte.com/) and has published several books on the field. Among these are *Futebol, Jornalismo e Ciências Sociais: interações* and *A Invenção do País do Futebol: mídia, raça e idolatria.*

David Manuel-Navarrete is a visiting researcher at desiguALdades.net (Free University of Berlin and Ibero-American Institute), where he studies the socioecological inequalities created by global tourism. He holds degrees in environmental sciences, ecological economics (Autonomous University of Barcelona) and geography (University of Waterloo). He has worked as a consultant at the United Nations Economic Commission for Latin America and the Caribbean (ECLAC) and as a research associate at the Department of Geography of King's College London. He is lead author of over a dozen journal articles and has also contributed chapters in several books .

Ruben George Oliven is professor of Anthropology at the Federal University of Rio Grande do Sul in Porto Alegre, Brazil. He received his PhD from the London School of Economics and Political Science and was a visiting professor at the University of California (Berkeley), Brown University, and University of Paris. He was the president of the Brazilian Anthropological Association and of the Brazilian Association for Graduate Studies and Research in Social Sciences. His research interests include national and regional identities, popular music, consumption, and symbolic meanings of money. He won the Erico Vannucci Mendes Prize for Distinguished Contribution to the Study of Brazilian Culture.

Anna Cristina Pertierra is an ARC postdoctoral fellow at the Centre for Critical and Cultural Studies, University of Queensland. She has a PhD in Anthropology from University College London, and publishes on the topics of consumption, media, and domestic practices in Cuba and Mexico. Recent publications include *Cuba: The Struggle for Consumption* (Caribbean Studies Press 2011) and, coauthored with Graeme Turner, *Locating Television: Zones of Consumption* (Routledge 2012).

Rosana Pinheiro-Machado is an assistant professor at the International Relations Department of the School of Higher Education and Marketing and Communication Management (ESPM-Brazil). She holds a PhD in Social Anthropology from the Federal University of Rio Grande do Sul, Brazil. She specialized in China and Latin American societies, where she has been carrying out multisited ethnographic research in the last ten years. Her interests are about capitalism in emergent economies, clientelism and guanxi, informal economy, legality and illegality, brands and consumption, human rights, and globalization. In 2010, her thesis was awarded The Best Thesis Prize in Brazil by the ministry of Education. She is the author of *Made in China* (Hucitec, São Paulo, 2011).

Michael Redclift is professor of International Environmental Policy in the Department of Geography, at King's College, London. His research interests include sustainable development, global environmental change, environmental security and the modern food system. Between 1973 and 1997 he was at [Imperial College at] Wye, ultimately as professor of Environmental Sociology. In 1987, his book *Sustainable Development: Exploring the Contradictions* was published by Routledge. He was the first director of the Global Environmental Change programme of the ESRC between 1990 and 1995, and has coordinated research grants for the European Commission (FM IV and V), and for the TERM programme of the European Science Foundation. He has also held grants from the ESRC/AHRC (2003–2005) and, in 2007, began research on a three-year study (with Mark Pelling and David Manuel) of coastal urbanization and adaptation to environmental risks in the Mexican Caribbean. In 2006, he was the first recipient of the Frederick Buttel Award from the International Sociological Association (RC 24). Recent books include *Chewing Gum: The Fortunes of Taste*, (2004, Taylor and Francis, New York) and in 2006 he completed a major comparative study for MIT Press: *Frontiers: Histories of Civil Societies and Nature*.

Megan Rivers-Moore has a PhD in Sociology from the University of Cambridge and is a postdoctoral fellow at the Women and Gender Studies Institute at the University of Toronto.

John Sinclair is an honorary professorial fellow in the Australian Centre, School of Historical and Philosophical Studies, at the University of Melbourne. He has been researching various dimensions of the globalization of media and communication industries over the last three decades, with a particular focus on television, advertising, and consumer culture in Asia and Latin America. His books include *Latin American Television: A Global View* (Oxford University Press, 1999); *Televisión: Comunicación Global y Regionalización* (Gedisa, 2000); the edited work *Contemporary World Television* (BFI, 2004); and *Advertising, the Media and Globalisation* (Routledge, 2012).

Joel Stillerman is associate professor of Sociology at Grand Valley State University. His work on labor protest, consumer culture, the informal economy, and middle classes in Chile as well as transnational labor activism in North America appears in *Journal of Contemporary Ethnography, Political Power and Social Theory, Qualitative Sociology, City & Community, Journal of Consumer Culture, Mobilization, International Labor and Working-class History, Social Science History, Revista Política, Revista Alamedas,* and several edited volumes.

Patricia Vega holds a PhD in History and a degree in Communication Studies, and is the director of the Centro de Investigación en Comunicación of the Universidad de Costa Rica. Her main research areas are in History of Communication and in History of Consumption. She is the author of several books and articles on these issues.

George Yúdice is professor of Modern Languages and Literatures and Latin American Studies at the University of Miami. He is also Director of the Miami Observatory on Communication and Creative Industries. He is the author of *Cultural Policy* (with Toby Miller, Sage, 2002);

The Expediency of Culture: Uses of Culture in the Global Era (Duke University Press, 2003); *Nuevas tecnologías, música y experiencia* (Barcelona: Gedisa, 2007); and *Culturas emergentes en el mundo hispano de Estados Unidos* (Madrid: Fundación Alternativas, 2009). He is or has been on the editorial board of *International Journal of Cultural Policy*; *Cultural Studies*; *Found Object*; and *Topía, Canadian Journal of Cultural Studies, Social Text.*

Index